GET BACK
IN THE
BOX

GET BACK IN THE BOX

BOX

Innovation from
the Inside Out

DOUGLAS RUSHKOFF

Collins
An Imprint of HarperCollins*Publishers*

HarperCollins books may be purchased for educational, business, or sales promotional use. For information, please write: Special Markets Department, HarperCollins Publishers, 10 East 53rd Street, New York, NY 10022.

FIRST EDITION

Designed by William Ruoto

Library of Congress Cataloging-in-Publication Data
Rushkoff, Douglas.
   Get back in the box: innovation from the inside out/by Douglas Rushkoff.
      p.   cm.
   Includes bibliographical references and index.
   ISBN-10:   0-06-075869-4
   ISBN-13: 978-0-06-075869-1
      1. Technological innovations—Economic aspects.   2. Business enterprises—
Computer network resources.   3. Internet.   4. Evolutionary economics.
I. Title.

HC79.T4R87 2005
658.4'062—dc22   2005049651

05   06   07   08   09   DIX/RRD   10   9   8   7   6   5   4   3   2   1

For my daughter, Mamie—the very best evidence
of a new renaissance

contents

preface

I'm supposed to start with something scary. You know, how the world is about to change very drastically and if you don't recognize this shift and reconfigure your business accordingly, doom awaits you. And after I paint that awful picture, I'm supposed to earn your trust so that you follow me "out of the box" and into a whole new way of looking at your predicament.

It's a great formula for selling books, but it serves you no good purpose. For the world is not about to change so drastically. It already has. The change has come—you're soaking in it. You don't need a trend forecaster to understand what's going on; you just need some eyes and ears.

After I've frightened you, I'm to tell you that there's a single path to salvation, and that I have it. Then I list a whole bunch of companies I've consulted with that have done exactly what I've said, to their great success (leaving out those that have failed using the same advice) and throw in a few case studies of other companies just to add some heft.

But—thanks, in part, to the change that has already happened— you no longer need to model behaviors that worked for others, or even to analyze the processes through which they achieved success in order to repeat them. That's a losing game, devised to disconnect you further from your own competence and make you even more dependent on the expertise of others. You shouldn't have to step outside your own intuition and experience to learn what worked for someone else in some other pursuit. That's *their* story. You get to write your own.

So, unlike most books aimed at businesspeople, this is not a series of lessons from the companies and organizations that got it right. For the landscape is littered with those who tried to follow the strategies that worked for someone else, what seemed like just yesterday. You—not someone else—are the expert in what you do.

To most businesses, this painfully obvious fact itself is a frightening prospect.

Just last year, I got a phone call from the CEO of a home electronics chain, asking if I could devise a new communications strategy for him. He had read one of my books on Internet culture and was wondering if I could help him make use of some of this "below the line" advertising he'd been hearing so much about lately. He wanted his marketing to be "less Saatchi and Saatchi and more craigslist." By this he meant he wanted to rely less on the expensive, high-concept traditional television advertising created by agencies like Saatchi & Saatchi, and somehow do his communications through bottom-up online communities, like the one that had developed around the craigslist online bulletin board.

As I reviewed the company's dossier, product line, and customer experience reviews, I realized this CEO had a much bigger problem than his ads. The chain had lost its way. It had alienated its core customer base by abandoning the electronics business and becoming more of an appliance store. It had pushed design and manufacturing offshore, leaving headquarters without talent who really understood electronics. As a result, the quality of store-brand products had deteriorated, leading customers to buy other brands at thinner margins. Finally, it had alienated its store managers through infantilizing incentives schemes, and their employees with oppressive "loss prevention" (antitheft) policies. Yet this CEO really thought a shift in marketing would change his whole business.

That's when it hit me: What this fellow needed was not simply to hire companies like craigslist but to *be* more like craigslist.

American companies are obsessed with window dressing because they're reluctant, no, *afraid*, to look at whatever it is they really do and evaluate it from the inside out. When things are down, CEOs look to consultants and marketers to rethink, rebrand, or repackage whatever it is they are selling, when they should be getting back on the factory floor, into the stores, or out to the research labs where their product is actually made, sold, or conceived. Instead of making their communications less Saatchi and more Craig, they should be *reconnecting with their core enterprise.*

I'm hard-pressed to think of two companies that embody the difference between these two approaches better than the Saatchis and Craig. Consider the rise and fall of Saatchi & Saatchi for a moment. It's typical of the kind of company that chokes as soon as it has broken from the pack, losing its way and forgetting its core value proposition. Without competitors at their side, many companies don't even know what they're about.

Sons of a prosperous Baghdad textile merchant, art patron Charles Saatchi and his brother Maurice, a Conservative party stalwart, founded Saatchi & Saatchi in 1970. The Saatchis took the conservative U.K. advertising world by storm with their provocative campaigns, a Rolodex full of high-society contacts, and a flair for self-promotion.

As the *Financial Times* put it, "The Saatchi brothers' expertise is in image-making. Their greatest triumph was in projecting the image of themselves and their company as the most dynamic force in worldwide advertising . . . they were great magnets for young talent—and made sure their company took full credit."[1]

Just a couple of clever ad campaigns led them to global prominence in the late 1970s. Their "Labour Isn't Working" spots for Margaret Thatcher became a new benchmark for political advertising. Their ad promoting the use of contraceptives featured a picture of a pregnant man. This edgy creative work, combined with the brothers' talent for schmoozing clients and the powerful, gave them the ingredients to build an empire.[2]

But this was their tragic flaw: their quest for empire overshadowed their desire to make good advertising. In the process, they transformed themselves from an advertising agency into a holding company, and subsequently allowed their core competency to wither.

Making use of a loophole in U.K. investment law, the Saatchis raised hundreds of millions of pounds by going public, which they then used to acquire as many other agencies as they could gobble up. For a brief moment, they were the world's largest advertising firm. But this didn't mean a lot. The Saatchis' wanton acquisitions had stirred up a feeding frenzy and merger mania in the advertising business, from which the industry has yet to recover.

The new way to acquire clients was to snap up the agencies that already had bookings with them. Instead of focusing on making great ads and pitches, agencies either became obsessed with purchasing their peers or establishing high stock valuations to prevent hostile takeovers. "Those agencies that are farsighted enough to grasp this will do well," Maurice Saatchi proudly told the *Wall Street Journal*.[3]

The cash-rich Saatchis set the standard for mismanaged capital and overindulgence. They had almost no interest in conventional management, making only halfhearted efforts at due diligence and, by all accounts, vastly overpaying for their acquisitions.[4] The Saatchis thoroughly convinced themselves they could go beyond advertising and provide pretty much any service to their clients. Maurice Saatchi had a vision for the firm to become a "one-stop shop selling advertising, management consulting and even financial services to corporate clients."[5] This led to their disastrous attempt to acquire Midland Bank, a failing British clearing bank, in 1987. Saatchi & Saatchi stock price was £50 a share at the time, but the bidding price for Midland was up to £3 billion.

The brothers were rebutted by a skeptical banking community and chastised by their shareholders for their cavalier behavior. Their bidding campaign almost led the firm to bankruptcy.

Saatchi & Saatchi's rampant expansion and indifference to costs eventually alienated clients and shareholders alike, driving the stock price down and leading to the brothers' dismissal from their own agency. The remaining, restructured, firm was renamed Cordiant after merging with the U.S. company Bates Worldwide; then Saatchi & Saatchi was separated out again for its original name value alone, and purchased by the French conglomerate Publicis Group.

As alienated from its core competency as ever, today's Saatchi & Saatchi seems more dedicated to selling itself than its clients. Charismatic CEO Kevin Roberts is spending most of the company's energy on a pet project of his called Lovemarks. In addition to being the title of his highly art-directed book, Lovemarks is an effort to rekindle the past glory of the advertising industry by conducting forensic examinations of brands people love—from Hello Kitty to Nelson Mandela. Of course, guiding people on a tour of winning brands is a process entirely different from building just one of them from the ground up. While platitudes such as "loyalty beyond reason" whet advertisers' appetites for effective campaigns, simply telling us what has worked for someone else is a far cry from delivering on that proposition. Saatchi's billings indicate as much.

If Saatchi & Saatchi epitomizes losing track of one's core competency, craigslist represents the opposite extreme: sticking to what one knows best. The enterprise began in 1994 as a simple email listing of local events, sent out by San Franciscan Craig Newmark to about 20 of his friends, all in the "cc" field of the message. His main motivation was to demonstrate how the Internet could empower people to help each other out. As the list expanded to more than 200 people, Craig got a friend to show him how to set up a real mailing list and Web page. He considered changing the name to SFEvents, but his friends all agreed he should call it what it already was: craigslist.

These friends realized something Craig didn't: it was people's trust in Craig, and his pure passion for serving others through technology, that gave the list its authority. By 1997, there were more than 3,800 subscribers to the list. Every day, another 800 people checked the online version—still just a long page of classified listings on Craig's personal Web site. Craig himself monitored the listings for abuse.

Internet giant Microsoft Sidewalk (now defunct) approached Craig to run ads on his site. He refused, citing an early cyberculture ethos: "While making money on the net was good, not everything had to be about money." Remember, now, this was the dot-com era, when people like Craig were becoming "paper millionaires." But, unlike those businesses that had been created for little else than their own acquisition, craigslist refused outside investment, fearing it would "destroy the spirit that we have."[6] There was something more profoundly important about building his business than money.

For both philosophical and practical reasons, Craig kept the interface on his Web list simple. No bells and whistles, no animation, no graphics—just text. The value proposition to users was not a style or brand, but trust: this was a community sharing information through its trusted host, Craig.

By 1999, craigslist was turning a profit by charging Bay Area businesses a modest $45 to run job listings on the site. Craig hired four people to help him comb the lists for integrity and manage the 180 new paid posts each day. Through the dot-com boom and bust, Craig maintained slow, steady growth, until by 2000, having grown solely by word of mouth (and, presumably, email) he was getting 8 million hits a month. Forrester, an Internet research firm, concluded that craigslist already outranked commercial job sites Monster.com and Careerbuilder.com,[7] which were charging 10 times or more what Craig charged per listing.

Soon, other cities wanted their own versions of craigslist. Even though his company grew slowly and organically, Craig realized that the realities of building the business were sidetracking him from his core expertise of serving his community. He hired a CEO to handle those aspects of the business, and continued to spend 50 hours a week on what had made him famous in the first place: customer service, answering emails personally, and patrolling the list for fake "no-fee brokers" and other spam.

Amazingly, it was the dot-com crash that pushed craigslist into the stratosphere. Thousands of former hi-tech employees were now looking for work, and solace. In Craig's words, "We provide a means for people to give each other a break, to help each other out. We're trying to, in our own small way, restore the human voice to the Net."[8]

By 2004, this formula had spread craigslist to over 40 U.S. cities, logging a combined 1 billion page views from 5 million individual visitors each month.[9] Since only prospective employers pay for the service, Craig has begun to count on his user base to help him patrol the tremendous databases for spam and abuses. In fact, he automated a process through which community members "flag" abusive posts; if enough users label a listing as spam, it is automatically removed. In a sense, his customers have become his extended workforce.

Oh yes, money. With a gargantuan staff of 15, craigslist achieved revenues that most analysts believe approached $10 million in 2004, simply by charging for job listings. By summer 2005, his 18 employees were serving more than 120 cities. For Craig, keeping operations lean is less a question of maintaining the bottom line than of maintaining focus. As he told CNN, "The biggest challenge is to stay small while growing much bigger, which is to say that, as organizations grow large, sometimes they forget important stuff."[10]

Indeed. Sometimes, as in the case of Saatchi & Saatchi—as well as that electronics chain I was supposed to advise—growth even takes precedence over the core business proposition. CEOs turn to marketers to "supersize" them, and when their businesses inevitably suffer, they turn to a new team of marketers to repair the damage. Exploring their own businesses, returning to what should be their core competencies, feels like opening a Pandora's box—when it should feel like coming home again. Businesses appear ready to do anything but what they actually do.

Over the past ten years, I've spoken with a lot of people about this conundrum, its historical context, and the ease with which so many businesses could transcend their reluctance to draw on their own expertise. Invariably, the Fortune 500 CEOs, billionaire entrepreneurs, and intellectual leaders with whom I engaged implored me to share these insights with the audience who needed them most: businesspeople. Their only advice was to write a book that tells the truth directly, unthreateningly, and with as few boring case studies and statistics as possible. That's why I'm making such a simple proposition: stop solving your problems from the outside in. Get back in the box and do the thing you actually do best. This disciplined commitment to your own core passion—and not a consultant, ad campaign, or business plan—is the source of true innovation.

The longevity and prosperity of any enterprise depends most on its participants' ability to maintain the wellspring of innovation. And the way to do this is to remember that you are always the source of your own best ideas. The most successful businesses for the next century will turn out to have been based not on infinitely repeatable Harvard Business School lesson plans, but on a combination of competence and passion. Dissecting an enterprise after the fact to see what made it work is akin to conducting an autopsy on a person to see what made him live. It's another version of Saatchi & Saatchi's Lovemarks. The very pursuit is symptomatic of the highly fragmented approach to business we're leaving behind.

So let's be clear: this is not a business book. Or at least it's not *just* a business book. For your career is not your job and your company is not its balance sheet. Your most personal choices are, in fact, your business choices. And your business choices may as well be your civic choices. Whether you realize it or not, your product purchases and brand loyalties express your politics, and your relationship to money says a lot about your understanding of time, of power, and of belief. It's all one dynamic picture.

That's why I'm going to ask you to look at commerce, communications, civics, and community as if they are all part of the same system—an ecology, really, of interdependent activities and needs. There is just one thing going on here. Pretending that each aspect of your existence or your enterprise can be compartmentalized is, itself, a product of the Industrial Age thinking I'll be asking you to abandon, and the surest path toward forgetting what it is you might have once, originally, hoped to accomplish.

For the same reasons, I'm hoping you'll suspend—at least for the plane ride it takes to read this book—the conviction that competition is the primary driver of innovation. It may have once been able to serve this purpose, but it is also a necessarily divisive force—turning potential collaborations into adversaries, and what could be meaningful play into grueling work. We find ourselves comparing and contrasting our progress with others, focusing on what we lack rather than what we have, and alienating ourselves from our potential allies in the process.

Indeed, as my lectures bring me from industry to industry, I find myself amazed by just how little fun most people are having. Whether separated from one another by policy, competition, or cubicle, the last thing that seems to occur to people is to have fun together—when it should be the first priority. Instead, managers feel obligated to reign over employees; executives think they must hoodwink their shareholders; sales believe they must strong-arm their clients; and marketers assume they must manipulate the consumer. All for the life-or-death stakes of the next quarterly report.

Yet if you've got this book in your hands and are capable of reading these words, then the chances of your ever going to bed hungry, ever lacking a roof over your head, even just lacking the ability to get your kids a proper education or medical attention are virtually nil. The same goes for me.

Except for a random catastrophe completely out of our control, we pretty much know for certain that we are both going to be just fine. So why do we motivate ourselves and everyone else in our lives by acting as if our very survival were in question? The language and logic of business are organized around the survival instinct, even when survival is not in question. This is inefficient, unprofitable, and, perhaps worst of all, depressing.

Instead of relentlessly pursuing survival even after our survival needs are met, we must learn how to do things because they fulfill us— because they are, in a word, fun. Fun is not a distraction from work or a drain on our revenue; it is the very source of both our inspiration and our value. A genuine sense of play ignites our creativity, eases communication, promotes goodwill and engenders loyalty, yet we tend to shun it as detrimental to the seriousness with which we think we need to approach our businesses and careers.

If we can switch our orientation to fun, and see it not as an anarchic threat that needs to be quelled but rather as the core motivator and source of meaning for all human thought and behavior beyond basic survival, we will enable ourselves to reach levels of success that were previously unimaginable. Our very definition of success transcends survivalist notions such as cash reserves, time remaining, or personal safety, into the realms of self-worth, meaning, connection to others, and greater purpose. Plus, it's better business.

In order to do this, however, we must radically reorient ourselves to the current social and business landscapes. We must learn to experience what is happening to us not as the collapse of our values and competencies—or, even worse, as an excuse to abandon them—but rather as their rebirth in an entirely new context. We must come to understand our age for what it is: a renaissance. Once we do, the rest will be easy. We'll have no choice but to discard old models, fears, and extrinsic motivators, and instead start to innovate from the inside out.

In short, what I'll be urging you to do in the following pages is to replace segmentation, repeatability, abstractions, competition, and effort, with integration, originality, foundations, collaboration, and fun. And to do this, all you need to do is rediscover your core passion and competency, and then pursue it relentlessly. It's that simple.

But I'm not supposed to tell you that.

introduction

RENAISSANCE NOW

There is no Next Big Thing. In fact, the more things seem to change, the better opportunity you have to stay the same.

Unfortunately, most of us tend to see change as something that must be kept up with. The never-ending river of culture takes a new twist and all of a sudden we're hiring researchers to conduct focus groups, and anthropologists to decipher the results. A new technology arrives and before we even know what it does, we've hired specialists to integrate it into our workflow.

How many of you remember the urgency with which businesses installed the brand-new Windows 2000 operating platform, only to go back to the more stable Windows 98 as quickly as possible? Newer didn't mean better. I bet you'd be surprised to learn that the International Space Station uses mostly pre-Pentium chips in its on-board computers, and a circa-1993 Windows 3.1 operating system.

And how many businesses invested in online storefronts as soon as the World Wide Web was launched, only to find themselves competing on price, cutting into their own margins, and burning through cash? Upstarts like Pets.com proved better at making ads than selling dog food, and once-profitable retail category killers like Toys 'R' Us ended up killing themselves by venturing into an online space they didn't understand. By focusing on conquering the Internet, these specialty stores also allowed their industry-specific expertise to languish, and offered potential customers of brick-and-mortar locations little if anything that Wal-Mart couldn't provide.

Other businesses respond to change with reactionary fear, which can be just as debilitating. The recording industry has incurred nothing but ill will and poorer sales by digging in their heels and fighting the rise of Napster and other peer-to-peer file exchange systems rather than focusing on the core value of their business: making and distributing music. The emergence of alternative distribution systems could have motivated innovation as easily as it induced paralysis; the industry could have used it as an opportunity to develop better, higher-resolution recordings that can't easily be shared, or to build more accessible downloading interfaces, as Apple did with its groundbreaking iTunes/iPod online music store combination.

Institutions tend to react to the destabilizing force of cultural change with panic and an impulsive need to make sudden, rash moves to one extreme or the other. Whether by being "reinvented" by an outside consultant or by putting up so many defensive barricades that all attention shifts to the periphery, these organizations end up losing sight of their core purpose and vision. In response to unfamiliar demographic patterns, a venerable institution like Judaism hires market researchers/pollsters to figure out how to make itself more appealing to the "MTV generation." Instead of figuring out what Judaism might actually have to offer kids living in a world dominated by MTV, the experts advise aping the styles, language, and ethos of the music station. Meanwhile, faced with pressure from competing clothing firms, the Gap imports a Disney executive with *no experience in clothing* to be its new CEO. On a shifting landscape, companies become mesmerized by the intangible priorities of branding or image, and begin to act as if all business processes were ultimately interchangeable. They are not.

Take the mismatched rivalry between America's two would-be satellite radio providers, Sirius and XM. While Sirius inappropriately applies the generic, out-of-the-box strategies of other businesses to the specific case of a new technology and market, XM got back in the box to reinvent both radio and the business model surrounding it from the inside out.

Although Sirius was first in space, first to IPO, and first to market, it quickly lagged behind its upstart rival, XM. The reasons are clear. While an impatient Sirius made the mistake of farming out its chip design to Lucent spin-off Agere Systems, XM assembled an in-house team of former Motorola engineers, and steamed ahead.[1] Without direct access to, or even knowledge of, their own research and development, Sirius suffered incapacitating production delays. XM, on the other hand, made its technologists central to the business and ended up innovating over and over again. And despite Wall Street's predictions that XM would forever lag Sirius, it actually made it onto the air almost a full year earlier.

XM didn't stop there. It pioneered the SKYfi boombox, MYFi personal receivers, and a variety of new distribution channels for satellite, including commercial jets and Internet streaming. XM's in-house technologists also gave it the ability to make its single best business move to date: a partnership to install XM-capable radios in General Motors and Honda vehicles. Marrying innovative technology development with innovative business strategy, XM CEO Hugh Panero invited the automakers to be part owners of the company, making them stakeholders in creating the success of XM. Panero's willingness to reconfigure XM's billing and accounting departments to mesh seamlessly with GM's (And why not? They're just spreadsheets!) was what ultimately won over the auto giant. Using similar strategies, XM has made deals to pipe its music into Starbucks, and has even convinced Microsoft to embed XM into its new Mediaplayer. Of course, knowing how your technology works makes you much more capable of imagining what your technology can do.

It's no wonder that Panero is at home strategizing for a satellite radio company. It's connected to his core passion and competency. Back in the mid-1990s, the battle-tested veteran of the cable-TV wars[2] was one of the few believers in subscription-based radio.[3]

Contrast this with Sirius, whose succession of CEOs have ap-

proached the underlying proposition of satellite radio with everything
from indifference to contempt. After witnessing his first series of
stumbles, the Sirius board replaced its company founder with Joseph
Clayton, the former president of the infamous Global Crossing. Used
to making waves by earning headlines, Clayton put image first, spending big on everything from a 15-year lease on a suite of offices at
Rockefeller Center[4] to a half-*billion*-dollar deal for Howard Stern (by
contrast, fiscally conservative Panero bought and gutted a warehouse in
a gritty neighborhood in Washington, DC). Bringing back memories
of the profligate dot-com days, the timing and publicity surrounding
the deal also led to charges of insider trading and an investigation by
securities regulators.[5]

Then, as if for no other reason than he had become available, the
board hired Stern's old boss at Viacom, marquee CEO Mel Karmazin.
Among satellite radio's foremost skeptics when he was at Viacom, a
$1.25 million annual salary from Sirius and $30 million more in stock
options[6] turned him seemingly overnight into a true believer.[7]
Reinventing himself as the coolest satellite executive on the block,
Karmazin gave reporters some stridently bullish predictions: He
boasted that his advertising revenue would grow from $1 million in
2004 to $100 million by 2007, and that satellite radio would grow into
a bigger industry than cable and satellite television, combined. Fueled
by hype, Karmazin's conversion earned almost as much ink as Stern's.
"We're making news," explained Sirius's PR department. "XM is buying ads."[8]

While Sirius used its deals to make headlines, XM used them to
help satellite radio realize its potential as a renaissance technology for
audio broadcasting; this meant reinventing the best and forgotten
things about radio in a new context. Panero talked to and hired people
who worked in broadcast radio before it was corporatized and homoge-
nized by Clear Channel and other conglomerates. Following their advice, and catering to their passion and core competency, he gave his DJs
and programmers total control over their choice of music and other
content. Karmazin, meanwhile, programmed his stations by category,
from the top, explaining to the *Wall Street Journal* that broadcasting's

creative side amounted to little more than "arts and crafts."⁹ Panero put
his faith and fate in the hands of a head of programming who pioneered
the artsy FM album format, to begin with, and who promised XM's
DJs, "We're not going to tell you what to play. You're going to tell us."¹⁰

With only a fraction of the subscribers required for the satellite
radio industry to succeed, it's too early to be placing golden wreaths.
But XM has already tripled the subscriber base of Sirius, earning
greater revenue with fewer costs. And it did so by celebrating the technology, industry, and people it was working with. It was native to the
space, populated by believers from the beginning, and not sidetracked
by out-of-the-box concerns.

Generic management just doesn't work anymore. Honestly, if our
chief executive could as easily be from a movie studio as a sneaker manufacturer, how can we take pride in, or even recognize, what's unique or
meaningful about the enterprise to which we're supposed to be dedicating a majority of our waking hours? We can't—which is why for
most people these days, work isn't an awful lot of fun. Our daily tasks
and the long-range strategies we're working toward have become completely untethered from our core values and competencies. It's a symptom of our era, felt across the full spectrum of our highly mediated and
highly marketed culture. Whether at work or play, producing or consuming, there's something missing.

Indeed, as all those depressing French cultural theorists predicted, twenty-first-century society has fragmented beyond our ability
to comprehend it, much less manage it. While our Industrial Age
processes were invented to simplify the once-daunting challenges of
mass production and mass communication, they did so at the price of
an immediate connection with our products and customers. The assembly line brought the many thousands of steps required for building
an automobile into one, simple process. But it also meant that no one
really knew in his bones how the whole process worked. The major
television networks made delivering messages to an entire nation, on
schedule, a snap. But it was really just a way of compensating for the
new distance between producer and consumer; beneath all the
sparkling brand images, a sense of alienation built up.

Now that the television dial has been expanded to a thousand channels, and commercial-zapping digital video recorders are on the rise, mainstream media audiences are hard to find. The Internet has further fragmented the public into affinity groups that shift almost as soon as they can be identified. Meanwhile, the spread of mass production techniques around the world has turned outsourcing of even the most creative and client-related tasks into a standard operating procedure, and almost every product into a commodity. While "demand" seems to be getting so much more varied and complex, what we have to "supply" the world with seems creatively, even spiritually, bankrupt.

Of course, with each new challenge come new experts, new studies, new solutions, and new technologies. Then each of these additions gives an excuse for the cycle to begin anew. But eventually, things get too complex for our hired generic managers to fix. And each overarching solution they do come up with only confuses things more, distancing us, our employees, and our customers or constituents further from whatever it was we thought we were offering them in the first place. Besides, our current situation is too complex to be solved with another temporary patch. We are simply pumping steroids into processes we don't truly believe in, and are hoping we'll have moved on from our current company or organization—or, better, retired—before this shortsighted strategy inevitably catches up with us.

We must face facts. We are living in a world with no discernible mainstream. Trends are mere quivers, while "best practices" and "repeatability" have grown synonymous with boredom and commodification. It's as if creativity and agency had been systematically removed from our lives and work, and replaced with performance metrics and short-term profitability. We work as if our lives depended on it, and feel utterly incapable of rising above our circumstances.

And then, onto this already alienated landscape comes a score of "next big things," from the Web and globalization to one-to-one marketing and nanotechnology, each with its own host of experts and neon-colored books, compelling us to reorganize our entire enterprises around them. We're supposed to hop onboard the next industrial revolution, even if this means trying to convince ourselves that what we really do know about our own fields of expertise is obsolete.

In truth, the only thing that's obsolete is our insistence on undermining our deepest goals by chasing yet another "next big thing." We end up taking dramatic leaps outside of our core competency and become even more vulnerable to the next round of assaults from the "new."

What we haven't taken into account is that the increasing complexity of our age, combined with the newfound interactive capabilities of our employees, customers, and collaborators, has led to a profound shift in our capacity to manage complexity. In fact, we don't have to "manage" complexity at all; we can instead embrace it for the abundance it portends. I maintain that we will succeed in this new reality not by hiring some stranger to reinvent us according to some zany new plan, but by engaging our core competencies. We're not going to grow by clinging to stale past practices, either, but by learning to depend on the intuition and creativity our values inform.

What if, just as a thought experiment for the time being, we approach this crisis moment not as the collapse of our access to innovation, but as its rebirth on an entirely new scale? Could a shift in our perspective beyond an Industrial Age mentality be the first step toward adopting a more appropriate path to innovation? Might our endeavors be more complex than the business plans we use to describe them? What if all this complexity is really just an opportunity to engage with our work and enterprises as living processes? Perhaps we are finally ready for all the creativity, skills, and humanity we sacrificed in the name of efficiency to be reborn in a new context.

History supports us in this view. The most innovative eras in our past, in fact, have come to be regarded as renaissances—literally, the "rebirth" of old ideas and values in a new context. Core values renewed from the inside out. Maybe that's why a renaissance embodies innovation on the grandest scale imaginable. So let's look for a moment at the last great renaissance in order to figure out just what happened, and then think about how to apply its best insights to our current innovation crisis.

Do you remember anything of what you learned about the original Renaissance—the one so big that we capitalize it? What were the main innovations? Well, how about perspective painting? Artists developed the technique of the "vanishing point" and with it the ability to represent three-dimensional scenes on two-dimensional surfaces. In a sense, they were contending with the newfound complexity of their age: people were beginning to see their world in greater dimensionality, and painting had to develop an innovation that rose to this occasion. It's not that flat-painting artists suddenly all became 3D sculptors. No, they incorporated a technology into their work that let them be painters for a new, more complex age. Painters reinvented themselves by becoming more aware of a core premise: that a flat image can represent the depth of our real world.

And why not? Everyone was seeing three dimensions where there had formerly been only two. Although cartographers had suspected the world was round for some time, it wasn't until the Renaissance that anyone actually circumnavigated the whole globe. This changed our relationship to both the planet we live on and the maps we used to describe it. The maps still worked, of course, but they described a plane instead of a sphere. Anyone hoping to navigate a course had to be able to relate a two-dimensional map to the new reality of a three-dimensional planet. Meanwhile, in more popular culture, people stopped thinking of the world as something one falls off, instead seeing it as something that could be encircled—even conquered.

Likewise, calculus—born at the end of the Renaissance—is a mathematical system that allows us to derive one dimension from another. It is a way of describing curves with the language of lines, or spheres with the language of curves. It allows us to understand the relationship between speed and acceleration, as well as work, power, and energy. The leap from arithmetic to calculus was not just a leap in our ability to work with higher-dimensional objects, but a leap in our ability to relate the objects of one dimension to the objects of another. It was a shift in perspective that allowed us to orient ourselves to objects and ideas beyond whatever world we were in. In other words, we didn't have to get out of the box in order to understand what was beyond it;

we could do it from right where we were—using telescopes, micro-scopes, maps, and new math.

The Spenserian sonnet, a new standard form of poetry, brought with it the first use of extended metaphor—itself a way of creating di-mensionality. Instead of just describing a thing or mood, the sonnet used one idea—say, a sunset—as a way of describing another one—like old age. Instead of describing something literally, the sonnet could add another dimension by making an extended comparison.

Perhaps the most profound new perspective came with the reader's newfound ability to have his own view on whatever he read. Gutenberg's invention of movable type and the printing press trans-formed the one-to-one communication of the manuscript into the one-to-many published volume. It was still just one text broadcast to the multitudes, but now it was subject to a multiplicity of individual perspectives. From then on, all people were able to enjoy their own per-spectives on their stories, their news, their religions and their world, and this newfound capacity led to everything from Protestantism and literacy to the Enlightenment and modern democracy. With the Renaissance, ancient Greek or even biblical ideals of humanism and the rights of the individual were reborn on a new scale.

All these examples of Renaissance innovation involve people ex-periencing a very particular shift in their relationship to dimension. Everyone's perspective is different; everyone's perspective matters. Originally, the Renaissance shift was seen as such a threat to existing authority that a new era of centralization was born. Both nation states, as we currently understand them, as well as corporations that would have the ability to operate between these nations, were products of this era. So was national currency, religion, and identity. But this massive centralization and administration of human affairs was less the charac-ter of the Renaissance than a reaction to it: institutions that respected the newfound autonomy of the individual needed to arise.

Understood this way, a renaissance is a moment of reframing. We step out of the frame as it is currently defined and see the whole picture in a new context. We can then play by new rules.

I believe we are currently living through a shift as profound as the original Renaissance. Our equivalents of perspective painting are the holograph and virtual reality, which allow us to experience not only three dimensions, but to move through them in real time. Even more amazingly, if you take a holographic plate and break it into many pieces, each fragment has a faint representation of the entire image. In this new understanding, unlike that of earlier philosophers and scientists who attempted to comprehend a collective organism, every part of a system in some way reflects the whole thing.[11]

We have not only circumnavigated the globe, but also orbited and photographed it from the moon. Thanks to television images of the Earth from space, we can all see the planet on which we live. And thanks to the atomic bomb, we can even conceive of blowing the whole thing up.

Instead of calculus, we have chaos math and fractals—new ways of understanding the relativity of dimension. Zoom in to any portion of a fractal image and you can readily observe its "self-similarity": every detail, in some way, reflects the whole. Meanwhile, chaos theory teaches us that any tiny part of a dynamical system, such as the weather or even the stock market, can be a "high leverage" point causing change throughout. Each part has an influence on the whole.

Where the Renaissance brought the extended metaphor, today we have the online web of hypertext, a universe of metaphors and connections that allows any idea to become linked to any other. And our equivalents of the printing press are the computer and the Internet; we not only can read, but we also can write documents that are available to the rest of the world. Again, any individual can now broadcast his point of view to the rest of the world.

Renaissances are great eras. They're opportunities, as the word "renaissance" implies, for things to be reborn in a new context. They are the springtime—reincarnations when the caterpillar comes back to life but more fully manifesting its core value and purpose as a butterfly. These are rare moments when we have the freedom and capability to redefine entire disciplines, arts, governments, religions, and industries in completely new ways.

Where we've gone so wrong, however, was to use all this increased perspective as a way of stepping out of frame. Just as our kids developed an ironic distance from the media that meant to persuade them, we developed an almost militarist detachment in our efforts to market them back into submission. The more guilty we felt about what we were doing, the further we detached from it, and the more lost we became. So rather than trying to understand the products we made or services we offered, we simply put them in different packages. We managed our brands instead of our products. We innovated by focus group consensus, removing our own creativity from the equation. Then we hired outside consultants to teach us how to "get out of the box," distancing us even further from the satisfaction and orientation to be found at the heart of our endeavors.

In short, the impulse in times like these is to step back from what we're doing and attempt to see the big picture, the long view, or the megatrend. We hire brand gurus and retreat into the woods with top management to "discover" a new reason for being, and end up with a Coke "C2" or a McDonald's "Arch Deluxe." Or we hire new accountants to rejigger our spreadsheets and turn us from an energy company into an Enron. We're convinced the answer is always to think abstractly, and end up solving our problems with generic managerial techniques rather than depending on insights intrinsic to the enterprises in which we're involved.

Instead of seeing renaissance, we see threats that need to be quietly managed, or "big think" ideas that need to be completely incorporated before our competition does. We are drawn away from what we do, and out into the business of business. We begin using the same language and strategies as any of the CEOs spouting off on CNBC, and then wonder why the competitive advantages we used to be able to depend on have withered away. The more complex things get, the more experts we hire. And no matter how much lip service we're giving to innovation, we're simply trying to prevent being run over by what we perceive to be a steamroller of change.

As I see it, we're still trying to coast, using the reductive strategies of the last Renaissance, while resisting the potential for innovation that this one offers us. If anything, the end of the Industrial Age might best be understood as the final chapter of the last Renaissance. Problem is, those innovations have already been exploited about as fully as they can be, and now we're applying them in situations that call for a new kind of innovation—one that works from the inside out, rather than the outside in.

The Renaissance gave rise to great fragmentation. Thinking dimensionally meant thinking abstractly. Understanding ourselves as individuals for the first time was tremendously empowering, but also isolating. It led us to institutionalize competition for the first time, and to perceive of the world as a rather ruthless marketplace. It's when we began mining natural resources for energy, centralizing our monetary policies, and formally establishing the division of labor.

For what was "reborn" in the original Renaissance were the high ideals of the ancient Greeks. The Renaissance innovations in the arts and sciences allowed some very old, long-suppressed idealism to rise back to the surface. The Greeks were the first true abstract thinkers, capable of applying logic to problems. They valued the intellect above all else, and saw the problems of our world as being errors in design. As long as human inventions failed to meet up to their abstract ideals, they would be destined to fail.

If we are enjoying another renaissance today, then which long-buried ideas will be reborn? Probably the ones that the original Renaissance suppressed: holism, feminism, and grounded creativity. The Renaissance was based so completely on logic and observable science, that people lost confidence in intuition and instinct.[12] So we turned to machines for support, security, and reinforcement. We used them to nullify our doubt. As those machines—eventually computers—failed to reckon with the extraordinary complexity of our age, the very modes of thinking they were built to subdue were again free to resurface.

So far, these repressed strains of thought and behavior have been emerging in crude and immature forms—mostly in the spiritual and environmental movements, and often as conspiracy theory and paranoia. But what if they were simply unrecognized, stray elements of a more culturally widespread creative resurgence?

If the original Renaissance invented the individual, then this one can reinvent the collective. In fact, the twentieth century could be viewed as a series of failed experiments in collectivism—from corporatization to communism—as our society has attempted to reorganize itself into a group.

These efforts were doomed to fail, but not because people couldn't organize themselves into groups. It's because the basis on which they were organizing was so one-dimensional. These top-down, regimented forms of group cohesion could not cope with the complexity of real human beings interacting with one another. Our newfound ability to embrace more complex dynamics changes all this. Instead of trying to get everyone to conform to a simple set of commands, a great manager, organizer, or leader strives instead to create an environment or provide the tools through which people naturally cooperate. The failed candidacy but successful campaign of Howard Dean, which utilized the Internet for a bottom-up collective action, represents one such early attempt at just this.

By understanding collective action less as a directed activity and more as an emergent phenomenon,[13] companies need no longer see an employee's personal interests and passions as interruptive to the work process, but as contributive. Firms can begin to see their competitors as collaborators capable of benefiting from each other's areas of expertise. AT&T's final solution to the wireless telephone conundrum was to work with Sprint's more fleshed-out network, rather than continuing to invest in a technological redundancy. Cooperation doesn't mean a spate of mergers and acquisitions, which tend to end up in reduced profits and innovation, but a more deliberate exploration of complementary skills and mutual interests. As Einstein sought to prove, everything is relative to everything else. It's all connected.

Of course, the idea that we're approaching a renaissance in which everything is connected to everything else can seem pretty daunting. Where to begin? It seems like there's a huge hurdle to leap or chasm to cross from one kind of thinking to another. (Quick! Hire more consultants!) Luckily, that's not the case.

The fact that everything is connected—that your career, ethics, shareholders, meaning, and passion are all part of the same thing—means you can start quite small. The rest will happen naturally. A tiny change made in your marketing strategy will trickle up and out to the rest of the company. British Petroleum's rebranding as "Beyond Petroleum" not only changed its public image; it also forced the company to live up to a new ethic. It made itself accountable. Becoming honest with your employees leads to honesty with your customers and shareholders. The walls dividing one set of behaviors from another no longer stand. Wal-Mart cannot be kind to its customers while being cruel to its employees—many of whom are the very same people. You can start anywhere you like; for if you do something, anything for real, it will take over your whole organization.

This is at once the most reassuring and intimidating quality of our age. Everything you do matters.

Our renaissance may be an opportunity to invigorate instinct and intuition but, contrary to popular belief, we are not born with these qualities—at least not in a useful form. If anything, the potential for innovation is dependent not on casting off our core competencies, but on seeing beyond the reductive models and disparaging contexts through which we understand our true capabilities. A renaissance calls not for newbies, but for experts.

You knew there would be a catch: experience counts. You can't play unless you've done the work to become a master.

Yes, a renaissance may be the quintessential "out of the box" experience. It is that sudden "aha" at pulling away from a picture long enough to see the frame around it. It's that moment in a Shakespeare play when the characters actually say out loud, "It feels as if we are characters in a play." But you can't seize this moment of innovative possibilities through more abstraction. You must experience your situation from beyond its normal context only to go back in again. As Alan Watts once said about using psychedelic drugs, "Once you get the message, hang up the phone."

Even if the original Renaissance encouraged looking at things abstractly, finding systems of logic to replace the unpredictability of emotion, and reducing the complexity of huge populations to manageable mass personalities, that doesn't mean ours should. Besides, the creativity unleashed by the original Renaissance, the multiplicity of perspectives, and the force of raw logic were, in their time, extremely destabilizing influences. Reason, observation, and science challenged the authority of the church and the superstitions that supported it. People got so good at astronomy, sailing, and mathematics that their results superseded all those faulty systems that had outlived their usefulness.

Learning what actually makes your business or organization work, and what makes it valuable to the world at large, is a similarly radical act on today's confused and abstract landscape. In a world where CEOs have become interchangeable, someone who actually understands his business from the inside out is a rarity! Even a threat.

Unfortunately, the business and career practices we invest in today fly in the face of our core competencies and values. Our obsession with focus groups does not mean we really care how people will respond to our products; it bespeaks a terrible disconnection between us and our own development process. True enough, someone who has run a car company by focus group may as well run a furniture company the same uncreative way. Their use in fashion or the arts (as, for example, when MTV execs test-market a new music style) are even more preposterous. What are producers and designers being paid for if not their creative capacity?

It should come as good news that techniques such as these have outlived their usefulness for all of us—whether we run a company, work for one, or work for ourselves. We are all being called upon to engage creatively once again. When everyone is developing their product line through focus groups, then how can one company distinguish itself from any other? A renewed reliance on our own expertise actually gives us the opportunity to differentiate our own work from all the crap that's out there.

A "renaissance perspective" gives us the momentary distance we need in order to see how our entrenched methods not only prevent us from recognizing best practices but also lead us to feel dissatisfied in our professions. We lose touch with whatever it may have been that led us into our chosen fields in the first place. It certainly wasn't to be bored, anxious, or miserable. But to adopt a genuinely creative—dare we say it, "playful"—approach to one's work is understood in today's confused environment as a form of distracting eccentricity and a threat to efficiency. We must change this view. We must come to recognize that real play is hard work and the key to innovation from the inside out.

Children have an innate mastery of business as play that we would do well to emulate, for it is much more compatible with the spirit of renaissance fueling this century. Many of us are able to hang on to the kids' perspective for quite a while. The ever-lengthening childhood of Americans, though a strain on parents, can even be understood as a sign of cultural development, since evolutionary theory shows us that extended childhoods tend to indicate a more advanced species.

Still, however long we might be able to maintain the player's perspective on life, invariably there's a moment in adulthood when we realize that the number in the checkbook matters. More often than not, that's precisely the moment when we could have finally chosen to stop worrying about it. Because once you're doing well enough at writing, thinking, painting, shoemaking, or accounting to transcend a hand-to-mouth existence, all of a sudden you have a nest egg to preserve and protect. The momentary celebration of having "made it" is quickly replaced by the urgency of what to *do* about it. Security is just another way of saying survival.

This is a dangerous moment for both individuals and businesses. It's the moment a sculptor spends two hours a day comparing mutual funds instead of sculpting. It's the moment a restaurateur decides he must learn how to franchise, even though his passion is crepes. It's the moment that an already wealthy clothing designer is convinced that his well-known fashions are more valuable as a means of borrowing money from the public (on the stock exchange) than expressing himself on the runway. It's the moment your company begins answering more to its faceless shareholders than anybody else.

For a rare few, who honestly find the business of their industries more fulfilling than the industry itself, this is fine. We may never know if Martha Stewart was a stockbroker with a catering brand or a caterer with an IPO. For the majority, however, a measure of success is what unnecessarily yanks us from whatever field on which we're playing into the much crueler reality of self-preservation. We are shifted away from our source of joy—and our true area of expertise—into an arena designed from the get-go to intimidate us into submission. So we succumb to instantaneous stock quotes and nine-dollar trades geared to stimulate an obsessive-compulsive relationship to the moment-to-moment fluctuations of our net worth. We surrender to the profit-based ethos of the corporations in which we're ensconced, losing track of whatever it may have been that attracted us to our chosen fields in the first place. We have, quite literally, sold out.

We can begin the rehabilitation of our creative capacity by consistently reminding ourselves that with just a little faith and determination, we will be just fine. Our lives and those of our families are not in jeopardy. Instead of focusing on what we still lack, we must take stock of what we already do have, in terms of resources, abilities, and pure will. We should immerse ourselves in the more playful and fulfilling aspects of our jobs and activities so that the apparent stakes give way to the moment-to-moment experience of engaging mindfully and spiritedly in our chosen fields. We need to remember why we chose them, in the first place. Once we do that, we are free to rise above the game board of business, and to see the principles underlying all this human motion and effort. It's an experience akin to what Michael Jordan describes happening to him when he's "in the groove" on the court: everything slows down, and he becomes aware of decisions everyone else is going to make before they make them.

This sensibility is readily available to anyone who can give up the game long enough to become its master. By learning to embrace the fun-loving, creativity-valuing stance of a renaissance perspective, we can lift our companies, organizations, schools, churches, and even ourselves and our families—whatever their current status—out of the struggle for survival and into the realm of play.

Sure, it's a bit easier in some career paths than others. As a writer and thinker, I've been allowed to pursue fun in one way or another for the past 20 years. But I wasn't doing this consciously in my own choices of how to work as much as in the way I chose my subjects. I sought out people, and subcultures, who were having the most fun. For they, I figured, in addition to being fun to hang out with, must be on to something. My pursuit of the world's most playful people brought me, long before my peers, to the hackers and freaks who developed the personal computer, the Internet, and virtual reality. By the late 1980s, I was writing articles and book proposals about cyberspace and hypertext, buoyed by the passion of the people I was encountering. Then I followed gamers, media activists, electronic music distributors, wireless enthusiasts—whoever was having the best time.

Article after article, book after book, I ended up "scooping" a scene or technology that would eventually hit the front page of the Business section. It had nothing to do with my prescience or trend forecasting—I'm not that smart—but rather my simple determination to spend time with and then write about people who were having fun.

That didn't stop the business media or the anxious CEOs of a few dozen Fortune 500 companies from deciding that I was an able futurist and media business guru, capable of taking them safely into the digital age and beyond. My track record predicting several "next big things" earned me profiles in periodicals from *Harper's* to the *New York Times;* regular seats on shows from CNBC's *Power Lunch* to *Politically Incorrect;* hundreds of magazine pieces; and, most lucrative and educational, regular speaking and consulting engagements.

I had become an unlikely business guru. And the more I spoke to corporate audiences, the more I realized I was sharing a single message. All of my consults came down to helping my clients discover that we weren't in a terrible crisis at all, but in the midst of a renaissance! My job became to convince them of the possibility for deep fun at the core of their industry, product, processes, or marketing. Even in the heady days of the dot-com boom, most businesses were still being guided by fear. (I remember telling one audience of real estate executives that as I walked among them in the lobby, I could quite literally "smell" their fear.) Slowly but surely, I would show my audiences how they could foster their own ability, desire, and curiosity to play with the rules in their industries, engage with the ideas behind them, and then retool them, instead of working within the unyielding structure of a bottom-line mentality. I reminded them of what they did, why they chose to do it in the first place, and how to be happy about it.

So that's largely what we'll do together through this book.

We've already begun the hardest part: accepting the possibility of a new renaissance, and recontextualizing our current creative dearth as the beginning of a new innovative age. The rest is simply proving to ourselves that genuine creativity is a result not of out-of-the-box thinking, but of true expertise.

We'll look at the opportunities afforded by the networked reality, and how the interactive age is not about putting old businesses or business models online, but about enabling and energizing the resurgence of the collective, social activities that were lost to the fragmentation of the Industrial Age. Then we'll look at the playful spirit that this collaborative mind-set encourages, as well as how to use it as fuel for creative exploration rather than having it be a cause of distraction.

This will lead us to where the barriers to creativity currently exist—and why they do. Sadly, the chief barrier tends to have less to do with any external obstacle or competition than with our own reluctance to engage in our own enterprises. We can only reinvent our industries from the bottom up if we understand them from the inside out. And this is where we get to the heart of the renaissance lesson: innovation is not extrinsic to your work, but the most intrinsic thing about it. *Get Back in the Box* is a call to reinvent yourself and your business, not based on some abstract plan but rather through the natural expression of your core competency. We'll look at some businesses and organizations that have successfully accomplished this, as well as some that thought they were doing this, but weren't.

We'll see how reinvention on this scale requires a willingness to challenge and even rewrite the most accepted tenets underlying our industries, and to invite our employees and even our customers to engage in that process with us. This is the real meaning of "open source," and the surest path to a sustained culture of innovation.

Finally, we'll look at today's artificially fragmented landscape of customers, employees, and shareholders, and how this false division leads to an "us and them" animosity. By seeing all of them, and ourselves, as part of the very same system, or even community, we break through this unnecessarily adversarial relationship. We even start to wonder how our enterprises might actually solve real problems rather than trying to "create need" for our services. Answering real needs becomes the simple but astonishingly effective solution to almost every business challenge in this seemingly complex era.

After that, just for fun, we'll look at an updated profile of the Renaissance Man, or Renaissance Person, and how the fifteenth-century's notion of an independently functioning, self-sufficient super-man isn't just obsolete in today's renaissance; he'd be a terrible and unsatisfied businessman. We'll meet a few of the most innovative players of this emerging era, people who have transcended their fear and transformed their expertise into what can only be considered new forms of wizardry. All because they had the courage to get back in the box.

Okay, now: down the hatch.

chapter one

THE NATURE OF
TECHNOLOGY

Yes, the Internet changed the world; but no, not in the way most people think.

Truth is, most people—especially people in business—still don't get the Internet. They tend to think of all our computers and networks as an extension of the industrialization and automation of the workplace and market, when they are actually the very opposite. They restore new life and unpredictability to pretty much anything they touch. That's because these technologies are not so important for any particular thing they can do, but for how they change our perspective on everything else.

To orient to the new interactive landscape of culture, commerce, and even consciousness, you don't have to understand how any single piece of technology works. But you do have to understand how the proliferation of all this stuff has worked to change the way people relate to everything from television and brands to business and, most of all, one another. The Internet is not a technological or even a media phenomenon: it is a social phenomenon. And in this sense, interactivity has changed everything.

Part of the reason why this is so hard to get is that most of us still think of technology and media less as ways of empowering people than as a way of controlling them. We invented technology, after all, as a way of defeating the rhythms of nature. Fire allows us to live in regions where the seasons would otherwise prevent us. Electric lights permit us to defeat the darkness of sundown. Airplanes let us cross 10 time zones in as many hours. We have alcohol and Ambien to defeat our natural sleep cycle, stimulants from caffeine to amphetamines to enforce our waking hours, and Prozac to adjust our emotional cycle to a life spent so disconnected from the circadian rhythm.

Of course, just as the use of drugs has diminishing returns, so does the use of technology to still the ebb and flow of nature. Unintended consequences, like side effects, tend to reinforce one another until we end up with a new set of circumstances as daunting as the one we were trying to control in the first place. But we hang on as long as we believe in the plan, and that there's an end to suffering in sight.

As long as each new technology we develop can serve to increase centralized authority over the unruly periphery, this can go on forever. The tremendous foundries required to produce metal canons, for example, kept the weapons of warfare in the hands of nation states. The complex and expensive presses required to print money, it is hoped, prevent anyone other than a central bank from issuing currency.

But somewhere along the way, many of the best new technologies found their way from the center to the edges. That's when the disconnected world of Ford and Sloan and the managed population changed into the connected world of Jobs and Gates and the new interactive culture they helped to spawn.

INDUSTRIAL OLD AGE

E ven if we wanted to avoid the new renaissance, we wouldn't stand a chance. For the big news is that we really have arrived at the end of the Industrial Age. It's just over. No matter what set of metrics we use to measure them, mass production, mass media, and mass marketing are all in decline. This is because the basic premise of the Industrial Age—that technology can or even should be used to reduce complexity and repress natural, emergent patterns—is obsolete.

Of course, we only developed such notions about technology be-cause—for a long time, anyway—they worked. Well. The Industrial Age was made possible, first and foremost, by the ability to find and ex-ploit new forms of energy and technology, usually just in the nick of time. Empires are subject to the law of diminishing returns, and can continue to expand only until the people or places they hope to domi-nate become too expensive to control. The Roman Empire, like that of Ancient Egypt, Mesopotamia, and even the Mayans, collapsed because the return on investment for foreign conquests declined, and the amount of effort required to keep their populations in line wasn't worth the price.[1] What made industrial society different—at least for a while—was our ability to find new energy sources when we needed them.

In fact, energy tells the story of the rise and impending fall of the industrial model. Before anyone knew to drill for fossil fuels, people burned wood for heat. In the process, they depleted many of the world's old-growth forests by as early as the thirteenth century. That's when Europeans turned to coal. Ironically, perhaps, it was the tremendous energy required to suck water out of mineshafts that inspired inventors like Thomas Savery and Samuel Newcomen to develop the steam en-gine.

Initially, however, they saw no role for this contraption in agricul-ture or industry, where the human body was still the primary energy source. Animals were occasionally used as beasts of burden, but they actually required more food than their human counterparts, as well as more direction. That's why, sadly, slave energy was exploited to build most of Egypt, Rome, and the early American empires: slaves were the most efficient form of energy available. Colonialism was, at its heart, a way of securing more of these human energy resources, even if it meant exploiting them from afar.

When slavery became untenable in the 1800s to Western society, it probably felt something like an energy crisis; its repercussions even

led to the Civil War. A reconfigured steam engine rose to this new occasion, accomplishing with coal what used to be done with indentured
muscle, and what we now call the Industrial Revolution began.[2] Coal
allowed for the mechanized factory, the locomotive, and, perhaps most
importantly, the steamships. With coal-powered boats, newly industrialized Western nations—predominantly England—were capable of
distributing their manufactured goods to their colonies, as well as enforcing military superiority and the trade policies that go along with it.
Legislation required the colonies in India to use mechanized looms, for
example, so that the ready availability of human labor in that region
could not compete with England's mechanical replacements.

The lesson of the Industrial Age, so far, seemed to be that whoever could monopolize energy resources would gain power. But this
lesson was overlearned. Nations and businesses were soon contorting
themselves in order to maximize on this principle.

It was the diminishing supply of whales, whose oil was used for
lighting and lubricant, that led to the invention of the oil well. Natural
gas and, eventually, electricity may have surpassed oil's use as a fuel for
light, but oil remained the primary energy source for engine fuel, leading to the development of the automobile, aeronautics, global travel,
and even the suburbs. The oil industry found uses for its precious resource in everything from pesticides and plastics to nylon and netting.
Accustomed from the coal era to serving as its own fuel source,
America tapped its underground reserves, poking and prodding the
continent's crust until John D. Rockefeller's Standard Oil controlled,
by some accounts, over 90 percent of the world's oil business.[3]

But just as Victorian England used coal power to dominate global
trade with rather oppressive military policies, Rockefeller used his monopoly on oil to introduce a set of unprecedented business strategies.
Predatory price-cutting strategies, kickbacks, takeovers, and industrial
espionage soon became the industry standard.

As the industrialized nations, such as the United States, come to
depend increasingly on oil, the techniques they use to maintain control
over those supplies become increasingly strained. International trade

and monetary policies are tilted to enforce free trade of the commodities we need—like oil, which must always go to the highest bidder—while protecting the ones we sell, such as intellectual property.

The economics of the Industrial Age, from Queen Victoria to Halliburton, have been predicated on the control and exploitation of natural resources. Industrial economies depend on energy monopoly, as well as some measure of repression. Nations whose chief export is oil have no incentive to educate their populations to develop skills, and those that control oil fields have strong incentives to quell competitive markets and the wealth they create.

Meanwhile, the ability of industrialized nations to maintain a favorable trade balance with those nations from which they are purchasing their energy grows increasingly difficult, particularly as more nations, such as China and India, begin to compete for the same barrels of fuel. As of this writing, energy imports account for a full 27 percent of the current U.S. trade deficit.[4] But that doesn't stop us from trying to keep this commodity-driven energy scheme in place by any means necessary.

It's no wonder. Everything from our automotive industry and land management to urban planning and foreign policy was based, in part, on generating demand for a commodity we thought we had in abundance and were looking to sell. And now that we are committed to using this fuel, we don't have any. Global discovery of oil peaked in 1964, and has declined since then. Current estimates on peak extraction vary between 2005 and 2020, depending on how much faith you have in new extraction technologies, but no one doubts that there are limits to the quantity of usable oil available to us.[5] Going to war over the remaining oil fields really wouldn't make much of a difference—it would just use them up faster.

Transition from oil to renewable energy sources such as solar, wind, geothermal, or the yet-to-be-imagined may be well within our reach, but would require as big a conceptual leap as the move from slavery to coal. Back in the 1800s, for example, incapable of imagining the modern extraction and exploitation of oil, leading British economists predicted dire consequences associated with the exhaustion of coal resources.[6] So just because we can't yet envision our way out of the energy crisis doesn't mean we have to revert to Shaker-era technology.

The important thing to understand, here, is the assbackwardness of all this. It's not an energy crisis at all, but a crisis of design and intent. The oil peak may mean the end of the Industrial Age as we know it. And while we might have the ability to fight on, dig deeper, and find yet another nonrenewable, polluting, and geopolitically destabilizing energy resource to depend on, the greater opportunity is to abandon the energy model we have been using. It no longer fits the reality in which we are living.

It's something we see a lot, these days: Systems are set in place for one set of priorities that are completely inappropriate for the next. But we come to accept them as given circumstances, and find ourselves utterly incapable of moving beyond them. Instead, we contort ourselves and our priorities to serve obsolete institutions, surrendering our ethics along with our creativity. Our "out of the box" thinking just gives us new tactics to extend the crisis (great ideas like taking the dollar off the gold standard to fix trade imbalances, or getting the World Bank to reclassify energy commodities). But these are just clever ways to avoid confronting on-the-ground reality and redesigning things from the inside out.

We think the rules are preexisting conditions set in stone, when they are actually of our own making. That's why it's so important that we stop struggling to rationalize and perpetuate them and instead review how they came into being and recognize the ways in which they no longer work.

MASS PRODUCTION, MEDIA, AND MARKETING

The most problematic legacy of the Industrial Age is not the machine itself, but the way we model and organize the rest of human behavior around it. Mass production, mass media, and mass marketing are all based on the premise that human beings can fall into place as cogs in highly mechanized systems and then behave with great predictability. Efficiency—of production, transportation, and transaction—becomes the highest priority. Over the past century, this strategy has succeeded in growing some of the largest and most profitable businesses the world has ever seen. But it may have reached it limits. Making matters worse, most of the so-called alternatives to Industrial Age thinking are really just extensions of it, albeit framed in new language. What we call "innovation" really isn't innovative at all; it's usually just another way of revving up, lubricating, or fueling the machine.

It's no wonder the mechanical model has come to dominate our understanding of business and human behavior. It has been the centerpiece of our thinking and culture since the Victorian era, when London's iron and glass architectural wonder, the Crystal Palace, was erected to house the 1851 "Great Exhibition of the Works of Industry of All Nations." This prototype of all "world's fairs" was intended to introduce the British public to the great benefits of the Industrial Revolution: the new products emerging from factories in Britain's many colonies. The fair was an early pitch for mass-produced goods.[7] What no one was expecting, however, was that these wonderful steam engines, cotton looms, telegraphy systems, and mechanical printing presses would prove to be the most popular exhibits,[8] and the new sensation of the age.

This cultural fascination for everything mechanical, combined with the massive efficiencies they enabled, was responsible for the widespread acceptance of the theories of the first great industrialists, such as F.W. Taylor and, later, Henry Ford. Taylor's 1911 work, *The Principles of Scientific Management*, focused executives on measurable quantities of seconds, units, and people. Coining the term "time study," Taylor used "stopwatch management" to gauge workers' efficiency at every stage of their tasks. He developed specific shovels for different materials, so that workers could dig and sort more efficiently. Like many of today's shareholder reports, successes were measured mainly in numbers of employees eliminated.[9] The only "human" factor in his business ideology was the notion of incentives. He believed that workers would cooperate better if they knew that better output meant higher wages. Everything would be perceived of as fair because it was all written down. Implicit in his system was the idea that organizations should be hierarchical, with management directing the factory floor through abstract systems of rules and impersonal relationships.

Fordism, named for assembly-line enthusiast Henry Ford, took the mechanical model a step further.[10] Workers were now to be seen as stationary moving parts within the factory machine, their objects of labor brought to them automatically by conveyor belt, and then shuttled off to another worker for the next step of assembly. Instead of one man assembling an entire chassis by himself—a process that took about 12 hours—a mechanized sequential labor force could do it in 93 minutes. People working in a completely coordinated fashion could be as finely tuned as the engines they were building. With the benefit of today's perspective, Ford's methodology can be understood as intrinsically dehumanizing. But, at the time, his determination to develop a strong separation between the conception and execution—management and labor—led to efficiencies and profit previously unimaginable.

Still, the disconnections inherent in industrialized culture extended beyond the division between management and labor to include the distance between consumer and producer. Consumers were used to purchasing goods from the people who actually made them. There had always been the face of the neighborhood chandler, baker, or cobbler behind the candles, bread, or shoes people bought. The rise of factory-made products and a rail system to transport them meant that consumers no longer knew exactly where their goods came from or, more importantly, the people who made them. The "brand" emerged to serve that function, to put a face on the oats, beverages, and automobiles we bought, thus elevating them from commodities to icons.

Mass media, most notably television, was developed to help stimulate the new mass market and create a sense of trust between people and the brands that were bidding for their attention. Marketing through media also became a kind of science, ruled by the same principles as the factory floor. Everything from spokesmodels to theme songs were tested on samples of potential consumers for their efficacy in eliciting a positive response.

This made us all, in one sense, parts of the machine. Goods were developed by an industrialist, manufactured in the factory, shipped via rail or interstate highway, and then sold to consumers who were prodded by commercial television.

The scores of manufacturing management, and marketing theories to emerge since then have all been geared toward making one part or another of this machine work more efficiently. No matter how humanistic in their wording, or how focused on giving people what they *really* want or need, these techniques are only "creative" in their ability to tweak the great engine of commerce. They all come down to manufacturing, shipping, and selling more stuff for less money and in less time. That's why, inevitably, Industrial Age processes hit a wall.

Efficiencies tend to diminish. Although new insights into manufacturing, marketing, and media have raised the Real GDP per capita in the United States from $5,301 to $27,331 (measured in 1990 dollars) between 1913 and 1998,[11] the vast majority of these increases are a result of doing things more efficiently, not necessarily more creatively.

Take legendary General Motors CEO Alfred Sloan, arguably the first celebrity CEO. His creative leap was simply to offer a wider range of products than Henry Ford, who believed he could produce the single automobile that was right for every American. Sloan's GM would acquire a number of different car companies, integrate their operations, and develop standardized car parts that could be used in any number of different brands. He used consumer research and complex mathematical modeling to predict the number of each brand of car that it should produce. Sloan's hallmark was an emphasis on what he called "decentralization," but his ideas would look to the contemporary manager like more command and control. Each unit of the corporation, division within it, and employee was considered capable of thought and feedback. So were consumers. But this feedback was all sent back to the top for "coordination," and valued only for its ability to improve the immediate rate of return. If there was anything truly unique in Sloan's thinking, it was applying the Industrial Age model not merely to supply, but to demand.

Once demand has been maximized, the only way for companies working in this way to improve returns is to find untapped efficiencies. Businesses that have already perfected their manufacturing processes by minimizing the need for labor have no choice but to further cut costs by sending overseas what work remains. This is no evil, in itself; no matter what protectionist politicians claim, global trade has proven itself beneficial to both parties, even if one country has greater competency in producing all the goods or services being traded.[12] Though while trade may be a positive-sum game economically, something is still lost in the translation: expertise.

Products are designed in San Francisco and then assembled in Brazil from parts manufactured in Singapore. Ads are developed in Chicago for customers in New York, who then depend on customer service reps working via computer from Bangalore. It's a miraculous feat of coordination and a testament to global cooperation. Still, it was not born out necessity or even an ethos of decentralization, but an unwavering drive toward pure efficiency.

Now I'm the last person to quote from the business lexicon of my grandfather, an immigrant fabric dealer, but there is something to be said for working your way up from the bottom: quite literally "starting with a broom in the stockroom," as he'd put it, and getting a sense of the entire enterprise. While a fragmented, decentralized organization may be able to benefit from the expertise of its highly diverse and scattered employees, the real opportunities for feedback of ideas are limited to an email here or there. And the assembly-line workers of Singapore are much less likely to present management with their good ideas when they don't even live in the same society in which the objects they are making are used—if they even know what they are. The reasons I'd argue not to ship your business overseas have nothing to do with protectionism or even politics. There's no need to levy a tax on outsourcing; one is already being paid in the form of lost creativity and fun. Really, a good enough reason to refuse outsourcing is that you'll miss the smell of the factory floor on your way up to your office. It's your business, after all.

Of course, if the work itself is thought of as "dirty work," then perhaps there's some rationale for shipping it as far from corporate headquarters as possible. But by the pure logic of efficiency, a corporate executive might as well job out all of his own baby's child care, since a babysitter could be secured for a fraction of what the executive could make on the job. (Changing one's own child's diapers is economically unsound.)

Likewise, by removing ourselves from our industries, we disconnect ourselves from the very source of true innovation. After a decade or so, no one remembers the entirety of the business model, much less the production cycle. Our firms become more like holding companies—in the business of business rather than in a business, themselves. Then we really are out of our sweet spot, and producing by spreadsheet. Reduced to the game of maximizing efficiency, company after company is robbed of any core competency or competitive advantage (or even just mystery and magic). With creativity no longer a viable path toward future growth, the only way to expand is through acquisition.

SELLING OUT

That's why there's no better gauge of the decline of an industry than a sudden spate of mergers and acquisitions. A period of innovation leads to a crowded field of players, who then acquire one another. The historical gluts of car, paper, and steel companies, agriculture, television networks, and Internet startups were each corrected by periods of merger and acquisition.[13] An all-time peak in mergers and acquisitions of $1.7 trillion, a figure equivalent to about 15 percent of the total U.S. GDP, occurred in early 2000—just four months before the dotcom bubble burst.[14]

Now, it appears, merger and acquisition are the only ways we know how to grow, anymore. And despite the axiom, bigger is not always better. According to a recent Booze Allen Hamilton study,[15] more than 50 percent of all mergers fall short of their stated objectives. Mergers tend to destroy value more than they create it.[16] To those in the know,[17] America Online's acquisition of Time Warner marked the end of the Internet company's growth potential. Indeed, subscription rates had actually peaked months before AOL cashed in its highly valued new media stock for Time Warner's temporarily depressed shares. Without a new creative strategy, AOL had nowhere left to go, so it cashed in its chips for a *real* set of assets.

The successive acquisitions in the Time Warner saga demonstrate how detrimental merging for the sake of merging can be. The "synergies" inherent in Time Warner's takeover of CNN, for example, only succeeded in removing the maverick, if hotheaded, Ted Turner from his flagship media property. The personality of the network vanished along with him, and to this day the programming on CNN is more the result of marketing surveys than personal vision.

AOL's purchase of Time Warner also led to a spreadsheet-driven decimation of the magazine division, Time Inc., once considered the crown jewel of the magazine industry.[18] Buyout offers were submitted to close to 1,000 Time Inc. employees in just the first round of "consolidations," leading over half the company's famed stable of editors-at-large to quit.[19] My own friends on the writing and editorial staffs of *Time, People, In Style,* and *Entertainment Weekly,* as well as a great majority of journalists on panels at union and guild events, began complaining that the atmosphere at their formerly revered publications had changed palpably. Story selection and other decision-making tasks had been taken away from the editors who traditionally handled them, and moved much higher up the publishing ladder—out of their sight, and presumably within range of the advertising division. Meanwhile, in an effort to cut costs, AOL made unpopular gaffs such as removing all water coolers and dismissing the entire mailroom staff, resulting in thirsty, disgruntled employees attempting to do their jobs amidst administrative chaos. Even without buyout packages, many writers and editors left *Time, People,* and *Sports Illustrated* for smaller publications such as *U.S. News & World Report, U.S. Weekly,* and *Smithsonian,* where they felt they could enjoy more autonomy.

Within just a few years, even the mainstream media became aware of the symptoms of death by merger. In February of 2005, the *New York Times* used its editorial page to chide Hewlett-Packard for its ill-fated $19 billion 2002 takeover of Compaq.[20] Had the paper questioned the deal three years earlier, fewer investors may have been taken in by HP's hubris in acquiring more than it could handle. Instead of the combined company becoming a competitor to Dell, as hoped, the entire deal resulted in a write-down, and the canning of flamboyant but ineffective CEO, Carly Fiorina. Likewise, Qwest Communications' well-publicized but ill-fated $56 billion acquisition of U.S. West in 1999 resulted in a company that, six years later, remains $19 billion in the red and apparently hungry for more acquisitions.

The *New York Times* now scolds companies like these for allowing mergers to take them out of the box. "The best thing Hewlett could do," *Times* editors remarked, "would be to get rid of the bells and whistles Ms. Fiorina acquired, and focus on its core—and enormously profitable—business: printers and cartridges."[21]

The other almost certain path away from core competency is to go public, which is really just another way of being acquired. A newly listed company is no longer growing organically, on its own steam, but extrinsically, on the expectations of others. Management is no longer responsible simply to employees and customers, but to shareholders. In short, the business has been sold; management's new role is to maximize short-term share value, as the metrics of Wall Street replace the original values of the company. An industry's former experts end up taking direction from investors with little or no knowledge of the field into which they've invested, who use their positions to impose often inappropriate one-size-fits-all management theories.

Mergers, acquisitions, and public offerings account for a significant proportion of economic activity in media, industry, pharmaceuticals, manufacturing, and even natural resources (in 1995, before the boom and bust, the value of mergers and acquisitions already equaled 5 percent of the GDP, and was equivalent to 48 percent of nonresidential gross investment).[22] Sure, this makes money for the brokerage houses. But it also indicates our inability to innovate in ways intrinsic to the businesses themselves, substituting new columns on the balance sheet and onetime tax losses for new growth. The mergers themselves further disconnect the on-the-ground workforce from management, who are now charged with running companies in industries at best tangential to their own areas of expertise.

INDUCING CONSUMPTION

As businesses and individuals lose track of their core passion and competencies, they tend also to lose their grasp on whatever made them unique. When all laundry detergents can deliver on the same basic promise of cleaning your clothes for pretty much the same price, they may as well be commodities. The only thing differentiating any of them is their marketing.

This is why brands ended up taking on a value of their own—beyond the product attributes they may have originally represented. The only thing distinguishing one box of cereal from another of the same type is the character on the outside. So companies turn themselves upside down, and put themselves at the mercy of their marketing departments or, worse, outside advertising agencies. The focus on the outside of the box has disconnected too many businesses from what they've got inside.

Back in the 1950s, a product might have had a very particular relationship with its brand, that brand might have had a particular relationship with a show, and a show might have had a corresponding relationship with its viewer. But the growth and subsequent fragmentation of the mediaspace, as well as the markets that media means to communicate with, have made that all but impossible. Everything became disconnected. But this only happened over time.

Advertising and the media it originally sponsored could well be credited with fueling America's great postwar boom. Television shaped the consumer class—initially the wives of GIs who had returned to find factory jobs—and created customers for all those products being churned out. Soap operas turned national detergent brands into cherished household staples, while family comedies and dramas paved the way for suburban living. We bought the idea that "what's good for General Motors is good for the USA," but we didn't realize that our new roles as consumers would also tend to be isolating.

A personal example: When I was a child, we lived in a middle-class urban neighborhood. There was one barbecue pit at the end of the block that was fired up each Friday evening and shared by everyone in a weekend-long barbecue party, which I remember to this day. As my father got better jobs, we moved out to the suburbs, where everyone could have their own grills in their individual backyards. Now, instead of barbecuing with the Joneses, we were barbecuing against them—or at least apart from them, in a typically suburban status war. The fun was gone. When every family has its own grill, more grills will be sold, increasing revenue for the grill manufacturer. But in order to create an environment in which everyone feels the need to buy his own barbecue, the spirit of community and the sharing that goes along with it must be surrendered to that of acquisition and competition. In short, people have more stuff but they're less happy—and the media that might be helping them figure this out is, instead, dedicated to exacerbating the problem.

As America's television audience fragmented even further into its demographic silos, consumers began purchasing televisions for every room in the house. Instead of watching TV as a family, each member watched his own programs. The expanded offerings of cable dial, at first, seemed like a boon for target marketers, who could now reach their intended segments quite specifically; but it also fragmented the audience beyond recognition. There was nowhere left to reach everyone at once. Advertisements on the main networks were no cheaper, but they were now reaching fewer people. And the problem of clutter—everyone trying to be noticed at once—made all advertising less effective.

Remote controls, videocassette recorders and, finally, digital video recorders like TiVo and ReplayTV now allow television viewers to watch the programs they want, when they want to, and the way they want to—which means without commercials. While earlier audiences of television could always be counted on to keep their end of the unspoken bargain, showing up when invited and sitting through messages from the companies sponsoring their entertainment, today's audience feels no such obligation. They are professional consumers, after all, and apply the same rules of efficiency to their media consumption that their bosses apply to corporate activity.

This trend has reached its extreme on the Internet, where each user creates his own content stream as he hops from Web site to Web site. More than merely assembling their own entertainment on the Internet, consumers are using it to become more savvy consumers of media and products. Sure, an ad for a brand might get their attention, but the statistics and user reviews of pretty much any product are also online for the asking. Too bad so many companies forgot how to make their own products.

So-called out-of-the-box thinking from the latest and greatest marketing wizards would have companies apply yet more mechanical models to this population of increasingly fragmented consumers. Instead of speaking to the mass market all at once, companies are supposed to communicate individually with 250 million markets of one. Databases, like those at Acxiom and Prism, contain enough information about each member of every American household to model the consumer probabilities for any one of them. Once cable and Web site operators get existing technologies up to speed, they'll be able to assemble and target advertisements for the individual viewers watching them, on the fly. Web banner ads are already called up automatically based on the IP addresses[23] of the individual visitors to a site.

This is not a new strategy, at all, but an application of direct marketing taken to extremes. Instead of looking objectively at the new landscape of media, it seeks to combat complexity with computing horsepower, while further fragmenting the marketplace in the process. It takes the focus of a business away from production or even demand,

and scatters it across a set of computer models through which no coherent purpose—other than maximizing click-through—can be ascertained.

I watched the CEO of a flower delivery chain who had been sold on such a scheme as he perused the segmentation and modeling data supplied to him by his Web advertising contractor. His eyes glazed over and his mouth opened slightly as charts he didn't understand were flashed on a screen at the end of the conference table. In the end, somewhat red-faced, he approved of the banner advertising campaign, but I could tell he had reservations.

"Do you think people really want to be hit with ads reminding them of a loved one's birthday?" he said. "I think I'd find it a little creepy." He went on to explain that, as he understood his customer, people liked to take credit for remembering such things, themselves, and then acting on them. He didn't want to turn a business known for delivering into one known for "nudging."

We see the same tendency to fight emerging complexity with forced predictability in all areas of business. Retail environments are concocted to manipulate consumers in ever more subtle but effective ways. Aisles, shelf heights, and even floor surfaces are redesigned to stimulate impulsive behaviors in shoppers. Studies showed that people will walk more aimlessly—and be more susceptible to manipulation—after losing track of where their car is located, so shopping mall floor plans force consumers to make at least three turns from the parking lot to the mall interior.

Even when natural social effects begin to emerge in this strategically dehumanizing shopping environment, they are immediately seized upon for their ability to sell goods. For example, security cameras at a major video rental chain revealed that customers unable to find the movie of their choice would often peer through a slot into the "just returned" bin to see if their selection might be waiting to be reshelved. Failing to find it there, customers often chose another movie from that bin—under the assumption that its recent circulation could serve as an indirect recommendation from another customer. Consultants[24] recommended that the video store exploit this phenomenon by "spiking" the bin with movies that hadn't been rented in a long time, in the hopes of imitating that effect.

These processes are all aimed at quelling the complexity of our time. Rather than celebrating the consumer's increasing sophistication and self-direction, retailers look for ways to redirect or thwart them. Depending on consultants, computers, and lingo no one understands, companies extend themselves well beyond their core values and competencies, way past even marketing, into the psychographic profiles of their target consumers. It's as if they were designing products by holding a mirror up to a focus group. The source of innovation is quite disconnected from their own expertise, sensibility, or passion, and turned toward trying to decipher the sensibilities and passions of strangers.

This out-of-the-box methodology exists not to extend the core proposition of a business or the wisdom of its leaders' experience, but rather to preserve whatever processes are already in place, however unwieldy or inappropriate they may have become. It reminds me of a classic out-of-the-box idea, Thomas Jefferson's dumbwaiter. Jefferson was well known for his misgivings about slavery, even though he kept many slaves throughout his life. His adoption of the dumbwaiter[25] seemed to embody this contradiction. While the device may have marginally relieved stress on slaves by saving them a few trips up and down the stairs, it's hard not to see its greater benefit being to Jefferson himself, who was now allowed to receive the meals his slaves cooked without having to confront them directly. His food arrived as if by machine—a *deus ex machina*. Rather than tackling the injustice directly, he came up with a way to keep it out of sight.

We are at a similar crossroads, and reminded of this daily as we confront the increasingly fragmented, meaningless, and just plain un-fun concessions we make to the mechanical, survivalist model on which so many of our career and business decisions are based. The Industrial Age was based on creating and feeding our machines. In the process, we have learned to become a lot more like them ourselves. Whether working in a factory, shopping in a mall, absorbing commercials on television, or managing investments into any of these activities, we are involved, primarily, in supporting industry. Most of us find no intrinsic value in these activities. In a recent Gallup poll, a full 71 percent of American workers said they are "disengaged clock-watchers who can't wait to go home."[26]

Not that we're fruitfully engaged when we get home, either. The few hours we have left are usually spent watching television, a medium where the only room left for creativity is to figure out how to make advertising look more like programming. Reality TV, devoid of metaphor, is simply an excuse to weave sponsorship opportunities into the show. The American Express effort, *The Restaurant,* was a thinly veiled commercial for the American Express Small Business card that the up-and-coming restaurateur uses whenever he gets into trouble. *Queer Eye for the Straight Guy* is little more than a series of product placements for men's fashion companies. Meanwhile, even commercial-free programming such as *Sex and the City* becomes an advertising opportunity for Absolut Vodka, whose brand managers were able to get an entire plotline woven around their label. It begins to feel as if television programming were simply one extended pitch dedicated to enhancing our productivity as consumers.

Completing the circuit are marketers who, equally devoid of genuinely new ideas, turn to science and statistics for answers on what to do next. What number-crunching by computer doesn't accomplish, brain scans will. Instead of developing products, advertisements, and packaging through a creative process, marketers test colors, words, and concepts on typical consumers. They're no longer doing this in traditional focus groups that still require a bit of human analysis, but by putting their test subjects into MRI machines, showing them pictures of ads or products, and then observing how various parts of the brain light up or don't. It's one big machine.

Even when innovation accidentally finds its way into production or marketing, it is valued not for the creativity it can unleash, but the efficiencies it can create. Individual problems are solved in isolation from whatever the core purpose of an enterprise may have been before industrial processes abstracted it well past the reach of our intuition or even our understanding.

Indeed, the mass media have been fragmented beyond recognition; the mass market has been replaced by several billion markets of individuals; and mass production of even the simplest products is now outsourced over a multiplicity of corporations and continents. In reaction, corporate consultants and motivational therapists may have taught us to think "outside the box" and "compete" even more fiercely, but these strategies have only served to distance us even further from the core values, competencies, and relationships that make us who we are. They take the play out of work, and rob us of our individual and collective creativity in the process. They turn what's left of our innovation into a giant bureaucratic game of prediction. It sounds more like the failings of centralized communism than of creative capitalism. Maybe that's why the people charged with judging the effectiveness of all this efficiency—stock brokers—suffer from a clinical depression rate of 23 percent, well over the national average of 7 percent.[27]

We've been on a pretty straight course toward a mechanized, completely predictable, and repeatable set of business practices since the Industrial Revolution, and maybe even a few centuries before. And though these practices have been responsible for a hell of a lot of progress until now, they appear to have maxed out. We must finally apply our inventiveness not to tinkering with these practices from the outside in, but to reconnecting with what it is we were hoping to accomplish in the first place, and then reinventing them from the inside out.

To do so, we'll have to rediscover what inspires us about our chosen fields, and what makes them applicable to the world around us. That's why this is all actually such good news for those of us left with even an iota of creative capacity and interest in other people.

chapter two

THE NETWORKED
REALITY

MEDIA STORIES

Just as technology has allowed us to control nature to some extent, media has always been applied to control populations. The "mass media" departments of universities around the world have nothing to do with exploring how the masses use media. They are public relations schools, teaching their students how to use media to communicate *to* the so-called masses. And from the first Greek tragedy to the newspapers of William Randolph Hearst right through to today's Fox News, the main vehicle used to shape both public and private opinion has been the story.

As Aristotle figured out over two millennia ago, stories work quite simply: create a character the audience likes and then let that character make a series of decisions that puts him into peril. Oedipus decides to pursue the king's murderer, or Bruce Willis decides to defeat a band of terrorists. The audience follows the character up an incline plane of increasing danger, and experiences empathy—the vicarious thrill of rising stakes. When the audience can't take any more tension without running screaming from the theater or turning off the TV, the storyteller comes up with a solution to the dilemma. Whether it's the gods descending from the rafters to forgive a Greek hero, or Bruce finding a new super-weapon with which to kill his enemy, the storyteller holds the keys to our relief. Excitement, crisis, climax, and relief. We might even call it the "male orgasm curve" of dramatic action. Once we reach the climax, we're allowed to go to sleep.

As long as the storyteller has a captive audience, he alone has the power to devise the solution. If a storyteller wants us to believe in a religion, then his god will be responsible for our relief. If he wants us to believe in a politician or product, then one of these will be the solution. I remember an ad from my childhood in which a middle-level executive endures the entire heroic arc in less than 30 seconds. First, his boss yells at him for losing an account, then he gets a phone call from his wife who just crashed the car, and finally he opens his bank statement to find he is overdrawn. Just when it seems his head will burst open from a migraine, the man pulls open his desk drawer to find whatever brand of pain reliever is being advertised. He pops the pill, and we watch a psychedelic animation of the pill moving through his system, providing instantaneous relief. Thirty seconds from start to finish. As long as we swallow the storyteller's pill, we're allowed to experience relief.

Engage the audience, put them in a state of tension, promise relief, and then—at the very last moment—deliver. It's a great formula for passing on values of any kind. But the heroic arc comes with an agenda of its own. One way or another, the structure of all these anxiety-producing sagas requires a suspension not just of disbelief, but of relief. The message of the structure is that we are required to postpone our joy. While this kind of story might be a great way to get entertained, it may not be universally applicable, and it's ripe for exploitation. What happens when it's applied to the way we approach everything from God to economics? It sets us up to postpone our happiness while instead longing for some future day when our problems will be resolved. In a sense, it takes our focus off the present and onto an all-too-distant future.

In extreme cases, like fundamentalist religious or political stories, the chaos of any given moment becomes an indication of some great impending apocalypse when justice will be done. I've seen cheeky bumper stickers that read: "In case of rapture, this car will empty." The passengers are literally looking forward to that scenario. When we are addicted to stories with endings, we'd prefer Armageddon to no ending at all.[1] Likewise, the more extreme stories we use to understand the economy—from communism to libertarianism—all involve a revolution and great suffering in order to bring about the great change that will set us all free. And when we use these grand narratives to understand the big picture, their bias tends to trickle down. We end up suspending our core values just to get through whatever we perceive to be the current crisis—postponing legitimacy and happiness until we get to those golf greens pictured in the 401(k) plan brochures.

We use stories to understand our world, orient ourselves, motivate our employees, communicate our brand values, and even tout our stock valuations. So our relationship to these stories really does matter. The biggest impact of the newly interactive mediaspace is that it has changed the shape of our stories and leveled the playing field on which they are created and disseminated. Thanks to the Internet, anyone can tell a story to pretty much anyone else. And while these stories, themselves, might not amount to much, the ability to write and share one changes a person's relationship to everyone else's.

LESSONS FROM THE MOON OF ENDOR

From an early age, I was fascinated by the way certain media enhance the authority of a storyteller. I came to understand this relationship between the content of a story and the technology through which it was being told when I was watching the movie *Star Wars: Return of the Jedi*. No, it wasn't George Lucas's storytelling but, in the true Renaissance fashion of frames-inside-frames, a story-within-the-story being told by his characters.

Luke Skywalker and Han Solo have been taken prisoner on the moon of Endor by some cuddly little creatures called Ewoks. As our two heroes struggle helplessly with their bindings, their two robots tell the captors a story. C3PO, the gilded mechanical man whom the Ewoks believe to be a god, relates in fluent Ewok how Luke and Han are fighting against an evil tyrant. As C3PO tells the wondrous tale of their space battle with Darth Vader, R2D2 projects holographic images of the pyrotechnic assaults. The teddy bear–like creatures' eyes glow in the campfire as they are mesmerized by both the great story and wondrous special effects.

By the time the two robots are done, the Ewoks not only release their captives, but fight a war on their behalf—a war in which many of them die. I couldn't help but wonder at that moment, what would have happened if Darth Vader had gotten down to Endor first and told *his* story with *his* special effects?

The principle in play here is that the more compelling or magical the technique of storytelling—in this case, the technology through which it is being told—the more likely people are to accept its content.

In ancient Greece, people may have gathered round the story-teller in the town square each day because they were interested to hear what would happen to Odysseus next; but what compelled them to listen was the seemingly magical ability of this human being to speak for so long in perfect meter! Likewise, the supernatural ability of priests to transubstantiate wine into blood went a long way toward confirming the validity of the gospel they preached.

In our own recent history, television held that same magical storytelling power. So magical, we must remember, that newscaster Walter Cronkite was able to cap off his evening broadcast with the absurdly authoritative "and that's the way it is." Absurd by today's standards, anyway. Could you imagine a contemporary anchorperson ending a broadcast with the declaration of its absolute truth? The best they can offer is the attempt to remain "fair and balanced," and we laugh at even that assertion.

What has changed? Not the power of news gathering; if any-thing, it has only improved. The difference is in our relationship to television as a medium. It no longer captivates us quite the same way it did. Just because someone can get his image into that little box doesn't mean he is speaking the gospel truth. In fact, the person in the picture tube could just as well be one of us.

This, and not e-commerce, WiFi, or Web-based stock trading, is what made interactivity the "next big thing." It broke down the story-teller's monopoly over the narrative.

The first main harbinger of interactivity was a tiny but awesomely powerful handheld device known in my family as "the clicker." Imagine if your father were watching that pain reliever commercial back in 1955 on his old console television. Even if he suspected that he was watching a commercial designed to put him in a state of anxiety, in order to change the channel and remove himself from the externally imposed tension he would have to move the popcorn off his lap, pull up the lever on his recliner, walk up to the television set, and manually turn the dial. That amounts to a pretty decisive action for a bleary-eyed television viewer resting after work. To sit through the rest of the commercial, however emotionally harrowing, might cost him only a tiny quantity of human energy until the pills come out of the character's desk drawer. The brain, being lazy, chooses the path of least resistance, so Dad sits through the whole commercial.

Flash forward to today. A kid with a remote control in his hand makes the same mental calculation: an ounce of stress to sit through the commercial or an infinitesimally small quantity of energy to move his finger a sixteenth of an inch and . . . he's free! The remote control gives viewers the power to break the storyteller's spell with almost no effort. Watch a kid next time he channel-surfs from program to program. He's not changing the channel because he's bored. He surfs away when he senses that he's being put into an imposed state of tension by someone he doesn't trust.

The remote control provides a way out. It allows a viewer to de-construct the story he is being told—in some cases even "pause" it—to avoid falling under the programmer's spell. If a viewer does get back around the dial to watch the end of a program, he no longer has the same captivated orientation. That's why kids with remotes can't really be considered to be watching television, at all; they are watching *the* television, "playing television," putting it through its paces.

Just as the remote control allowed a generation to deconstruct the content of television, the video game joystick demystified its technology. Think back to the first time you ever saw a video game. It was probably Pong, that primitive black-and-white depiction of a Ping-Pong table, with a square on either side of the screen representing the paddle and a tiny white dot representing the ball. Now, remember the exhilaration you felt at playing that game for the very first time? Was it because you had always wanted an effective simulation of Ping-Pong? Did you celebrate because you could now practice without purchasing an entire table and installing it in the basement? Of course not. It had nothing to do with the power of the simulation (tell *that* to today's video game designers). You were celebrating the simple ability to move the pixels on the screen for the first time. It was a moment of revolution! The screen was no longer the exclusive turf of the television broadcasters.

Thanks to the joystick, as well as the introduction of the VCR and camcorder, we were empowered to move, even make, the pixels ourselves. The TV was no longer magical—at least not someone else's magic. Its functioning had become transparent. Just as the remote control allowed viewers to deconstruct the content of storytelling, the joystick allowed the audience to demystify the technology through which these stories were being told.

Finally, the computer mouse and keyboard transformed a "receive only" monitor into a two-way portal. Packaged programming was no longer any more valuable, or valid, than the words we could type ourselves. The addition of a modem turned the computer into a broadcast facility.

We were no longer dependent on the content of movie studios or TV stations, but could create and disseminate our own content. The Internet revolution was a do-it-yourself revolution. We had deconstructed the content of media stories, demystified its modes of transmission, and learned to do it all for ourselves.

Now *that's* mass media.

SCREENAGERS

In the old days, the only law of physics that applied to the mediaspace was gravity: some person at the top of a glass building decides on a message, and that message is broadcast down to everyone else. This new interactive world was different. With all those interactive devices like faxes, camcorders, modems, and monitors proliferating everywhere, the datasphere got very complex very quickly. Now there were opportunities for feedback everywhere. And people took advantage of them.

The entirety of Internet culture might best be understood as an unintended consequence. Though our technologies and media were mostly developed to exact or even enforce control over the unpredictability of nature and populations, the distribution of all these tools to so many people turned out to have the opposite impact. All because they went both ways instead of just one.

The universe of media and messages got so complex that it began to behave like a natural system itself. To fully grasp the operating principles of this new media universe, we must look at the Internet less as an investment opportunity than as a life-form. That's the way we used to see it in ancient times, anyway. Until 1991, you had to sign an agreement promising not to conduct any business online just to get access to the Internet! Imagine that. It was a business-free zone.

How could such rules ever have been put in place? Because the Internet began as a public project. It was created to allow scientists at universities and government facilities to share research and computing resources. Everyone from the Pentagon to Al Gore saw the value of a universally accessible information-sharing network and invested federal funds to build a backbone capable of connecting computers around the world.

What they didn't realize was that they were doing a whole lot more than connecting computers to one another. They were connecting people, too. Before long, all those scientists who were supposed to be exchanging research or comparing data were exchanging stories about their families and comparing notes on movies. People around the world were playing games, socializing, and crossing cultural boundaries never crossed before. Since no one was using the network to discuss military technology anymore, the government turned it over to the public as best it could.

The Internet's unexpected social side effect turned out to be its incontrovertible main feature. Its other functions fell by the wayside. The Internet's capability to network human beings proved to be its very lifeblood. It fosters communication, collaboration, sharing, helpfulness, and community. Sure, it was the nerdiest among us who learned of the Internet first. Then came those of us whose friends were nerds. Then our friends, and so on. Someone would insist he had found something you needed to know about—the way a childhood friend lets you in on that secret door leading to the basement under the junior high school.

Can you remember that first time you watched that friend log on? How he turned the keyboard over to you and asked what you wanted to know, where you wanted to visit, or whom you wanted to meet? That was the moment when you got it: Internet fever. There was a whole new world out there, unlimited by the constraints of time and space, appearance and prejudice, gender and power.

It's no wonder so many people compared the 1990s Internet to the psychedelic 1960s. This was the movement in which I came of age, and I still refer to it with the same reverence that hippies remember the summer of love. It seemed all we needed to do was get a person online, and he would be changed forever. And people were. A 60-year-old Midwestern businessman I know found himself logging on every night to engage in a conversation about Jungian archetypes. It lasted for four weeks before he realized the person with whom he was conversing was a 16-year-old boy from Tokyo. Grandmothers were creating support groups, Arab and Israeli kids were sharing peace strategies on bulletin boards, and Chinese activists were sharing stories of prisoner abuses around the world.

It felt as though we were wiring up a global brain. Techno visionaries of the period, such as Ted Nelson—who coined the word "hypertext"—told us how the Internet could be used as a library for everything ever written. A musician named Jaron Lanier invented a bizarre interactive space he called "virtual reality," in which people would be able to, in his words, "really see what the other means."

The Internet was no longer a government research project. It was alive. Out of control and delightfully chaotic. What's more, it seemed to promote an agenda all its own. It was as if using a computer mouse and keyboard to access other human beings on the other side of the monitor changed our relationship to the media and the power the media held. The tube was no longer a place that only a corporate conglomerate could access. The Internet was *our* space.

The Internet fostered a do-it-yourself mentality. We called it "cyberpunk." Why watch packaged programming on TV when you could make your own online? Who needs corporate content when you could be the content? This was a world we could design ourselves, on our own terms. That's why it fostered such a deep sense of community. New users were gently escorted around the Internet by veterans. An experienced user delighted in setting up a newbie's connection. It was considered an honor to rush out to fix a fellow user's technical problem. To be an Internet user was to be an Internet advocate. Whereas traditional media communities had always tended to form around what people watched, Internet communities seemed to have more to do with what people created, and how they contributed to the extension of the Internet ethos.

It's also why almost everything to do with the Internet was free. Software was designed by people who wanted to make the Internet a better place. Hackers stayed up late coding new programs and then distributed them free of charge. The early interactive mediaspace was a gift economy. People developed and shared new software with no expectation of financial return. It was gratifying enough to see one's own email program or bulletin board software spread to thousands of other users. It's easy to forget—and it's rarely brought up at board meetings—that, in fact, most of the programs we use today are based on this shareware and freeware. Internet Explorer and Netscape are bloated versions of a program originally created at the University of Illinois and given away. Streaming media is a dolled-up version of CUSeeMe, a program developed at Cornell. The Internet was built for love, not profit.[2]

People became the content, a shift that had implications not just for the online community but for society as a whole. For the notion of a group of people working together for a shared goal rather than financial self-interest was quite startling to those whose lives had been organized around the single purpose of making money and achieving personal security. The Internet was considered "sexy" simply because it inspired young people to work hard for something other than money. People who developed Internet applications in this way were pejoratively labeled "hackers," and their antics were often equated with those of Wild West outlaws, hippies, Situationists, and even communists. But their organization model was much more complex and potentially far-reaching than those of their countercultural predecessors.

A new story was being written. Online communities sprung up seemingly from nowhere. On the West Coast in the late 1980s, one of Ken Kesey's Merry Pranksters, Stewart Brand, conceived and implemented an online bulletin board called The Well (Whole Earth 'Lectronic Link). Within two years, thousands of users had joined the dial-in computer conferencing system and were sharing their deepest hopes and fears with one another. Famous scientists, authors, philosophers, and scores of journalists flocked to the site in order to develop their ideas collaboratively rather than alone. Meanwhile, as the Internet continued to develop, online discussions in a distributed system called USENET began to proliferate. These were absolutely self-organizing conversations about thousands of different topics. They themselves spawned communities of scientists, activists, doctors, and patients, among so many others, dedicated to tackling problems in collaboration across formerly prohibitive geographical and cultural divides.

If adults were acting like kids again, kids were acting like the new adults. I came to call this new generation "screenagers." Although they weren't all online activists quite yet, the early exposure of young people to new media changed the way their old media had to work, too. Broadcasters addressing an audience growing up in a world where any story could be deconstructed, and any technology demystified, were forced to create shows that acknowledged the viewer's newfound power. Sometimes at their own peril.

Beavis and Butt-head, for example, originally an obscure segment on an artsy, evening MTV animation show called *Liquid Television,* almost single-handedly brought down the immensely popular rock video format. For these two animated characters, far more than iconic teen troublemakers, served as armchair media critics, deconstructing MTV's videos in real time. The show's simple formula consisted of playing videos while two boys told jokes about them. In their own, crude way, they exposed the marketing tactics nested in MTV's thinly veiled advertising-as-content model. A kid who might normally be wowed by the beautiful girls in a video has a very different experience of that video after Beavis has panted along with him, or Butt-head has explained that the girls were hired to make the rock star look cool. In the boys' words, "This sucks. Change it."

Shows like *The Simpsons* arose to challenge the traditional story format and present a new structure more compatible with a screenager's sensibility. Each *Simpsons* episode might have a traditional narrative arc, but only unsophisticated viewers actually care whether Homer survives a nuclear accident or keeps his job. The more media-savvy viewer, for whom the show is written, is involved in a very different narrative. *The Simpsons* isn't a single story as much as a series of media satires. Each scene is a send-up of a media or cultural institution. One scene satirizes an Alfred Hitchcock film, the next one a presidential campaign ad; and the next one cleverly mocks the ethos underlying Disneyland. The reward for the viewer is not the great release at the end of the heroic arc, but the joy of making connections between the scenes they are watching and the things being critiqued. It's not a post-ponement of joy, waiting for the hero's great reversal; it's an instantaneous sense of recognition, a way to make sense of the increasingly complex landscape, and a series of "aha" moments that comprise the viewing satisfaction for the screenager.

Created not to capture the screenager, but to appeal to his new sensibilities, shows like these, as well as their many followers, from *Mystery Science Theater* to *South Park,* shift emphasis from the great prize at the end of the story to the immediate task of making sense. This is a more highly dimensional experience of the story. You don't have to wait for the end; you experience its essence in one moment. Right now. Instead of being told what to think or feel, the viewer is charged with making the connections—the links between one world and another—and, in doing so, trains himself for the networked world growing all around him. As in any renaissance, the ability to gain perspective is all that matters.

THE BACKLASH

Cultures tend to react romantically to any industrial surge. The first factories in England are believed to have spurred the Romantic movement in the arts and poetry. Without those dehumanizing factories and coal mines, we'd have no reaction in the form of William Blake, Mary Shelley, odes to wine, vampire stories, puffy shirts, or the entire Gothic revival. Likewise, the highly scientific, early computer age—the mainframe and punch-card universe—also gave rise to long-buried cultural strains.

But in the case of cyberculture, rather than rejecting the new technologies, youth and counterculture members embraced them. And why not? Unlike the technologies of the Industrial Age, these new ones didn't simply imprison people; they afforded them unprecedented access and power. As a result, companies and institutions that were dependent on Industrial Age models of command and control found themselves in the awkward position of trying to limit the impact of the technologies they had themselves developed.

The clicker, the joystick, and the mouse represented a tremendous threat to business as usual.

Studies in the mid-1990s showed that families with Internet-capable computers were watching an average of nine hours less television per week. Even more frightening to those who depended on the mindless passivity of consumer culture, Internet enthusiasts were sharing information, ideas, and whole computer programs—for free! People were turning to alternative news and entertainment sources, ones they didn't have to pay for. Worse, they were watching fewer commercials. Something had to be done. And it was.

It is difficult to determine exactly how intentional each of the mainstream media's attacks was on the development of the Internet and the culture it spawned. Certainly, the many executives of media conglomerates who contacted my colleagues and me for advice throughout the 1990s were both threatened by the unchecked growth of interactive culture and anxious to cash in on these new developments. They were chagrined by the flow of viewers away from television programming, but they hoped this shift could be managed and, ultimately, exploited.

While many existing content industries, such as music recording, sought to put both individual companies and entire new categories out of business (such as Napster and other peer-to-peer networks), the great majority of executives did not want to see the Internet entirely shut down. (It was, in fact, the U.S. government, concerned about the spread of pornography to minors and encryption technology to rogue nations, that took more direct actions against the early Internet's new model of open collaboration.) But corporations played their part in fighting the trend toward interactivity.

A review of articles quoting the chiefs at TimeWarner, NewsCorp, and Bertelsmann in the 1990s reveals an industry either underestimating, obfuscating, or simply misunderstanding the true promise of interactive media. The real attacks on the emerging new media culture were not orchestrated by old men from high up in glass office towers; they arose almost as systematic responses from an old media culture responding to the birth of its successor. It was both through the specific, if misguided, actions of some media executives, as well as the much more instinctual response of an entire business culture to a threat to the status quo, that mainstream media began to work to reverse the effects of the clicker, the joystick, and the mouse.

Borrowing a term from 1970s social science, a business strategist addressing a new media economy audience at the Aspen Institute declared that we were now living in an "attention economy." His idea was that attention is a scarce resource, and the only limiting factor on how much money can be made online. Internet-as-business publication *Wired* magazine was quick to give this idea additional attention, and it took hold. True enough, the mediaspace might be infinite, but there are only so many hours in a day during which potential audience members might be viewing a program. These units of human time became known as "eyeball-hours," and pains were taken to create TV shows and Web sites "sticky" enough to engage those eyeballs long enough to show them an advertisement or, better, make a sale. That's where all those flashing Web banner ads came from.

Perhaps coincidentally, the growth of the attention economy was accompanied by an increase of concern over the attention spans of young people. Channel surfing and similar behavior became equated with a very real but variously diagnosed childhood illness called attention-deficit/hyperactivity disorder (ADHD). Between the years 1990 and 2000, major *New York Times* articles on ADHD increased from 5 to 52.[3] Meanwhile, prescriptions for Ritalin (the most common of the amphetamines given to children with this diagnosis) have gone up 700 percent since 1990.[4] Oddly, there is no known biological basis for ADHD; and researchers I've been working with blame an environment oversaturated with sticky advertising for many of the behaviors being attributed to the mysterious disease. In any case, in our attention economy, children who refuse to pay attention are much too quickly drugged with addictive amphetamines before the real reasons for their adaptation to the onslaught of commercial messages are even considered.

The demystification of media, enabled by the joystick and other early interactive technologies, was quickly reversed through the development of increasingly opaque computer interfaces. Whereas early DOS computer users tended to understand a lot about how their computers stored information and launched programs, later operating systems such as Windows 95 put more barriers in place. Although these operating systems make computers easier to use in some ways, they prevent users from gaining access to or command over its more fundamental processes. Now, to install a new program, users must consult the Wizard. What better metaphor do we need for the remystification of the computer than a wizard with a big pointy hat? The subtle communication is: "Don't touch. You are not qualified to go behind the screen. Leave it to the magicians." In such a computing environment, computer literacy no longer means being able to program a computer, but merely knowing how to use software such as Microsoft Office.

Finally, the do-it-yourself ethic of the Internet community, enabled by the mouse and keyboard, was replaced by the new value of commerce. The communications age was rebranded as the information age, even though the Internet had never really been about downloading files or data, but about communicating with other people. The difference was that information or content, unlike real human interaction, could be bought and sold. It was a commodity. People would pay, it was thought, for horoscopes, stock prices, and magazine articles. When selling information online didn't work, businesspeople instead turned to selling real products online. Horoscope.com and online literary journals gave way to Pets.com and online bookstores. The e-commerce boom was ignited.

This wouldn't have been possible had the interactive and essentially two-way quality of the early, text-only Internet not been supplanted by the flat, image-laden World Wide Web. Just as Windows encouraged people to use computers in a more passive fashion than they had before, the World Wide Web encouraged Internet users to behave more like traditional consumers. Hands off the keyboard and onto the mouse. Pointing and clicking replaced thinking or typing, as the opaque interface of the Web made the Internet increasingly one-way and read-only, more conducive to commerce than communication. The Internet was reduced to a direct marketing platform.

Few e-commerce companies made any money selling goods, but the *idea* that they could was all that mattered. When actual e-commerce didn't work, the Internet was rebranded yet again as an investment platform. The Web was to be the new portal through which the middle class could invest in the stock market. And which stocks were they to invest in? Internet stocks, of course! Like any good pyramid scheme, everyone was in on it. Or at least they thought they were.

News stories about online communities such as The Well, or even discussion groups for breast cancer survivors, were soon overshadowed by those about daring young entrepreneurs launching multimillion-dollar IPOs. Internet journalism, written by option-holding employees of media conglomerates, moved from the culture section to the business pages, and the dot-com pyramid scheme became the dominant new media story.

A medium born out of the ability to break through packaged stories was now being used to promote a new, equally dangerous one: the great pyramid. A smart kid writes a business plan. He finds a few "angel" investors to back him up long enough to land some first-level investors. Below them on the pyramid are several more rounds of investors, until the investment bank gets involved. Another few levels of investors buy in until the decision is made to go public. Of course, by this point, the angels and other early investors are executing their exit strategy. It used to be known as "carpetbagging." In any case, they're gone and the investing public is left holding the soon-to-be-worthless shares. Tragically, but perhaps luckily, the dot-com bubble burst, along with the story being used to keep it inflated. The entire cycle—the birth of a new medium, the battle to control it, and the downfall of the first victorious camp—taught us a lot about the relationship of stories to the technologies through which they are disseminated.

The whole ordeal may have given us an opportunity for renaissance. For back here in the real world, the Internet is doing just fine. Better than ever. The World Wide Web, whose rather opaque platform ascended primarily for its capability to serve as an online catalogue, has been adapted to serve many of the Internet's original, more technologically primitive functions. USENET discussions have been reborn as Web-based bulletin boards such as Slashdot and Metafilter. Personal daily diaries known as Web logs have multiplied by the millions. Blogger.com provides a set of publishing tools that allow even a novice to create a Web log; automatically add content to a Web site; or organize links, commentary, and open discussions. In the short time Blogger has been available, it has fostered an interconnected community of millions of users. These people don't simply surf the Web; they are now empowered to create it. Rising from the graveyard of failed business plans, these collaborative communities of authors and creators are the true harbingers of a cultural, political, and perhaps even business renaissance.

TASTING THE APPLE

When Satan gave Adam and Eve the apple, he was doing something very much like Steve Jobs did by marketing us his Apple: both fruits of knowledge are really just paths to the attainment of literacy.

The first great renaissance moment in Western civilization, in fact, can really be attributed to the invention of the common alphabet. Until that moment, people accepted their world quite as it was. The gods were thought to control everything. The calendar was measured in a circle, as there was no understanding that things could ever be changed. One season the gods might grace us with rain, peace, or fertility; the next, they might not. Human beings simply accepted the story as written, and had nothing to do but pray.

Nobody even really knew what writing was. Hieroglyphics—literally, "priestly writing"—was reserved for priests and a few kings. With the invention of the 22-letter alphabet, everything changed. Now, people no longer needed the time required to learn thousands of hieroglyphs. These 22 symbols could be recombined to form any word, or even to invent a new one. People got into the box of language, so to speak, and wrote a new religion that gave human beings a role in human affairs.

There's a great moment in the Bible that has confounded scholars for centuries. God tells Abraham, his first prophet, that he will be the father of a nation of priests. Many have concluded that this means the Jews were supposed to be holy priests. What the text might be implying is that Abraham will father a nation of people who, like priests, can read and write. No longer passive recipients of the story, they will be free to write their own. Instead of simply looking forward to the rewards of death—as their many pre-Judaic cults insisted—the Hebrews would celebrate their ability to effect change in this life. Moses and his father-in-law went ahead and wrote the new laws of the land. *L'chaim*—the famous Hebrew toast meaning "to life"—was akin to a revolutionary ethical stance, and an affirmation of the real present over the fictional future.

The Renaissance, too, was an expression of newfound literacy. Texts that had, once again, been relegated to kings and clergy were being made accessible, thanks to the printing press, to much larger populations. And as we saw, the idea that each person has his individual perspective on the world started to matter.

But while the original Renaissance may have transformed populations from passive recipients into active interpreters, today's renaissance brings us another leap forward. We are no longer just interpreters, with our own perspectives; we are authors.

Unlike the printing press, which allowed a select few texts to reach wide distribution, the Internet allows pretty much anyone to reach wide distribution. The book was a great boon to individual interpretation; the Internet is a boon to individual expression. Whereas the original Renaissance gave us the ability to circumnavigate the globe, our current one gives us the ability to blow it up. Our new painting techniques show the importance of a unique perspective on a scene; the holograph and fractal show how each tiny piece of a system can reflect, and even change, the whole thing.

A networked culture is a culture of authorship. It's one where a videotape of a black man being beaten by white cops can iterate through the media and then result in full-scale urban rioting in a dozen American cities. It's a world filled with high-leverage points, both creative and destructive. An unknown Internet reporter named Matt Drudge can launch the Monica Lewinsky scandal. A teenage day-trader can earn his college tuition from his bedroom PC. An angry Russian adolescent can disseminate a worm that grinds the entire Internet (and the businesses depending on it) to a near halt.

The easiest way to grasp the three stages through which our renaissances have brought us, and to apply it to the real world of business today, is to consider the experience of any computer game enthusiast.

At first, a gamer will play a video or computer game by the rules—right out of the box, so to speak. He'll read the manual, if necessary, then move through the various levels of the game as best he can. Mastery of the game, at this stage, means getting to the end—making it to the last level, surviving, becoming the most powerful character, or, in the case of a simulation game, designing and maintaining a thriving family, city, or civilization. And, for many gamers, this is as far as it goes.

Many gamers, though, after they've either mastered this level of play or gotten stuck, will venture out onto the Internet in search of other fans or user groups. There, they will gather "cheat codes" to acquire special abilities within the game, such as invisibility or an infinite supply of ammunition.

When the gamer returns to the game with his new special abilities, is he still playing the game? Yes, but now he's playing as a cheater—from outside the original confines of the game. Like a Renaissance art lover who is now aware of the frame around the painting, the gamer now has wider perspective. He is playing the game with an arsenal of his own techniques—not just the ones supplied by the manufacturer on the original CD, but the ones he can find on the larger landscape of the Internet.

What does the gamer do when he tires of his own invincibility in the world of the game? If the game is any good, and there's a big enough community of players, he'll go back online and learn how the game was programmed. The enormously popular shoot-'em-up game Doom, in fact, owes much of its success to its creators' decision to release the operating code of the game to the public. Now, instead of just playing the game out of the box, or even using special codes, players assume the roles of programmers and develop their own versions of the game world.

Some kids decide to change the location of the game, from its original dungeons to, say, an interactive map of the corridors of their own high school (much to the chagrin of parents and teachers). Other kids change the very principles of the game, so that instead of shooting bullets at one another, the players might be casting spells, turning each other into magical creatures. They reorient to the game as its new authors, and have no hesitation about rewriting it from the ground up.

So gamers move through the same three stages as our society: from passive recipients of the rules to individuals worthy of breaking them to authors capable of rewriting them. They deconstruct the content of the game, demystify its interface, and then turn the game into a do-it-yourself creative expression. In their path toward innovation, they're not getting out of the box at all, but burrowing deeper inside. Learning the game as well as—or, in some cases, better than—the people who developed it in the first place!

This is the template we must use to understand the interactive age. It's not about extending the techniques of the assembly line into the homes and offices of our customers and employees. Rather, it's about finding ways to get behind or, better, in front of this wave of authorial, self-determinist energy.

The most successful entrepreneurs of the interactive industry—from Steve Jobs and his "think different" Macintosh to Bill Gates who asked us, "Where do you want to go today?"—have understood that they are not simply allowing their customers to be reached, but to reach out, themselves. It's empowerment on a scale significantly greater than any product has provided a customer since, perhaps, the apple itself. And to those who refuse to grasp its implications, just as dangerous.

NETWORKED ENTERPRISE

Okay, so computers and networks offer everyone more opportunity to assume the roles of authors in an increasing variety of venues. What about when "everyone" includes your own customers and employees? Don't panic; rejoice.

Your best choice is to turn every interaction people have with your company into an opportunity to express and extend this newfound capability. By doing so, you will allow your enterprise to be experienced as an enabling rather than a restricting force in their lives. You will also stand to benefit from the immense outpouring of creativity that both customers and employees produce, often with no expectation of anything in return.

In short, by recognizing this renaissance for what it is, rather than attempting to squash its complexity, you can exploit the unstoppable energy of this era as a source of innovation. By embracing the creative capacity of those whose actions you may have formerly sought to control, you allow a different sort of coordination to emerge. Yes, networking, self-determination, and autonomy lead to a certain amount of chaos. But, as our renaissance is teaching us, chaos is not disorder, at all, but a way that systems reach higher states of complexity and self-regulation.

Thanks to computers and the systems theory they enable, the ocean, the weather, and even the media and the stock market are understood as systems with behaviors. Scientists no longer explain the tremendously sophisticated organization of everything from slime mold to anthills as a result of a hierarchy. The queen ant does not direct her minions. Rather, the many categories of worker and task arise from the bottom up, as a result of evolution. The upshot of emergence theory is this: individuals residing on one scale start producing behavior that manifests a scale above them.[5] Molecules create cells, ants create colonies, people create neighborhoods, cells create organisms . . . and, of course, customers create markets and employees create companies.

Behaviors on one level of experience, when allowed to manifest fully, lead to organization on a higher dimensional level. It's pure renaissance.

The caveat is that part about allowing them to manifest fully. People can't be coerced to emerge at a higher level of organization. They can be forced to stand in a line or behave in a certain way, but the result is a less coordinated collective, incapable of responding to anything without orders from central command. The most complex, stable, and self-regulating organizations in nature, from the coral reef to the rain forest, organize from the bottom up.

What all complex systems have in common is that they are highly networked. While members of these systems may not be taking direction from a centralized authority, they are in constant communication with one another. Each member is capable of listening to his fellows and, more importantly, feeding back his own observations to the rest. A message from one organism in a coral reef can spread hundreds of miles, from member to member, in a matter of hours. This is how the entirety of the reef can "decide" it's time to reproduce or hibernate.

Emergent order only happens when a system becomes chaotic enough to reach the next level of organization. Like a pot of water brought to a boil, it all looks pretty messy and bubbly right before the system changes state and reaches new order. Of course, putting a lid on the pot and weighting it down doesn't prevent any disorder; it only prevents the new, higher level of organization from emerging.

But this is precisely how most businesses respond to the challenge of a networked office and marketplace. Instead of promoting the cross talk and feedback required for a higher level of organization to emerge, managers use technology to reduce complexity by monitoring and restricting the behavior of employees. Taking their cue from the stopwatch management theories of the past, they count keystrokes and treat office cubicles like boxes on a spreadsheet. Technology is used to regiment the workplace instead of liberating it.

Meanwhile, customers are reduced to their purchasing profiles. We may see our customers as individuals, but only insofar as we believe that if we can only crack each consumer's personal profile, we will be able to appeal to his own needs and wants. We want to market one-to-one. We even see this process as empowering to the consumer. As a renaissance of his autonomy. What more could he want than to have his individual desires addressed?

Kevin Roberts, chairman of Saatchi & Saatchi, and a world-renowned expert in the way people relate to their roles as consumer, epitomizes this view: "The consumer is now in total control. I mean she can go home, she's going to decide when she buys, what she buys, where she buys, how she buys. . . . Oh boy they get it you know, they're so empowered at every age. They are not cynical, they are completely empowered, they're autonomous. All the fear is gone and all the control is passed over to the consumer. It's a good thing."[6]

His perspective is perfect for the last renaissance, but completely inappropriate for this one. The only way the consumer feeds back is through purchasing decisions. The consumer self-expresses by buying Tide instead of Cheer. This is not authorship, at all; it's equivalent to deciding which of two sitcoms to watch. The idea that consumer empowerment is the right to choose between existing products is indicative of a top-down model of technology, and a broadcast model of media. Yes, every individual has his own perspective on the great problems of laundry detergent, pain relief, and every other consumer dilemma. But simply having one's own opinion and brand of choice is no longer an adequate expression of who we are.

Participants in today's renaissance, empowered by the proliferation of networked authoring tools, no longer define themselves by their perspectives, but by their contributions. That's why it's so futile, say, to think we can fulfill people's deepest needs by reengineering a brand or corporate identity that is more compatible with one new value or another. It's not about reflecting their perspectives; it's about giving them the chance to reflect and express it, themselves.

And there's no better place to practice this new ethos, and watch it play out, than on the Internet. On each of the main landscapes of business, the Internet can be used either in a vain attempt to restore order or to encourage authorship and the innovation that comes with it. The Internet gives us a new way to relate to our employees, our customers, and even our products—as well as the ideal laboratory for experimenting with strategies applicable to the renaissance society into which our interactive technologies have helped bring us.

NETWORKED WORK

Coming out of the era of Alfred Sloan, it's no surprise that early computer theorists first imagined all the ways that computing technology would alter the factory floor. What might have been less expected, however, was their common concern that computers might not liberate the worker at all, but force him into competition with robots! Norbert Wiener, the computer scientist who coined the word "cybernetics," understood that the way we choose to apply our technologies could turn our workers either into more autonomous agents, or simply into automatons.[7]

Despite these warnings, managers who brought computers into the workplace saw them, primarily, as a way to further control and monitor the actions of their workers. IBM Rolm telephone systems, among the first computerized switchboard systems, also gave managers the ability to monitor their workers through the speakerphone microphone. Employers from the U.S. Postal Service to AT&T used computers to monitor everything from keystrokes per minute to minutes per customer service call. As such practices became commonplace, these same companies' health facilities became jammed with workers complaining of stress, headaches, and sleeplessness.[8]

More recently, cell phones and home access to email have become excuses for managers to keep employees tied to the job. A study by the Radcliffe Public Policy Center revealed that 83 percent of workers would prefer more distinct boundaries between work and nonwork time.[9] Study after study is showing that Americans are working harder, worrying more, sleeping less, and having more trouble balancing work and life. In fact, over 70 percent of men between 21 and 39 say that, if given the choice, they would give up pay for more time with their families. Instead of helping employees author the lifestyles they want, and create the boundaries they are looking for between work and time off, more and more hi-tech companies, like Microsoft and Google, are attempting to encompass the entirety of their employees' lives. When they're not installing work-related software on their employees' home computers, they are creating campuses with games, dining rooms, and even gyms, so that workers can spend 12 or more hours a day on the job.

Computers have been used to emphasize the priorities of the assembly line, and the allure of Internet culture has been exploited to emphasize the workplace as the central location in a person's life. These strategies are ultimately inappropriate for the networked era, because they do not enhance an individual's opportunity to author or innovate.

Using networking tools for surveillance discourages their most important function: networking. These technologies must instead be used to promote collaboration and cross talk, so that individuals can become parts of teams that eventually emerge as the component parts of the company organism. Work-from-home cannot be seen as a way to impinge on more of an employee's time; it's a way to offer an employee more autonomy over where he wants to get a particular task completed. At Princeton University, the "honor code" allows a student to take an exam anywhere he wants to—in his dorm room, the library, or in the classroom with everyone else. The level of trust granted the student is paid back in more developed responses to the exams; and less energy is wasted on paranoia and proctoring. The students are treated like free adults—not convicts.

It turns out most people don't really like to telecommute, anyway. After reaching a peak in 1990, telecommuting rates have been falling ever since. Whereas people who work alone can run businesses out of the house, those who work for an organization find they are "out of the loop" when they don't come into the office. Other studies have shown that people prefer to go to the office in order to work with others—if they don't already perceive of the workplace as an oppressive environment. Face-to-face contact and informal discussions, according to one university study, strengthens corporate cultures. Without them, "ritual and specialized language can no longer be maintained. Geographic dispersion is the primary factor contributing to a weakened culture." [10]

Rather than turning the workplace into a panopticon,[11] computers can enhance the ability of people to interact with one another and with the outside world, as never before. Firewalls be damned. Adobe Systems, the software company responsible for Photoshop, has encouraged a porous relationship between its developers and its users. As a result of the free flow of information, the user community ends up developing a great many of the "plug-ins" for Adobe's programs, and takes delight when its efforts are integrated into the next release, for the benefit of all.

Palm Computing understood that its operating system for handhelds would reach wider adoption if the Internet community felt it was a platform for authoring, not just for keeping names and dates in order. Rather than requiring its employees to maintain secrecy on software developments, Palm opened its code to the public. A worldwide community of developers—some amateur, some professional—developed around the device, and new uses for it were invented that no employee would have thought of by himself.

The makers of Doom saw their own employees as the ideal test subjects for their product. Rather than dictating every development pathway, they let their employees play with the game. The in-house community's desire to play networked versions of the game, and to reprogram different levels, led to the innovations that made this title one of the best-selling in history.

Of course, the challenge for an office using open networks and collaborative "groupware" is that people tend to bend communications tools to social uses. It's how we got the Internet, after all. That's why in an environment where people are empowered to act in pretty much any way they want they'll choose to collaborate on the projects you need them to. You don't do this through direct command, but by creating a networked environment where certain kinds of interactions are enhanced, and thus encouraged.

I advise workplaces to adopt a collaborative ethos where everyone is allowed to call upon pretty much anyone for the help they need. In a networked environment, random collaborations should be free to emerge. But they need not be exactly random, nor should they. Groupware—basically, collaborative software through which an entire team can work on the same project or document—should list the particular qualifications of everyone in the company, as well as their willingness and availability to help someone needing to learn or utilize that skill. This way, a worker who needs to figure how to embed video in his PowerPoint presentation can simply look up who knows how to do it.

Yes, conflicts will emerge, but working through those conflicts properly will define the organization, itself, from the bottom up. Let that employee who is being called upon decide for himself whether this is the best use of his time. Superiors become the judges who resolve disputes and forge compromises, rather than the authorities who predetermine everyone's best activities. Employees who are feeling overwhelmed by requests for a particular skill can feed back the need for a PowerPoint class for the rest of the company. By granting your employees the responsibility to determine best practices from the bottom up, you will allow them to experience their collective stewardship of your company as a privilege.

THE NETWORKED CONSUMER

The misuse of technology in customer relations is so easy to spot that it has become fodder for late-night television comedians. When comics describe the hassle of, say, navigating a computerized switchboard in an effort to get some customer service, they are revealing something about the public's sense that there's something amiss in this application of microchips.

There is. While the replacement of an employee with a computer might save the company a bit of money, it costs the customer in time lost to the machine. On some level, the customer realizes that he's not the only one going through this nightmarish process, that he is, in a sense, competing with everyone else to figure out which menu selection might bring him to a "real" customer service representative. Multiply the three minutes wasted times a few thousand customers, and you're no longer looking at a computerized switchboard; you're looking at a substantial shift of labor from a company to its customers.

No, not every consumer is busy calculating the balance sheet of labor hours lost to management. Nonetheless, it is now common for consumers to exchange tips online about how to "hack" through to a live customer service representatives by selecting the option for "new customer" instead of "troubleshooting." So well do they understand the misplaced priorities of business. And in a world where your customers have the daily experience of technology as a liberating force, they are less likely to look kindly on those who use it against them.

The danger for most marketers entering the computer age is that, like bad managers, they see these tools as ways of updating and reinforcing the automated, captivating practices of the past. Instead of acknowledging the way human beings are moving beyond their predictable identities as members of single consumer tribes, market researchers claim that, with their state-of-the-art computing skills and algorithms, they can keep up with the complexity of our shifting populations. They cannot succeed, nor should you hire them to try.

For decades, market research firms like Claritas and Acxiom have kept detailed records on a great majority of America's households. (In fact, all but two of the 9-11 hijackers were in the Acxiom database!) All those warrantee cards we fill out, our credit card purchases, travel profiles, real estate transactions, and more, are concatenated and analyzed. Once the numbers are crunched, we're segmented into one of about 70 consumer tribes. According to Acxiom, I'm probably a "shooting star"; 36 to 45, married, wake up early and go for runs, watch *Seinfeld*, travel abroad, no kids yet, but undergoing fertility treatments. No, I won't tell you how much of that is true, but the intimacy of their observations is off-putting, even frightening.

And no matter how many market segments these companies develop, they still amount to a tremendous oversimplification of the marketplace, and strategies that contradict the overwhelming ethos of our renaissance to promote complexity and boundary crossing.

The data from companies like Acxiom are responsible for the offers that arrive in our mailboxes, as well as the language that's used in them. This is the data a telemarketer's computer uses to direct him to which of a hundred different possible scripts to use when speaking to each of us. And from a consumer's perspective, I don't know which is worse: for them to miss the mark or to hit it too precisely. Is it comforting that the junk mail universe has discovered you are overweight, or have a fertility problem?

On the Web, companies that assemble banner ads in real time based on what they know about each visitor now use "click-through" data to fine-tune their offerings for the next Web surfer with the same profile. More advanced and privacy-challenging versions of the software can make use of real customer profiles—such as those associated with credit card numbers or accounts with other merchants—and then assemble ads directed precisely at their individual target.

The problem with these strategies is that they are directly opposed to the liberating potential of networking for the consumer. Taking their cue from early *Wired*'s attention economists, these marketers hope to increase the stickiness of their offerings, seeking to entrap the user in an ever-narrower series of choices, drawing them down, inevitably, to the Buy button. One Web company, Realmedia, goes so far as to advertise stickiness as a virtue. It's print ads feature people the size of insects, stuck on giant rolls of flypaper, or snared by a hook at the end of a lure. The slogan? "Nothing attracts like Realmedia."

Stickiness is not attraction; as the advertisement suggests, it is a form of captivity. The experience of a Web banner is that of an obstruction on the windshield one is using to navigate through the Internet. Stickiness is a roadblock. Placing ads on the Internet slows the actual experience of obtaining and sharing information. The sponsor of such ads will not be seen as a benefactor, but as an impediment. This is not a good way to establish customer relationships.

Free email programs engage another form of stickiness: they can't be forwarded. In an effort to ensure that users of Yahoo's and Hotmail's free mail services see all the ads that are intended for them, users must retrieve their mail directly from the Yahoo or Hotmail site. Unlike most mail services, which allow the user to forward email automatically to work, home, or even a temporary address, the free services—and even a few pay email accounts like AOL and MSN—are fixed right where they are. What these providers don't realize is that this reduction in usability and freedom will make customers less likely to use these services—once they figure out how they have been disabled.

The next frontier of stickiness will be the wireless arena. We have yet to see whether Verizon will be able to maintain its own sticky policy of preventing its cellular customers from leaving the closed Verizon universe. Photos taken on Verizon cell phones, for example, can't be uploaded to a computer or sent to a non-Verizon subscriber without going through Verizon's own Web site—for an additional fee. Users can't download programs or games except from Verizon's own vendors, and communications features such as Bluetooth have been partially disabled on Verizon's version of Motorola and other phones, to prevent users from exchanging files, songs, or videos with people subscribing to competitors' phone services. Verizon is able to enact such policies because, as yet, it has the best coverage in the United States. But numerous Web sites and online groups have already been working hard to "crack" the locks Verizon has put on its phones, and to defame the company wherever possible.

Cell phones also pose the next challenge, and probable hazard, for marketers. Since young people are spending an increasing amount of time talking to one another, rather than watching television, companies looking to reach them have charged their advertising agencies with penetrating this new conversational environment. To do so could, again, be a crucial error in judgment. If a marketer has done his job right (and we'll look at this job in the next chapter), those kids will already be talking about his product. To interrupt the conversation with an ad is to defeat word of mouth.

This doesn't mean marketing, of one sort or another, can't happen online or even on phones. It just won't look like advertising or be based on the reductive, sticky tactics of yesterday's marketers.

Amazon.com's best marketing strategy costs it almost nothing, because its users take care of it. By creating a forum for customers to rate and write reviews of any book in the system, Amazon turns an otherwise ordinary online bookstore into a community of book critics.

The consumer is recognized as the ultimate arbiter of a product's quality, and the online store becomes a vehicle for millions of pages of individual expression.

When Amazon was first coming onto the scene, I remember a good amount of concern about bad reviews. Isn't it a problem for a bookstore to allow for its customers to say bad things about some of its products? In hindsight, such concerns seem laughable. Of course, it isn't a problem; it's one of the site's greatest attributes. It displays a true understanding of "transparency"—the idea that all processes are kept out in the open. It generates the kind of customer loyalty that stickiness advocates can only dream of; when a customer has what amounts to a body of work associated with a single Web site, he'll become an advocate of that site everywhere he goes, even using other sites and conferences to link to his reviews on Amazon. Finally, it takes the onus off Amazon to market its products. The only thing Amazon needs to communicate is that it is putting its resources behind this renaissance in literacy.

Of course, eBay is the other great example. Instead of offering any product of its own, eBay simply enables the transactions of others, and systematizes the process by which people can trust one another enough to send checks and items to each other through the mail. eBay is a listing service but more importantly, it is a ratings system. eBay's participants have no motivation to rate merchants after a successful sale, except for their knowledge that it makes the community a better place to do business in the long run. By encouraging an ethos of trust and responsibility, eBay comes to represent these values in the greater online community. No advertising necessary.

IT'S THE PEOPLE, STUPID

The greatest danger for any business looking to enter the interactive mediaspace is that, like any business in an increasingly transparent marketplace, the Internet can turn almost any product or service into a pure commodity.

For once a business puts itself online, its goods, services, and, most of all, prices, can be compared quite mechanically against anyone else's. Shopping aggregators, like Yahoo Shopping and Epinions, do this automatically. Once a shopper knows the product he wants, he types it into one of these engines, and the list of online retailers offering the item is presented, in order of price—including shipping and handling. A ratings system of stars indicates whether other consumers have found the merchant to be reputable, and the consumer goes to the least expensive one. That's transparency.

But it also spells doom for companies that have no competitive advantage other than to shrink their margins down to nothing. Without a real strategy for taking advantage of interactivity, and doing so in a way that complements rather than stifles the customer's sense of agency, most businesses would do well to stay away lest their cost structure deteriorate irreparably.

The Internet has seen a number of battles between companies providing complementary goods and services. They attempt to turn one another into commodities. By 1998, some companies were offering free computers to anyone who signed up for an Internet service provider (ISP) contract. Meanwhile, computer manufacturers were giving away a year of ISP service to anyone who would buy one of their computers. This only succeeded in turning both products into potential commodities in the minds of consumers.

Hi-tech companies that can't find any true competitive advantage usually try to compensate through a version of stickiness called "loyalty incentives." The worst of these are currently being employed by the most commodified of technology businesses: the cell phone providers. In return for a discount on a phone, customers must sign up for lengthy contract terms with stiff penalties for early cancellation—often up to $300 or $400. The wording on these contracts is so opaque that the American Association of Retired Persons (AARP) is currently considering either taking action against providers on behalf of its members or offering its own low-cost cell phone service, with more transparent terms.

One practice, now in use by a variety of cellular companies, allows customers of the same network to call one another for free. This leads the customer to become a de facto salesperson for that company's services, since it is in his own best interests to turn his friends and family into toll-free calls. But while such techniques might work with utilitarian, cost-conscious customers, they feel coercive to others. Those who don't want to be in the position of wireless mercenary tend to conclude that they are paying a premium for their unwillingness to go with the program.[12] Besides, technology is being used, once again, to corral people into predictable, mapped groupings.

The greater effect of the Internet and the mentality that comes with it has been to break down the bonds of customer loyalty. An America's Research Group study showed that the number of customers who believe that brand names are "extremely important" for choosing holiday gifts has been decreasing by about 10 percent a year.[13] Advertisers are beginning to find that their ads tend to benefit their whole category more than their own offering within it.

That doesn't mean the Internet can't still be used to a business's advantage. I consulted to Dell Computers as it was attempting to migrate its home and small business customers from phone orders onto the Internet. It was a tough transition for the company because it didn't want to end up head-to-head against retailers that offered products that were indiscernibly different on the surface, for very discernibly lower prices. Meanwhile, Dell was losing market share to Gateway, which had made quite a splash with its "cow" campaign and homespun brand image. In the home user sector, Gateway seemed friendlier.

The answer I gave the Dell executives was to migrate not just their product line, but their competitive advantage online, as well. Dell made its name on ease of ordering. A single phone call to a knowledgeable sales rep, and you'd get the computer you'd need. So we worked on a new Web site, appropriately (but rather uncreatively) called Dell4Me, through which users could enter the sorts of needs they had from a computer, and then receive a recommendation for a whole system. Unlike other sites that spoke only in gigabytes and megahertz, the

Dell4Me site would humanize the technology on offer, rather than technologizing the humans coming to shop. We demonstrated Dell's competitive advantage—knowledgeable human customer service—in the online environment. Dell's sales quickly retook the number-one position in that category.

If any company could be thought of as offering a commodity in the Internet space, it would be Intel. What's more a matter of mega-hertz than a computer chip? Even ads for computer chips just show one computer doing some calculation faster than another. But Paul Otellini, the company's president, COO, and next in line for CEO, shocked Intel insiders and the greater industry by insisting that Intel's competitive advantage lay not in chip speed, but creativity. Its new direction will be to integrate features like long-range wireless networking into its chips.

What seems to outsiders like an admirable journey outside the box, however, is actually a perspective formed by working within the company for 20 years. Otellini headed everything from the sales department to the chip-making division. His experience in both areas taught him that the company's research and development had become too reliant on simple speed increases from engineering. Intel's true legacy and competency wasn't just increasing speeds of chip operation; it was increasing the applicability of computing power across a wide variety of purposes. So he listened to what customers were asking for— better communications capabilities—and decided to push the research division in that direction.

It's the simplest lesson of the Internet, and one that Internet companies seem to be the last to get: it's the people, stupid. We don't have computers because we want to interact with machines; we have them because they allow us to communicate more effectively with other people.

TRANSPARENT AUTHORITY

Most businesses are still looking at this renaissance through the lenses of the last one. They can't help but want to reduce complexity and create order.

Restoring order, however, whether in the office, marketplace, or production floor, means enforcing obsolete policies, restricting creativity, and putting up walls between people. In an age of innovation, this is just putting one's head in the sand. Worse, thanks to the transparency of the networked age, everyone can see you doing it. Resistance is futile.

Our interactive networks are responsible, at least in part, for the liberation of the consumer and worker alike. We evolve from controllable cogs to human beings behaving with agency. As this process is just beginning, we are all the more conscious of the people and institutions that are standing in the way.

We reward Amazon.com because it makes the book-buying experience transparent. We can see what real people, just like us, think about the books we are considering purchasing. Going "meta" on this evaluation process, we can judge the value of a particular review by seeing how many other users found it "helpful." We can even look up the reviewer's other postings, to judge for ourselves whether we agree with his perspectives. Once we've read a book, we can join in the community and establish our own reputation by writing reviews, ourselves.

But Amazon's transparency goes beyond that. Much to my own chagrin, Amazon serves as an aggregator for used booksellers around the country. Pretty much anyone who has a copy of one of my books and wants to sell it can fill out a simple form on Amazon. It'll then list the availability of used copies of my books, right on the book's main page. Click on a link, and the customer sees the used copies, listed in price order, with customer ratings of the reliability of each vendor.

Amazon positions itself not just as a bookseller but as a promoter of reading—even if it means undermining the sales of a particular title, or the number of new books my publisher can print. In the end, Amazon promotes the expression of its online customer-authors more than that of the authors whose books it sells. And in a bottom-up renaissance, it wouldn't be any other way.

Even the phenomenal success of peer-to-peer networks like Napster and Bittorrents might best be understood as an exploited creative culture using its newfound power to reintroduce some measure of transparency to opaque and excessively greedy businesses. Once the record industry decided to charge more for CDs than vinyl, even though they cost less to produce, the entire music consumer base had been alienated. Napster was a way of making the music industry transparent and accountable. It was as much a media story as a computer service, which slowly revealed the practices of conglomerates that often shut artists out of the profits on their own music. This was file-sharing's real function. These programs really aren't that much fun to use; it's simply payback. It's the exposure of an industry that was unfair to consumers and, worse, stifled creative authorship.

Besides, back in the real world, sales of ringtones actually far exceed the sales of music files through services like Apple's iTunes. Why? Because ringtones aren't just listened to, they are played for others. Not everyone has the ability to write a song or even "scratch" like a DJ, but a great many young people still want the experience of authorship and self-expression that communications technologies suggest. So while they may not write novels, they do participate all afternoon in "instant message" sessions with their friends. And while they can't compose a symphony, a two-second strain of their favorite song is worth more to them in the form of a programmable ringtone than it is as a private, play-only file.

The Internet was never about the computers or the content they carried. It was about elevating people to the role of creators, and letting them interact with one another in this new capacity. Companies that allow and, hopefully, even encourage this to happen will find themselves giving birth to entire cultures that transcend the boundaries between what they formerly thought of as employees and customers. They'll reach a level of organization beyond what they could have implemented by design. And they'll find an emergent stability that far exceeds anything they could have enforced from above.

Then maybe, just maybe, they'll finally get it.

chapter three

SOCIAL CURRENCY: WHAT PEOPLE REALLY VALUE, AND WHY

T hanks to the emergence of the Internet and its networked culture, a whole lot about our needs—both as consumers and as
workers—has been put into perspective. Success has a variety
of definitions and dimensions, and many of them are changing.

For instance, the most respected kids in the culture of computer
games are not the ones who play the best; they're the ones who program
the best. For they, even more than Nintendo champions, give the rest
of the players something to talk about, something to play with, and
something through which they can connect with others. The driving
force behind all of the authorship and creative energy of the networked
age is the need to create what I've come to call *social currency*.

Networks are great, but until we can move through them ourselves, we'll need proxies in the form of ideas, images, words, and other
constructs that can be exchanged through our wires and screens. Even
in the real, physical world, our engagements with one another are almost always predicated on something else. A party starts with a few
good jokes to break the ice. "Invite Sam," we remind ourselves, "he tells
good jokes."

Those jokes are social currency. And Sam's reliability at offering them when they are needed make him a valuable addition to any gathering. It's not that the jokes are so great in and of themselves. Rather, they provide everyone an excuse to listen, to laugh, and build conversations around them. They're like a jumpstart. A medium through which we can interact.

Observe yourself the next time you're listening to a joke. You may start by listening to the joke for the humor—because you really want the belly laugh at the end. But chances are, a few sentences in, you will find yourself not only listening, but attempting to remember its whole sequence. You'll do this tentatively at first, until you've decided whether or not it's really a good joke. And if it is, you'll commit the entire thing to memory—maybe even with a personalized variation, or a mental note to yourself to fix that racist part. This is because the joke is a gift—it's a form of social currency that you'll be able to take with you to the next party.

So is the great majority of the media we watch and even the products we buy. HBO understood this well enough to base an entire season's advertising campaign on the "water cooler" effect. In a series of fake ads, the water cooler industry thanks HBO for giving workers something to talk about the next day at the water cooler. The message of these ads was clear: watch these shows to gain social currency.

In today's commercial landscape, cluttered as it is with messages of personal gratification and consumption, the HBO campaign revealed a deeper understanding of our social needs than meets the eye. Not only did it recognize our desire for connection with other people—especially at work—but it recognized our awareness that accumulating social currency was the surest route toward achieving these connections.

I first developed these ideas in a spirited, if overly optimistic, book called *Media Virus*, which I wrote in those breathy days just before the emergence of the World Wide Web. I argued that all our media are connecting up to one another, forging a "datasphere" in which we are all connected, too. Thanks to interactive media from phones and faxes to the early Internet, everyone was becoming capable of providing "feedback"—launching ideas that could spread through this new mediaspace like viruses.

Media Virus became something of a media virus itself. Many business authors, consultants, and advertisers caught on to the idea of cultural contagion and came to believe that a savvy marketer needed to find only a few key individuals who could provide the right word of mouth (or word of Internet), and a campaign would propel itself. This led to an industry of "viral marketing," where hip advertising agencies find people they consider to be cool or trendy, and then induce them— or pay them—to hawk a particular brand of shoe, book title, or camera phone to their friends and followers.

But they've got the horse and the cart reversed. People don't engage with each other in order to exchange viruses; people exchange viruses as an excuse to engage with each other. Media viruses, and their massive promotional capability, are all dependent on the newfound collective spirit of our age and the increasing need for social currency that has resulted. It's not about convincing a few key individuals to sell products; it's about creating products that provide everyone the currency they need to forge new social connections. Sure, if we analyze the movement of an idea across a community, we'll be able, retroactively, to determine which individuals gave it the most word of mouth.

If we want to understand or even replicate this effect, however, we must instead learn to see people not as individuals looking for power or social status, but as parts of a group looking for cohesion. Media viruses were made possible by the emergence of a networked mediaspace. They are an emergent phenomenon—a life-form, of sorts, native to this new interactive landscape. Viruses exploit what we have in common and, when we have little in common, help to create shared experience. The best products and brands in this environment do not serve to help people stand out; they have much more to do with helping people fit *in*.

That's why, in spite of growing fears that we are living in a materialistic society, social currency almost always wins out over pure ownership as a motivator for buying. Long gone are the Howard Hugheses, who own massive collections of cars or artworks that never see the light of day. For the majority of consumers, their cars, electronics, and even their sneakers are ways of communicating to and connecting with other people. In an almost Darwinian competition for survival, products that serve as social currency succeed, while the ones that don't, fail.

Take the codependent rise of bubble gum and trading cards. The first real trading cards—produced just after the Civil War—were just conduits for advertisements. Called "trade cards," they had a picture of a politician or baseball player on one side, and carried an ad on the back, usually for a sporting good or something tangentially related to the theme on the card. By the turn of the century, trading cards doubled as a promotional giveaway and a "stiffener" in packs of cigarettes. But as tobacco companies diversified into candy during the Depression, they stumbled upon the trading card's true aficionados: kids. And their consumers taught them that these cards were about more than just selling gum.

When my father was growing up, bubble gum companies like Goudey, Bowman, and Topps competed for young customers by offering free trading cards inside their packages. Little pieces of cardboard with the images of baseball players proved the most successful, and soon children were buying whole packs of baseball cards with only a single stick of bubble gum. Topps won this competition, eventually buying out Bowman altogether, because it emphasized the cards more than the gum.

Today, baseball cards are sold without any bubble gum at all. Despite gum's textural attributes, baseball cards proved to be the "stickier" content. Why? Because cards provide a richer media experience. Not only can collectors look at pictures, but they can compare and analyze the statistics of each player as chronicled on the back of the card.

More importantly, this depth of data allows the card to serve as social currency. Children can debate the merits of one brand of gum over another for only so long, but they can talk endlessly about the players whose cards they've collected. They can even trade them, make up games like "flipping" to gamble them, or just peruse one another's collections. Before the Internet, baseball cards were also the best way to support one's arguments about a player with verified stats.

Unlike gum, the cards aren't really ends in themselves; they are the basis for human interaction. Johnny got some new cards, so the other kids come over to see them after school. The cards are social currency—the excuse to get together.

In an era like ours, where the ravages of fragmentation and isolation are felt more than ever, consumers and workers alike are looking for forms of social currency that can help them relate to one another and reforge the bonds of community and intimacy. Producers unaware of the principles of social currency seek to make products and experiences that substitute for or even impinge on people looking to do things together. Businesses producing products and services for those living in our renaissance culture, on the other hand, do so with full knowledge that they are simply providing ways for people to experience one another.

We don't need advanced degrees in psychology or marketing to understand why memories of a community barbecue pit in Queens are so much richer than those of a private backyard grill in the wealthy suburbs. It is because a cookout is a great excuse for people to come together, and even elicits a collective memory of shared experiences—after all, we've been cooking around campfires since before recorded history. It's not the grill, the charcoal, or even the food, but the gathering itself that's important.

That's why the idea that the digital age should have taught us that "content is king" is so wrong, both on the Internet and in real life. The lasting lesson of the Internet is that the best reason people purchase stuff in a networked culture—whether it's real objects or electronic content—is to share it with other people. In short, the things we buy are means to an end; they are all media through which we can interact with other people.

That's right: media. We tend to think of media as the conduits—the television or radio or Web site—that deliver some form of content. But the delivered content is, itself, a kind of medium. Content is just a medium for the interaction between people. The many forms of content we collect and experience online—from images and videos to music files and clever opinion pieces—are really just forms of ammunition. They are excuses to send an email, or something to have when the conversation goes quiet at work. Better, they can be a good excuse to start a discussion with that attractive person in the next cubicle: "Hey! Did you see that streaming video clip at streamingvideoclips.com? Let me come over there and type in the URL for you."

Think of this the next time you curse that onslaught of email jokes or infinitely forwarded news articles cluttering up your inbox. The senders think they've given you a gift, one that might be enough to engage your attention and provoke an interaction. If the joke or article is good enough, this means the currency is valuable enough to earn them a response. Even amateur Web authorship, such as it is, amounts to little more than a way for people to share the social currency they've collected through their lives. A Britney Spears fan site or a collection of illegally gathered MP3s of popular songs are both ways of enticing people to visit and, hopefully, leave a message in a guest book. A great myth of the Internet is that people want to share the stories of their own lives. But a quick check of Web content on personal sites reveals a different picture: people will share anything they've got—usually in the form of prepackaged, unoriginal content—in order to make contact with others.

Social currency makes it easy to see why certain products work and others ultimately fail. Napster, though heralded as a revolution for online music, will be chalked up as a failure—and not just because the music industry made them a deal they couldn't refuse. Napster doesn't offer its users a genuinely social component. In fact, by making all of its users anonymous (its original design required this because it was, in effect, an illegal file-sharing scheme) Napster pulled social currency out of the music equation. The Napster universe was entirely about acquisition. Yes, it required an underlying ethic of sharing, but the experience was about hoarding music on one's hard drive.

The iPod, on the other hand, allows for an entirely different form of sharing that is growing increasingly popular among young people around the world: the creation and dissemination of "podcasts"—music mixes, speeches, even original music, formatted for the iPod and distributed online. In another trend, students and office mates working on shared networks often open their iTunes libraries to the entire con-nected community, allowing friends and associates to listen to or download one another's libraries, learn about new music, and, more importantly, sample one another's tastes. The interaction is geared less toward getting music for free than it is toward learning about one an-other: Did you know Joe over in accounting has great taste in old jazz? The engineers at Apple's iPod division regularly receive emails from college students, telling them their playlists have won them new girl-friends.[1] In another exchange of social currency, scrolling through one another's iPod-archived photo albums has become a regular party ice-breaker, giving people a chance to learn what they have in common—children, vacation spots, or even cultural perspectives.

Of course, the principles of social currency also apply to the things people consume offline, in the real world. A print ad for a snazzy new Bang & Olufsen telephone says it plainly: "All phones enable con-versation, but few provide the topic." In other words, the reason to own this phone is that it is a conversation starter. At their most effective, all consumer purchases work like this. When you were a kid, did you buy records simply for the pleasure of listening to them? Or was it a way of getting *other* kids to your house to listen to them *with* you? "I've got the new Stones record; come on over after school." Do we read books for the sheer pleasure of interacting with the text, or are we also giving our-selves the social currency we'll need for the next cocktail party? When you come upon a particularly brilliant passage, or even jot something down, do you do this purely as a "note to self" or because someday you might want to share this idea with someone else?

Mass production, and the attendant need to induce consumption on a mass scale, has fooled marketers and manufacturers alike into thinking that the best way to sell people things is to play to their sense of individuality. You should buy this item because you deserve it. You are special. You alone matter. An army of one. This strategy, combined with forecasts of continued "cocooning," has led too many businesses to think that the consumer's chief drive is to re-create a womb. As if by getting us to regress to an oral fixation, we'll buy the most stuff.

It's an ethos that translates to business in the form of books such as Spencer Johnson's *Who Moved My Cheese?*, which see the world as a zero-sum game of fixed commodities. The characters don't learn how to make cheese, only how to find what's out there, by reading the "writing on the wall." It's a consumerist perspective on innovation, and the final chapter in a business philosophy based on finding what's waiting out there in the dark of the maze, rather than expressing and creating from what's inside. Even as producers, we are reduced to consumers, competing for sustenance in a maze of someone else's making.

We seem to take for granted that everyone simply wants a bigger piece of the pie. As the saying goes, he who dies with the most toys, wins. But this logic just doesn't square with people's behaviors. Sure, there will always be customers who buy the supersized meal or grotesquely proportioned SUV, and there will always be employees who leave a job for nothing except a bigger paycheck. But, to put it simply, these aren't the happiest or most productive people around, and catering to the survivalist impulse by which they live is no path to innovation. It's a road to isolation, obesity, and some of the worst attributes associated with American consumption.

That's classic first Renaissance. The home is a castle or, better, fortress. Each family barricades itself inside, to venture out only for provisions. Unlike earlier eras in American history, all attention is turned inward. Instead of a front porch where we can welcome guests, we have a back deck for private dinners. Instead of watching TV together in the living room, we each have a TV in our bedroom.

We've reached the endgame of that scenario, and it isn't pretty. Many of us have consumed ourselves into isolation and depression. The number of people in civic organizations has been in a freefall since 1960, and is now as low as it has ever been in U.S. history.[2] Meanwhile, studies have shown that people belonging to just one group, of almost any kind, are half as likely to die over the next decade as people who belong to none. Although most Americans are not reading those studies, the Internet has exposed its users to the direct experience collaboration and connectivity, and many are looking for these experiences offline, as well.

Successful businesses are learning how to offer them.

THE EXPERIENCE ECOLOGY

The retail industries form the very frontlines between producers and consumers, and have been charged—perhaps unfairly—with stimulating and guiding the purchasing power of ordinary people. Dutifully, the store architects, salespeople, and brand managers responsible for maintaining the demand side of the economic equation devised marketing schemes, shopping environments, and persuasion techniques to get consumers to buy. Only recently, however, have a few of them begun to realize that it's not their products consumers want; it's the experiences that these products, or the brands they represent, can offer.

You wouldn't know this looking at most retail spaces today. Retail architects generally apply one of two manipulative strategies on consumers. The first, called "atmospherics," was developed beginning in the early 1970s, as a merger between the sciences of perception and psychology. Taking their cue from experiments done on gamblers in casinos, store designers sought to discover which colors, textures, lighting, music, and even scents could stimulate the highest volume of sales.

Shopping malls rose in popularity among retailers for their capability to create closed and completely controlled environments. National chain stores could develop a single design strategy and employ it across the country. All sorts of shopping phenomena were discovered through trial and error. Hardwood floors that allow the clicking of heels to resonate make female shoppers feel more powerful—perfect for selling higher-priced kitchen appliances and other items for the place where she needs to feel in charge. Muzak discovered that shoppers need to be brought through very specific cycles of increased pacing, rather than trying to get them to shop at full speed all the time.

These almost Pavlovian techniques were supplemented, in the 1990s, by a slew of more advanced methods, advanced by former anthropologists like Paco Underhill of Envirosell. His infamous "butt-brush theory," for example, states that women inspecting an item will stop and move on the instant another passerby accidentally brushes against her butt. That's why he advises that items a woman needs to inspect be placed in wider aisles. Designers of this stripe look at the consumer as an impulsive creature, capable of being led, or at least coaxed, into buying more stuff if treated just right. They're the ones who suggest putting candy down where kids can reach it, keeping checkout counters at clothing stores huge and clear so that customers will feel inadequate presenting just one small item to the cashier, and trying to get customers in housewares departments to take shopping carts because they will be twice as likely to buy something.

Yes, all this seems more like common sense than social science. But the sum total of all these observations and recommendations amounts to a manipulative, mechanical approach toward the retail environment, where customers are to be stimulated and directed like cattle. The actual experience of shopping, as well as its social components, are subordinate to how much each customer can be coaxed to charge up on his Visa.

This emphasis on efficiency actually kills the fun of shopping, and prevents a culture from rising out of the experience. Customers are shuttled through stores as if being conveyed through the assembly line on a factory floor. Shopping is treated as a means to an end, rather than an end in itself—an activity to be returned to, for the sheer joy of it, again and again.

That's why we'd expect the other main camp of retail designers, the theme architects, to rise to the occasion of shopping. But while the designers of these theme environments may be picking up where theme park legend Walt Disney left off, they are so foolishly sidetracked by the need to sell that they, too, degrade the overall experience of the brands into which they should be welcoming consumers.

The first theme environments were devised by *Wizard of Oz* author L. Frank Baum, for the bridal area of Wannamaker's. His idea was to turn the entire department into a kind of cathedral to the bride—an entire universe of values all dedicated to the perfect wedding. This way, the bride-to-be was to be intimidated into doing everything possible to fit into that world.[3] That means buying products. Department stores of all kinds followed with themes for every department, with the intention of making customers feel out of place. Salespeople were instructed to speak in fake, upscale Cary Grant accents, and to match the tone and décor of their department with their dress and grooming.

Today, nearly every store is a theme store. Niketown, in New York, is more than just a temple to the sport shoe: it is an environment that serves to make people feel incapable of reaching the values of the shoe brand. Huge (multistory) portraits of sports legends combined with an ambient soundtrack laced with sports sounds create a self-contained universe: 60,000 square feet on five stories, all dedicated to overwhelming consumers with the importance of a single brand. The customer is to be overwhelmed by the environment, reduced to a childlike state, so that he will then be more likely to transfer parental authority to the salesperson or the store itself.

With the preponderance of national "superstores," consumers no longer need to go to the mall, or to a New York flagship, to experience the intimidation of a theme environment. The latest permutation of this technique is the "untheme" theme store, like Home Depot or Staples, where the store is designed to look like a warehouse. Customers walk down cement aisles with oversized metal shelves. Forklifts, palettes, and the general unavailability of sales help complete the simulation of an environment meant for professionals or contractors.

Theme environments, like those designed to trigger sensory cues, are daunting places to shop. Few people feel like empowered parents after making their way through the multitude of choices in a superstore like Buy Buy Baby, or like capable athletes after picking a tennis racket from among the multitudes at Sports Authority. Yes, the intimidation strategy may work to upsell the customer on a few extra items, or even a higher-quality main purchase. But the overall effect is torturous. This is why, today, most Americans consider shopping a form of work.[4]

Oddly enough, the few ways in which malls and other retail environments actually succeeded were seen, at least at first, as their failures. Kids in the suburbs, victims of zoning laws that isolated commerce from recreation, had no natural places to hang out. While young people living in towns or cities could socialize by the candy store or comic shop, the suburbs had no such meeting places along the main routes where retail was supposed to happen. With the first shopping malls came the first place many suburban kids had to congregate, enjoy an inexpensive meal, or even take in a movie. In such an environment, shopping could be elevated to a social experience.

And while age limits, parental supervision rules, and curfews were set to keep teens from disrupting more serious shoppers at work, the lessons of the social reality of the mall were not lost on the most forward-thinking retail designers.

Starbucks was one of the first major retail companies to recognize the power of a brand, a storefront, and a product to serve as social currency for urbanites desperate for an excuse and means to congregate. By the 1980s, when Starbucks was making its move, conventional wisdom dictated that the key to making money in chain restaurants was to push customers through as fast as possible. Fast-food restaurants were busy testing color schemes and seating styles for their capability to speed up diners' consumption of food and make room for the next.[5] Starbucks went against traditional wisdom, and made its storefronts into lounges, encouraging people to stay as long as they wish. The stores quickly turned into major meeting and gathering spots.

Starbucks was not getting out of the coffee business, at all. It was getting further into it. A futurist named Andrew Zolli likes to think of coffee as having gone through three main stages. First, it was sold as a bean. When beans became a commodity, it was sold as one brand of coffee grind or another. Finally, now, coffee is sold as an experience—a form of social currency. Starbucks realized that coffee, more than providing people with a boost, gives them the ability to socialize.

That's why Starbucks created its own culture around coffee. It has its own style, customs, and even its own language. Try ordering a small coffee, and you'll be told it's a tall breakfast blend. The words that first intimidate eventually form the basis of a shared identity for the Starbucks community. Almost anywhere in the world, Starbucks means a place you can sit down in the presence of fellow coffee drinkers and relax, work, or meet others. It's a new town square. While the merits of corporations filling in where churches, schools, or civic clubs have failed us can be debated (and will be in Chapter Seven), the fact remains that Starbucks owes its success to promoting its shops as platforms for social interaction—and elevating its brand to a form of social currency.

Almost any retail environment can turn itself into a social space, as long as the values of the place are married in some way to the values of the product being sold. A retail space only makes sense as a provider of social currency if hanging out in that space actually means something significant about the customer. The piano lounge in the lobby of a midtown New York Chemical Bank branch did attract a few senior citizens at lunchtime, but had nothing to do with the core values of banking. Commerce Bank, on the other hand, is the fastest-growing bank in the Northeast because it has reinvented the culture of banking around the way real people use and save money. It is open on weekends, has eliminated intimidating dividers between customers and tellers, and has even installed free change counters called "Penny Arcades" where families, whether bank members or not, can exchange their coins for paper currency.

Barnes & Noble reinvented bookselling from the inside out by turning its superstores into a new kind of public library. Facing widespread public outcry in the mid-eighties for moving into the established territories of independent booksellers, Barnes & Noble faced a tremendous challenge. This faceless national brand, nonetheless, created a new culture around books by leveraging the social currency that a bookstore could offer people in otherwise anonymous urban and suburban communities. B&N opened cafés within its stores, and allowed shoppers to read books and magazines while they sipped beverages.

Although they weren't explicitly encouraged, customers were free to read entire books without ever paying for them. The magazine racks were spaced wide apart, so people could sit down on the floor or in a nearby couch and read to their heart's content. New customers walking in for the first time are still shocked by the scene: Is this a bookstore or a pickup bar? But that's precisely the point. Those who are initiated into the culture of B&N understand that the store is a social hub. To be there confers upon one the status of book reader—a leg up in an otherwise competitive social scene. Being a reader means having something in common. "Have you read the new Philip Roth?" It's a form of social currency.

Guitar Center, today the world's biggest music instrument retailer, began as a single shop in Hollywood in 1964. Unlike most musical instrument shops, Guitar Center created a professional atmosphere. This was easy, as most professional rock musicians are out of work most of the time. While your guitar salesperson may not have played with Bruce Springsteen, he may very well have played in a band that opened for Bruce Springsteen at one time.

Guitar Center is more than an opportunity for kids to buy guitars; it's a place to try out pretty much any piece of musical equipment there is—and to play on it for hours. Moreover, it's a way for an amateur musician to interact with professionals, and for professionals to interact with one another. Rather than offering itself as a brand proposition, Guitar Center gets out of the way and turns its stores into round-the-clock music socials. The shops break down the barriers between sales clerk and customer, and provide a place where musicians of all levels become part of the same culture. The store unifies, much in the way music does.

Stores work best when they provide social currency for people who need it. The brand of the store becomes less about selling product than conferring legitimacy on the space itself. That's why the owners of American Girl Place—still my favorite example of social currency on the sales floor—have always maintained strict limitations on the number of shops that could be opened across the country. American Girl Place is a special kind of doll shop. It's a destination spot, a tourist attraction, and, most of all, a way for mothers and daughters to connect through a brand.

Again, let's set aside for the time being whether facilitating an intimate mother-daughter interaction is an appropriate role for a corporation to take on. The fact is, women and their daughters are experiencing something very special in these branded environments, and they're doing so not because they're being strategically upsold on more doll clothes and accessories, but because they are being offered various forms of social currency through which to interact.

At American Girl Place, the doll is not an end in herself, but a means of interaction. The doll can be brought to a hair salon or a dress shop, where the mother can supervise a daughter's makeover at the same time a girl supervises her doll's. The most strikingly ingenious touch is the café, where mother, daughter, and doll can enjoy afternoon tea together while they tell each other stories. For those who might need some stimulus to connect, the store provides little cards at each table, with suggestions for conversations. It may sound silly, but it works. I once interviewed a woman who had visited the American Girl Place Café in New York, along with her daughter and her mother-in-law. When they were asked to each share a story with the others about losing a doll, the woman remembers, she finally forged a connection with her estranged mother-in-law. When a branded environment can help people connect with one another on this level, its owners have nothing to worry about.

Perhaps the best example of a branded experiential environment is the Apple Store. Unlike Levi's, Calvin Klein, or even Sony, which have all created flagship brand temples in New York and other major cities, Apple's little cathedrals are even more thought out. In the words of cult brand anthropologist Douglas Atkin:

> As you enter, you are faced with a stunning but simple glass staircase. On the first floor, there are side chapels dedicated to the worship of digital photography, mp3s, and sleek laptops. Upstairs is the confessional—the Apple bar—where past mistakes are corrected and absolved . . . Worshippers' doubts are heard and some truths and answers are given here, too. Along the galleries are the ecclesiastical libraries of software, and the sacred texts—the manuals and user guides. And everywhere, ministering quietly and reverentially, are the black clad acolytes, always on hand to explain the doctrine of loading software or give instruction on downloading music. At the top of the stairs you enter an inner sanctum. Congregants quietly gather there on slick pews facing a

pulpit to the left of a giant flat screen exploding with color and life. The pastor of the day . . . will preach on the doctrine of OS X, the uses of Adobe Photoshop, the salvation of FinalCut.

Off to the right of the entrance is the altar, the last stop for a member's hour of supplication. A long smooth plinth of light colored wood, cash registers accept offerings from the dedicated, mediated by the smiling deacons.[6]

Like the best of churches, the Apple Store works because it fosters a true culture. It's not just a static representation of a cathedral—a mere monument or photo opportunity. It is a working church, providing meaning, counsel and, most of all, a parish to its believers. Everyone who hangs out at the Apple Store understands they are among fellow Apple users, and part of the Apple cult. They are bound by the symbolic system of the Macintosh, iPod, and other carefully branded Apple products.

And the store itself allows Apple users to exercise a bit of their privileged status as members of a special community. Like B&N regulars who know that the magazines can be brought to the coffee shop, Apple users know that the many computers on display are all hooked up to the Internet, and available for checking email or even doing a little iChat. For those in the know, an Apple Store is really a free cybercafe, with the benefit of being surrounded by fellow Apple users. Sure, the Apple Store is a store, and many new attractive products will be tantalizingly displayed. To a committed Apple user, however, this amounts to a public service. The more one knows about what Apple is up to, the higher one's status in the community. Information is social currency.

THE OBJECT OF BRANDING

However much attention goes into their design, Apple's products are less valuable to customers as objects than they are as enablers of experience. They are a form of social currency, making connections between people not just technologically but also philosophically. In our renaissance culture, just as retail space must shift emphasis from selling and to social interaction, so too must brands shift focus from the products and to the opportunities for bonding and community they offer.

As we saw earlier, brands arose as a way to compensate for the dehumanizing effects of the Industrial Age. The more people had previously needed to trust the person behind a product, the more important the brand became as a symbol of origin and authenticity. Products associated with fraud, such as beer and liquor that could easily be fermented with sugar or diluted with water, had always depended on the reliable reputation of a locally known brewer. Maybe that's why the very first brand, registered in the United Kingdom in 1875—the same year that the Trade Mark Bill passed—was Bass Ale's Red Triangle. It was the first registered symbol used to represent a product.

As various products became commodified, however, supply eventually surpassed demand. Branding came to serve less as a mark of authentic connection to some human producer than as a mark of distinction all by itself. As customers realized that one detergent or box of frozen peas was pretty much the same as any other, brand identity became less about guaranteeing quality than providing additional value. Leo Burnett, founder of the Chicago school of advertising, was the first master in this pursuit, inventing characters from Tony the Tiger to the Green Giant. These manufactured spokes-creatures didn't embody a product's attributes as much as they broadcast the brand's attributes, which were entirely less tangible.

Over the last several decades, all these brands have become something of commodities, themselves. Do we want the cookies made by elves in a hollow tree, or those brought to the supermarket by a little man in a lab coat? They all taste the same, and one commercial is pretty much as entertaining as another. Why pick one cookie or computer over any other?

Today's marketers believe that the way to capture and retain customers is by engaging in a conversation with them. The strategy is to create a brand so compelling and layered that people want to have a relationship with it. Detroit's brand managers believe that kids will develop loyalty to one car brand by the time they are 10, and then—if properly engaged over the years—maintain brand "fidelity" throughout their adult lives.[7] Homemakers are conditioned to pick one brand of fabric softener over another because they are endeared to the market-research-generated bear that appears in its commercials. Such surface distinctions are no longer enough. The commodification of brands, combined with the widespread use of brands as social connectors, rather than ends in themselves, has made this strategy obsolete.

In an age of interactive media, customers don't want to communicate *with* brands or their spokespeople, anymore. They want to communicate *through* them. Brands for this era can become a form of social currency, offering opportunities for affiliation and, at best, even authorship.

This is new. Until just the last decade or so, products and brands served as substitutes for connections with other people. While brand names provided a sense of accountability and recognition, the products themselves gave a bit of comfort on an increasingly alienated suburban landscape. Americans had fewer friends and civic relationships, but they had more cars, appliances, TVs, and other objects with which to fill their homes and lives. Products substituted for people, as divorced midlifers established relationships with their sports cars, and latchkey children were greeted at home by televisions instead of parents. The Bauhaus ethos that mass-produced objects could fulfill our need for functionality and meaning reached its apex in a consumer culture where people were defined by the many manufactured things they bought.

But the last few consumer products off the assembly line—computers, cell phones, and other interactive technologies—shifted the focus off themselves or their creators and onto the connections they could make to other people. That's when the overwhelming need to communicate more effectively arose, and where the new opportunity for brands made itself apparent: to serve as social currency.

Choosing a brand, today, is more like joining a club. It conveys not simply a willingness to be associated with that brand's values, but a desire to associate with the people who have already joined. Those brands that can appeal to people on this level—as social facilitators and meaning systems—rise to the level of secular cults. The best brands today are not merely names on products consumers can own, but cultures to which people feel they can belong. And cultures begin with real people.

The most primitive form of brand culture begins where the spokesmodel strategy left off. While the big brands were busy conducting focus groups to determine which celebrity to artificially link to their products, entrepreneurs like Mary Kay, Martha Stewart, and even George Foreman were busy launching products based, to varying degrees, on their own expertise.

Although these brands don't necessarily give people the opportunity to connect to one another, they do provide a sense of connection to their creators. The customer can sense Martha's design process as they examine the embroidery around her towels. An aspiring cosmetics saleswoman reads about Mary Kay's rise from poverty and feels she can follow in the self-made millionaire's footsteps. Cooking a burger on a George Foreman grill creates a sense of connection with the happy, retired boxer and the indulgent but healthy lifestyle he seems to represent.

In these cases, the products begin to serve as media themselves, between the customers and the people who really did develop them. After all, not every kid buys a record just to play it for his friends. There are occasions when playing the music creates a sense of connection not just to other listeners, but to the musician himself. For a brand to become an invitation to an entire culture, though, it must also provide a way for everyone involved to forge connections to one another. This requires the brand to develop itself into a form of social currency.

The Body Shop, for one, took a category most people associated with surface beauty, and turned it into an entire meaning system.[8] Founder Anita Roddick's "Body Shop Charter," a list of rules and values that the company would practice and preach, raised bath soap to a cultural ethos. It was a brilliant positioning. While products like bath oils and scented facial cleansers had always evoked a certain guilty self-indulgence, Roddick was capable of transforming them into instruments of selflessness and global change.

She began by selling potions made by indigenous peoples she met on her global travels, and along with them, the stories of the Africans or Nepalese whose ecofriendly recipes she was using. "Stories about how and where we find ingredients bring meaning to our essentially meaningless products," she explained to a journalist early on, "while stories about the company bind and preserve our history and our sense of common purpose." The retail business began as a single shop in Brighton, England, frequented mostly by hippies, vegans, and environmentalists. This self-selecting group became the core cultural proposition of the brand. To buy from the Body Shop meant to be part of its crunchy, caring, holistic, and herbal subculture.

As the Body Shop story and culture spread, the business grew into a powerful global brand. By developing her original charter over a period of 18 months, in collaboration with her employees, Roddick was assured of developing a corporate culture and marketing strategy that matched the ethos she was selling to her customers. Her employees weren't just selling soap, anymore, but spreading a culture that embraced animal rights, labor standards, hemp agriculture, and the environment.

To buy a Body Shop product was to join the Body Shop movement. This brand no longer belonged just to Anita Roddick, but to everyone who supported breast cancer research and micro-loans to Third World women. The brand served its culture by providing its members with a flag for their shared values. When a company recognizes its ability to provide social currency for its customers, it elevates its brand from simple accountability for a mass-produced good to a complex and ongoing meaning system to which a person can belong.

The danger in creating such a meaning system, of course, is that eventually the customers are as central to the brand's identity as its founders are. And because they see themselves as having signed on to a proposition, they don't take kindly to what they see as a brand's betrayal of these values. In the 1990s, a well-researched article in *Business Ethics*[9] revealed Roddick's founding myth as, in fact, a myth (she copied

the idea from a store she saw in San Francisco) and her ingredient pro-
curement as environmentally and ethically unsound as any of her competitors'. Brand loyalists fled the Body Shop in droves. Roddick
managed to salvage her brand by admitting her sins and recommitting
to the ethics she initially announced in her charter. But the lesson was
clear: the culture of a brand must be lived from the inside out, and for
real.

Brand cultures work by turning their customers into advocates
and missionaries. This may sound far out of the box—as if a business is
to trust its marketing to outsiders. As the ultimate enactors and beneficiaries of the brand culture, however, it is the customers who are in
charge and most *central* to the brand's experience. A business can set
the stage, but the customers must act the play.

In that sense, the best thing a company can do is provide the tools
for a culture to form, and then get out of the way. BMW motorcycles,
though much less known than Harley-Davidson, nonetheless have a
rabid cult of followers. Belonging to a BMW motorcycle club means
being able to announce what city you'll be touring to and knowing a fellow BMW rider will be willing to house you overnight. It's an exclusive
club, for riders who see themselves as a special breed of bike aficionado.
BMW has offered to get more involved in the development of their organization, but the riders have refused. BMW got the message; this may
be something it started, but it's not a culture it can, or should, control.

Whereas BMW may have stumbled upon the secret of social currency by accident, other brands of all kinds have been mining it quite
intentionally. It's just a matter of getting deep inside a product or service, beyond the point of purchase or object value, and into the extended social experience that affiliation can offer.

Virgin, JetBlue, and Southwest Airlines, for example, have each
created distinctly different but tremendously successful cultures
around an activity as rote, uncomfortable, and fraught with anxiety as
air travel. But all three understand that this is an interactive process.
The brand can lay out clues and hints, but the customers must form the
actual culture.

Virgin had a head start, since Richard Branson's brand already enjoyed a clear identity through his record shops and label. Branson looked at every aspect of air travel, from arrival at the airport to the words written on a toothbrush case, for their opportunity to convey the insiderly, cheeky spirit of his music industry brand. The planes were painted with Vargas-like images of girls, the flight attendants wore retro outfits, and even coach passengers were told to keep their headsets as a gift. To fly on Virgin felt as though one had discovered something and was now a member of a club. We might have to do business, but we do it in the style of the rock performers who might be traveling on the same flight.

Southwest went in the opposite direction, using homespun humor and self-effacing charm to push through air travel's status as a boring commodity. It would be a no-frills carrier, taking passengers from point A to point B and making no apologies for it. Southwest would celebrate it. The single bag of peanuts flight attendants give passengers is labeled "The Frills." But this doesn't mean the experience of flying Southwest is painful. On the contrary, by turning its brand into a lowbrow but friendly culture it gives its passengers the gift of one another.

Every plane is laid out in the same configuration, with some seats facing one another. Open seating leads to something of a rush for the best place, but it ends up favoring the loyal customer who knows where to go. It also forces passengers to develop social relationships fast, as they exchange places to accommodate couples and families. On many flights, the attendants ask the passengers to clean the plane before landing, or even help distribute beverages. Southwest is a friendly, participatory airline, where pilots and flight attendants tell bad jokes over the PA system, and customers are invited—even required—to participate in their flight experience. In a testament to openness, a reality show about Southwest's workers and flyers, called *Airline,* completes the picture, candidly exposing the real but almost always humorous challenges that Southwest employees and flyers face every day.

It's not for everyone, but that's part of the charm. Those who do see themselves as Southwest family are as loyal to their fellow Southwest fans as they are to the airline. Hundreds of articles and even a few books have been written about the Southwest loyalty formula, as if incorporating the airline's style of employee retreat or customer service phone scripts could reproduce its success. It's much simpler than that: just build a real culture from the inside out.

It begins with honesty, and follows naturally from there. JetBlue distinguished itself by facing up to the lie in modern American aviation: that "we love to fly and it shows." In February 2000, founder and CEO David Neeleman started the airline with a simple strategy focused on "bringing humanity back to air travel" by offering passengers low fares, friendly service, and a high-quality product.[10] He put free TVs in every seat, made the whole cabin one class, and found employees who could bring themselves to be nice to passengers for an entire flight. Saving money by using some less-frequented airports allowed the airline to splurge on entertainment and customer service. JetBlue succeeded in making its airline and its marketing fun.

As a result, the experience of JetBlue was different enough from other East Coast point-to-point airlines to serve as a brand identity: cheap chic. Wealthy vacationers and business travelers alike became loyal customers—and vocal ones. Being in a single cabin class makes the usually privileged traveler feel like part of the regular people, but without any sacrifice in quality of experience. Again, an airline's flyers began to think of themselves as belonging to a club of fun people who are "in the know."

Moreover, as a measure of social currency, to be a JetBlue flyer means having a great recommendation for any friend or family member who needs to fly, as well as reasons why flying to John Wayne Airport is finally just as convenient as landing at LAX. Unless, of course, it's a person who just isn't fun. In that case, there's no reason to let him in the club.

Airlines were already in the experience business, though, whether they liked it or not. People fly together, and a cabin filled with passengers is already a temporary microculture. How does one turn a product like a car or computer into an experience—especially when everyone knows it will eventually break down? And how does a branded object become a way of connecting, when you might very well use the product alone?

Apple did it with the computer. The original maker of personal computers is still the industry leader in terms of brand experience and customer loyalty. Apple users are so dedicated to the cause of the company that they regularly volunteer to demonstrate new products at CompUSA and other retail outlets. That's right: they volunteer their time to pitch the virtues of Apple to strangers. Others belong to MacUser, MacAddict, and MacEvangelist groups, to support one another in everything Apple—and more. To what does Apple owe this intense loyalty?

It is a culture. An ongoing proposition. The products aren't ends in themselves, but invitations to a new and particular way of living, as well as a new and particular form of inclusion. It is a cult of individuality—of thinking differently. The company initiates this spirit through its products, and then reinforces this experience of a brand culture through its marketing.

Apple products can be customized, enhanced, and upgraded easily. In a sense, Apple is not a product at all, but a system one belongs to. It's more of a subscription, really. Everything is modular—camera, programs, music player, displays—so that users can upgrade and personalize continuously. The brand experience doesn't begin and end with an object; it mutates and evolves along with the customer and his needs. To "get" this is to get Apple—to think differently, and be part of the club. From there, users make their own customizations, naming their hard drives, and placing totems on the tops of monitors and graphics on their desktops. Other computer brands have followed suit, giving users control over the "skin" of their computer, but none has made itself a culture based on the right to think for oneself, separate from the pack.

Apple's commercials seem to exist less as a way of advertising products than providing existing customers with an enhanced experience. Those arty billboards in the street, showing a silhouetted iPod user dancing to a tune of his choice do more than publicize the existence of iPod; they reinforce what it can feel like to walk down the street wearing an iPod. To be one of those cool, silhouetted, but stridently individualist Apple people.

The fact that Apple exists as a counterculture within an entire universe of Windows PC users is significant. Windows' dominance energizes Apple's base, even helping to define what a Mac user is by the negative example of conformist Windows users (just as Wal-Mart helps define Target, or SUVs define Mini). Apple isn't a computer; it's a lifestyle choice. Steve Jobs is not in the computer business or even the operating system business; as the name on his suite of Macintosh programs, iLife, suggests, he's in the digital lifestyle business. Whether enabling people to do videoconferencing via iChat, download and listen to songs through iTunes, giving them professional-quality digital music production with Garageband, or offering a full-featured video editing system with iMovie, Apple is building the tools that a digital culture needs to grow.

Apple's management team is no longer really at the helm, separated from its customers on one side and its employees on the other. Steve Jobs may be at the center of the cult of Apple, but it is the cult leader's job only to articulate and embody the mission of the brand. It's up to the employees and customers, alike, to build out the culture. The employees do this by developing new authoring tools; the customers do this by using them to tell new stories and relate to one another in new ways.

A brand culture can even have more to do with the employees than it does the customers. One of Wal-Mart's greatest liabilities, in fact, is its well-publicized poor treatment of its employees. In smaller towns, where Wal-Mart's employee base represents a significant portion of the local community, this translates directly to ill will. As these stories trickle up through media, they poison the brand culture, making Wal-Mart patronage a social deficit rather than a form of currency.

The American automobile industry was facing a similar challenge in the 1980s. Japan had surpassed the United States as the world's top automaker, but union restrictions here were preventing automobile companies from adopting more innovative approaches to manufacturing. All they could do was lay off employees as they sold fewer cars. Meanwhile, the car-buying experience had become characterized by the aggressive sales techniques of master dealers Mike Kay and Remar Sutton (who has since switched sides to become a consumer advocate). Prospective customers knew they were going to be subjected to a battery of manipulations as they haggled their way to a deal that would be anything but fair. The American automobile industry had become synonymous with unemployment lines, the decay of cities like Flint, Michigan, and overbearing salesmen.

Somehow, the notion that what's good for General Motors is good for the USA was no longer enough consolation for the company's real culture. That's why, in 1984, a small group at GM, led by its CEO Roger Smith, decided to embark on a venture with its adversary, the United Auto Workers, to figure out a way to build a car that could compete effectively with the Japanese. This new venture became the Saturn brand and culture. It was a radical reinvention of the way automobiles were produced and sold.

Tellingly, it all took place without study, research, or even very much consultation.[11] Because it happened so fast, and from the hip, no one even checked for previous trademarks on the name Saturn. A few months later, Saturn was launched as a wholly owned subsidiary of GM, with an entirely new approach toward making and selling cars.

Both because GM wanted the new company to be untainted by GM's practices and because the brand would be competing directly with GM, Saturn set up shop in a rural area near Springhill, Tennessee. Not many wanted to be a part of the new venture, but those who did choose to sign up all shared the common belief that a radical, even heretical approach to making, distributing, and selling automobiles was called for.

These engineers, plant workers, marketers, and executives formed the core culture of this new brand. As experienced automotive industry members, they had full knowledge of what worked and what didn't in the existing systems. As a self-selected band of heretics, they had the courage to reinvent American car culture from the inside out. And so they did. By 1991, the first Saturns were hitting the showrooms. Instead of dealerships, Saturns were sold in "stores." The entire culture of haggling was scrapped, and replaced with a single sticker price. No negotiation necessary.

Instead of training salespeople how to manipulate buyers in windowless haggle chambers, Saturn taught its salespeople about the nature of trust and community. This work eventually evolved into the now-famous notion of a "Saturn Family." Workers, salespeople, and, finally, customers were all part of the same interdependent culture. The success of this strategy with consumers said as much about the existing car culture as it did about Saturn. People who needed new cars had been putting off their purchases for years merely because they wanted to avoid engaging with a car dealer! This was especially true for women, younger drivers, and minorities, who felt particularly disadvantaged on the showroom floor.

The Saturn Family was not just a commercial. It was real. People who went through the experience of buying one said they could feel it. The cars were all right, but the buying experience and the follow-up customer service and repairs were unique for their time. It made customers into loyalists who wanted to share this experience with others.

But they also wanted to reinforce their sense of community with their fellow Saturn Family members. That's why 45,000 of them showed up (with their cars and families) at the Saturn plant in Tennessee for the first Saturn "Homecoming," in 1994, to interact with Saturn workers and watch the cars being made. (Amazingly, and contrary to all expectations, plant productivity actually *increased* during the two days of the Saturn Homecoming.)

Saturn drivers from all across America, even as far as Taiwan, spent their family vacations at an automobile plant. Why? Because Saturn was more than just a pleasant buying experience. It represented a new approach to hard times. It evoked good, old-fashioned American values of pitching in, sharing responsibility, and breaking down the alienating walls between worker, salesperson, and consumer. As the economic downturn of the 1980s taught Americans, we're all in this together. Saturn rose to embody this ethos by rebuilding the car industry from the inside out in a manner consistent with the values of its workers and customers.

Viewed more cynically, as I have, myself, in articles and documentaries, the Saturn effort was brand masquerading as a social experiment. The mass pilgrimage of customers to an automobile plant would be laughable were it not experienced as so very meaningful to everyone who participated. Besides, the Saturn experience of family and fairness was felt and lived throughout the organization, from team spirit and fair labor practices at the plants right through to customer service and free automobile safety and maintenance workshops for owners. Some dealerships hosted days at theme parks or other destinations for their customers. Ten thousand customers showed up for a Saturn-organized social day at Carrowinds in North Carolina.

Moreover, like the extinct civic organizations whose communal function Saturn means to restore, the company offered customers and employees the opportunity to extend the ethos of the brand into the nonautomotive world, as well. Saturn dealerships became the organizing points for community action and development. Plant workers, salespeople, and customers worked side by side building playgrounds in poor neighborhoods, with seed money from the Saturn Corporation. No matter how cynical we may be about corporations usurping the traditional roles of churches, Boy Scouts, or Kiwanis clubs, it's hard to argue with several hundred completed playgrounds in communities that lack the resources to provide for themselves. This was more than a brand attribute; it was a brand serving as the ideological motivation for civic engagement.

In spite of the brand's connection with consumers, Saturn ultimately failed on the level of engineering innovation. Unlike its sales, distribution, and marketing divisions, Saturn's automotive research and development still took place at GM, and the parent company was incapable of providing Saturn with models current enough to compete with the Honda Civic or Toyota Corolla.

Saturn was eventually reabsorbed back into GM, as an upscale brand to take the place of the retired Oldsmobile line. With its operations moved to GM's headquarters, it is hoped Saturn will get the attention it deserves in the form of new product development. The $3.5 billion worth of resources put into Saturn's new products for 2005[12] attests to more than GM's faith in the Saturn brand. GM wants Saturn to survive because it is hoping to incorporate the best of Saturn's culture into its own dying one. GM is already restructuring its sales divisions to be more like Saturn's.

In the same way that a bit of yogurt can culture a whole new vat, the living thing that is Saturn can infect the entirety of GM. Just as for its customers, for GM, the brand experience of Saturn is now more important than the brand itself.

chapter four

THE PLAY IS
THE THING:
FOLLOWING THE FUN

Successes like those I just described do not originate in focus groups or consumer research. Social currency is not something constructed by a cynical marketing department and then broadcast through some preselected trend leaders, but something that emerges out of a living culture. It's a form of agreement, a collaborative process, a way of making meaning together. It's something real.

Cultures such as Saturn, Apple, and Virgin tend to emerge spontaneously, as the organic expression of a passionate CEO or the tight-knit group of innovators at the core of a company encountering the equally passionate energy of a customer base. It's a live, unpredictable and even messy affair between a whole bunch of people figuring out how they might have some fun or find some meaning together.

That's right: the driving force of our new renaissance society is play.

Sure, groups can organize around a variety of things: fear, patriotism, even hatred. But these are more suitable for armies than cultures. They require blind allegiance to a single idea on the commands of a leader, and are compromised by feedback or cross talk. They can't handle complexity, freedom, or natural evolution. And because they tend not to be fun, they require enforcement. That means additional resources must be spent just maintaining cohesion, which eventually leads the whole enterprise or movement toward diminishing returns.

Play, on the other hand, allows for engagement on an entirely more voluntary and complex level. Participants in a successful brand culture are not cajoled or coerced into membership, but simply invited. Even the spread of media viruses—the word of mouth promoting products and ideas through cultures—is a form of play. The reward, as in a game of "telephone," is seeing what the whole collective has wrought. We pass on tidbits of social currency because it's fun. The mediaspace becomes a kind of play space, where the object of the game is to get the most Web "hits" for one's homemade animated video, or to see if a media prank can get coverage on the national news.

In a renaissance society driven by the need to forge connections, play is the ultimate system for social currency. It's a way to try on new roles without committing to them for life. It's a way to test strategies of engagement without being defined by them forever. It's a way to rise above the seemingly high stakes of almost any situation and see it as the game it probably is. It's a way to make one's enterprise a form of social currency from the beginning, and to guarantee a collaborative, playful, and altogether more productive path toward continual innovation.

And this play begins at work.

Establishing a playful career or company isn't as easy as it looks. It doesn't require expensive consultants, trips to the woods, or the reinvention of a company's culture based on some abstract ideal. But it does mean going against much of what we've been taught about competition and survival—not just in business school, but for the past five centuries! Still, just as people have stopped relating as individuals to their brands and opted instead to become members of brand cultures, producers in a renaissance era must come to think of their companies as collaborative minisocieties, whose underlying work ethic will ultimately be expressed in the culture they create for the world at large.

Such cultures are created from the inside out. Only a truly playful enterprise will be capable of attracting others to the party and then keeping them there.

Playfulness is at the heart of business. Sure, it may have been lost, along with the rest of innovation, to the gods of efficiency and scale. But our renaissance has reintroduced play into human affairs. Coming to understand the new and increasingly welcome role of play in our culture will give us clues on how to incorporate this ethos into our work and businesses. It's only working if it's fun.

MAN, THE PLAYER

I'm not the first to discover the play principle at the heart of any truly successful enterprise. My own grandfather, in fact, was sent to America in 1914 when he was just 12 years old, with specific instructions from his father to earn enough money to bring his four brothers, two sisters, and parents over as soon as possible. He pushed a cart on the Lower East Side in New York and sold rags to other immigrants. But rather than take a survivalist's fearful attitude toward his fledgling business, young Morris Weintraub saw the whole thing as a game. A child, himself, he was unable to see it any other way. He learned about fabric, searched for new angles on how to get it at rock-bottom prices, made friends with the child of a man who was developing a new form of rayon, and became his neighborhood's exclusive purveyor of this exotic textile. To Morris, it was just a great big game. Three decades later, the Weintraub brothers had the biggest retail textile chain in New England. And Morris kept buying fabric into his eighties, all because, in his words, "it was so much fun."

I suppose I followed in his footsteps—not as a textile merchant, of course, but as a follower of fun. In my career as a writer, futurist, and consultant, I've been able to predict some of the biggest cultural and business trends simply by seeking out the people who were enjoying themselves the most. And I did this because I wanted to have a good time myself. The secret of my own success, and that of the people, organizations, and businesses I've studied, has been to follow the fun.

It's an idea I've traced back to a few European philosophers of the 1930s, who went so far as to suggest that play is the fundamental human pursuit, underlying everything else we do. A great Dutch thinker of that time, Johan Huizinga, hoped that human society would someday dedicate itself openly to play. He argued that play was not just some ritualized version of life, but its truest expression. Dogs don't play in order to practice for the hunt. Rather, they hunt in order to give themselves the time and energy to play. Likewise, human beings must learn to understand play as central to our ability to live mindfully and meaningfully.[1]

Unlike the totalitarianism that was sweeping Europe, this play imperative celebrated human autonomy. No one can *do* play to a person; it must come from within and then be enacted by individuals engaged with one another. It was an ethos incompatible with the repressive regimes of midcentury Europe, in which human behavior was to be controlled from above. Fascism, for example, directed the human spirit toward the state, while communism sought to eliminate the individual and his innately destructive personal ambition. Of course, the totalitarian ideologies won out, and even after fascism was defeated, the notion of people freeing themselves from their sense of duty and obligation, and instead losing themselves in an orgy of play, was hardly a sensibility befitting a society that so recently went off the edge. Even in America at that time, play proved difficult as people surrendered the costumes and customs of their own cultures to the melting pot of solidarity, assembly lines, and the Protestant work ethic that supported them.

By the 1950s, however, people in the wealthiest and most technologically advanced parts of the world—the United States and Europe—rediscovered elements of play, and attempted to incorporate them into their lives. The hippie movement, with its emphasis on communal love, tapped into the spirit of play, albeit on a personal level. So did the free sex parties of the 1970s, which tried, yet mostly failed, to introduce play into the institution of marriage. The effort of antiwar protestors to levitate the Pentagon was as mischievous as it was provocative. The prankster activists of this era understood how playfulness could trigger the perspective required to think of important issues in new ways.

Fearing anarchy and revolution, our postwar government couldn't help but crack down on such play. Tricksters like Timothy Leary, Abbie Hoffman, Ken Kesey, and Lenny Bruce were each in his own moment bugged, beaten, and booked by the enforcers of a social order that couldn't yet contend with the threat that play poses to a status quo based on the gravity of negative consequences.

A decade later, their ideas and tactics were revived, embraced, but ultimately distorted by the New Age movement. A champion of rising above the fear for survival, Joseph Campbell advised spiritual people to "follow your bliss." He reassured them that "the universe would conspire" to support them in choices made from a higher level of consciousness. Most people who found their source of bliss, however, much too quickly rushed to determine a way to profit off it. Great ideas were immediately shrouded in mystery or cultism, and became pyramid schemes, from EST to Herbalife. The discovery of a modality that really "worked" meant becoming a yoga instructor, healer, or guru oneself, and working up the pyramid of payers to the realm of paid professionals, who meted out their playfulness for a price. Teachers and advisors developed markets for insights, artificially creating scarcity for playful experiences that were actually in abundance. In the mad rush from personal bliss to business plan, the fun was lost. As a result, the train to bliss derailed wherever bliss was actually found.

Meanwhile, the ascendance of marketing as an art form in the late 1970s and 1980s also gave new life to the cause of play, but the ethos of fun was always surrendered to the greater context of turning a profit. Although many television advertisements turned out to be entertaining, the industry from which they emerged was more concerned with creating the illusion of fun than actually having any. Agencies went public, got absorbed by conglomerates, and ended up as crippled by short-term bottom-line considerations as the corporations they were supposed to liberate with their creativity. Even 1980s character Gordon Gekko's widely celebrated, if misguided, proposal in the film *Wall Street* that "greed is good" was an effort to bring the player's mentality into the world of investment banking. He just had the ends and means reversed.

The other problem with all of these fledgling efforts at reintroducing play is that they were so limited in their scope. A person might have a blast at the rave party or prankster protest one night, but then has to get up the next morning and go to work in a real world that respects none of the insights gained. Teenagers might be permitted a certain degree of latitude in their relationship to hard reality, but after a few years of playful college antics, it's "welcome to the machine." Until very recently, play could only happen in some very particular and temporary time and place—a fraternity, a commune, an underground social scene, or an "old boys" club like Bohemian Grove or a Yale secret society. And when it did occur, it was so distinct from workaday reality that it took extremist, even perverted forms.

The repressiveness of existing regimes, the overwhelming cultural emphasis on money, and the built-in limits of our prospective playing fields have stunted the emergence of Huizinga's society based in fun. Luckily, thanks to our renaissance, these conditions have changed.

Whatever anyone's problems with American empire, it has also firmly established liberal democracy as the dominant global ethos. Real repression—on the order of midcentury European totalitarianism—is no longer an acceptable public policy. Western civilization has moved on, at least in the way we understand our own values, and our universalism is penetrating the world's repressive and fundamentalist strongholds—both abroad and at home.

Meanwhile, interactive technologies gave us widespread access to the world's formerly restricted playing fields. Computer hackers, themselves extraordinary exemplars of the player mentality, shared with us the greatest gift of the digital age: connectivity. The advent of networking has facilitated the first truly global mediaspace and marketplace in which play on a mass scale can take place. No, it's not a giant game of networked Doom I'm talking about, but a sense of fair play and equal access that pervades almost all levels of society.

In many cases, such as investing, journalism, or marketing, the opportunity to play in the formerly restricted big leagues is actually facilitated by the existence of the Web. Internet columnist Matt Drudge can break a scandal worthy of impeachment; an unknown Web blogger can push for—and win—the resignation of a Senate majority leader; or a passionate shopper can share her best "finds" on a mailing list that becomes a major Internet brand, Daily Candy. Each node is, potentially, a high leverage point to the whole system.

In other cases, the Internet serves more as a lens through which we can gain new perspectives on entrenched and unfair systems. The dot-com boom and bust, as well as scandals from Enron to Worldcom, played out in real time on everyone's computer screens. Thanks to cable business channels broadcasting the entire saga in real time, millions of Americans came to regard Wall Street as a Ponzi scheme that was forever unwinnable. As we learned to accept the utter worthlessness of our stock option packages and leveraged retirement plans, as well as all the false hope on which they hinged, we started to wonder just what to do with our lives. We are now, for once, open to answers that don't start with a dollar sign. As for the answers that *do* start with a dollar sign, we are much more likely to engage with them in the spirit of play.

FLOW: THE ZEN OF PLAY

Repression has been lifted, the playing fields opened up, and the financial imperative lessened: Why are so many of us still so unsatisfied with our jobs? It's precisely because we have the freedom to behave otherwise that our current circumstances have become intolerable. Now that play is a possibility, work as we formerly understood it just won't fly.

Those charged with cracking the whip have been among the first to break ranks. CFOs, for example, who bear the brunt of the business world's short-term bottom-line obsession, are exhibiting some of the lowest rates of job satisfaction even though they are among the best-paid executives. A *CFO* magazine study[2] revealed that a full 68 percent say pressures had increased on them in the last two years, and 63 percent believe this stress has had a deleterious effect on their health. According to a recent *New York Times* article[3] on the subject, CFOs are leaving their jobs in droves—usually to start their own smaller businesses or private enterprises. They are giving up money to have a greater sense of autonomy over their work, and their time.

A Harvard Business School professor told me that more than half of his students leave their corporate jobs within two years, disgusted not just by the company for which they worked, but "the whole world of business." Invariably, they choose jobs or start their own companies in order to participate in projects they feel offer meaning and fun.

In a recent study of American workers by the Radcliffe Public Policy Center, 64 percent said they would prefer more time to more money, and 71 percent of young men said they would give up pay for more time with their families.[4]

Employers are busy installing foosball tables, hiring chefs, and building gyms for their increasingly disgruntled employees, but these are just ways of trying to make a bad situation more tolerable. A foosball table is not the sign of a fun place to work; it's a glaring symbol indicating that work is not fun and employees need a break. Why would they rather be playing foosball than doing whatever it is they've been hired to do?

Many have argued that it's immature and idealistic to believe that everyone, or even a majority of people, should be allowed to enjoy their jobs. In the words of one dark *New York Times* OpEd piece, "We're still just means of production. . . . Work is often more bearable when we don't, in addition to money, expect it always to deliver happiness."[5] The same might be said for life, particularly when our duty to perform an economic function extends from what we can produce to what we can consume. Both work and life should be much more than "bearable."

Luckily, renaissances celebrate immaturity and idealism. The growing field of "neotany" looks at the extended childhoods of species as a sign of their development. The longer an infant is helpless, the more advanced the species to which it belongs. Fish are fully developed from birth, dogs depend on their mothers for a few months, and human beings are helpless for several years. Likewise, the extended time for youth and exploration our society now offers (a full 90 percent of American residents now graduate high school, and more than a third make it through college) means more time for practice, development, and play. Growing up should not mean an end to this freedom to expand and innovate. It can be its rebirth in an entirely new context: that of playful work.

True, most attempts at incorporating play into our work have failed so profoundly that many individuals and managers are loath even to try. We associate fun at work with those crazed motivational specialists of the 1980s and 1990s who led bizarre companywide workshops, or conducted private career counseling that had more to do with putting affirmative slogans on one's refrigerator than learning to love a path of work as the pursuit of play.

Real play is not silliness. Think of the last time you skied down a difficult slope, piloted a plane, wind-surfed, dived off a high board, or did any other daring feat. You were doing it for fun, but you approached the challenge with the utmost seriousness. Yes, it was a rush and absolutely purposeless; but it was serious business, too.

The heightened sense of perception and the "high" associated with such acts of daring are what have made "extreme sports" such as skateboarding, surfing, and motocross so popular among kids of this renaissance era. While competitive team sports evoking the battlefield are losing ground, individual sports that push a kid's personal limits are all the rage. This is because they are completely immersive experiences that provide significant challenges. This sort of experience has become known as "flow," and is equally applicable to work as to play.

Mihaly Csikszentmihalyi's groundbreaking exploration into the psychology of optimal experience, *Flow*, found that deep satisfaction with work had less to do with the job at hand than the way in which that job is approached. He defined flow as "the way people describe their state of mind when consciousness is harmoniously ordered, and they want to pursue whatever they are doing for its own sake."[6]

Among his subjects were members of a small mountain community in the Italian Alps who found their seemingly simple work of milking cows, herding sheep, or carding wool continually interesting and challenging. When asked what they would do if they didn't have to work, they invariably laughed and responded that they would still engage in the same tasks. This *was* their fun. In their community, just like those of many other societies where people are deeply satisfied by their work experiences, very little distinction is made between work and "free" time. All time is free time, since everyone is in charge of his individual choices. Everything is being done for its own sake. For the fun of it.

Of course, the freedom to engage in work this way is largely a function of scale. The villagers of the Italian Alps are not competing with agribusiness just yet. Without a quota of work to complete, a 74-year-old Italian woman Csikszentmihalyi encounters is free to take the longer scenic route from hill to barn in order to prevent erosion of the valley. On the way, she can enjoy the foliage or stop to tell a story to her grandson. Of course, her appreciation of nature is part of what motivates her to do the "extra work" necessary to preserve it, leading to a more sustainable ecosystem in which to raise her sheep. So, in a sense, having this fun *is* a good long-term business strategy.

Csikszentmihalyi studied a wide variety of people who experienced their work as a natural and joyous part of the lives—factory workers, solo artists, members of family enterprises—for the qualities they had in common. A welder from South Chicago named Joe Kramer typified his findings. Joe, by then in his midsixties, had repeatedly turned down offers of advancement because he liked doing what he did. Though Joe worked at the "lowest rung" in the company hierarchy, everyone in the company agreed "he was the most important person in the entire factory."[7]

What made Joe so valuable was not that he steadfastly kept to his welding station. It was that his natural curiosity had led him, over time, to learn how every piece of machinery in the plant worked. He could fill in for any worker, and even repair any machine in the plant that broke down. Not that Joe was a workaholic, either. At home, he created two community gardens out of rough abandoned lots, and even developed a way to make rainbows out of sprinklers and lights.

According to Csikszentmihalyi, Joe has a rather special personality, in that he can create "flow" experiences for himself even under circumstances most of the rest of us would find difficult or even boring. But the secret to Joe's success was his ability to find *increasing complexity* in the tasks before him. A person in "flow" is continually making new observations and confronting new challenges. These challenges are intrinsic to the work at hand, and experienced in the moment—not afterward.

Surprisingly, given our conscious attitude toward our jobs and careers, Csikszentmihalyi's studies show that even modern Americans find themselves in "flow" much more frequently at work than elsewhere. Although we claim we want more leisure time, we are much more likely to find an opportunity for genuinely fulfilling engagement and learning at work. Unfortunately, however, most work environments are not yet set up to maximize these experiences, and our attitude toward work keeps us from experiencing or remembering nearly any of it as fun. The overall message we get from our workplaces is to produce more, complain less, and ignore stress.

But workers, and even independents, actively participate in the perpetuation of this sad myth of work as a form of suffering. When I was in college, I made friends with a sanitation worker named Peter who experienced his duties in "flow." He had spent many years developing and perfecting his technique of lifting cans with one arm and swinging their contents into the truck in one smooth motion. He made up games for himself and the others on his truck to play, involving elaborate choreography and other meaningless challenges.

Problems arose, however, when he and his truckmates ended up finishing their routes two or three hours earlier than their schedule demanded. Returning to the depot earlier got them into trouble. Did they really finish the work? Once they were able to convince their dispatcher that they weren't shirking their responsibilities, they got in trouble with the union. The quantity of work demanded of a seven-hour shift had been negotiated. To do more than one's part constituted a violation of solidarity, since it raised the productivity bar for all. By the time I met Pete, his gang of four had been dispersed throughout the system—not for their techniques to be shared with others, but for them to be quashed.[8]

It doesn't take a union to turn "work" into a dirty word. We condition this attitude into ourselves by insisting on equating pain with gain. We are suspicious of ourselves when answers come too easily—feeling as though we've cheated. Those of us who secretly may love our work nonetheless feel guilty socializing with friends whose work we assume is more grueling than our own. So we complain about the hard hours, carpal tunnel syndrome, or exorbitant taxes on independent contractors. In the process, we may even convince ourselves we hate what we do. Everyone does, right?

We reinforce this attitude by "rewarding" ourselves after having completed a particularly difficult task—as if completing that task weren't a reward in itself. Most stress-reduction specialists now advise people to take regular breaks and sabbaticals, or recommend that managers begin offering massage, playrooms, and other workplace "perks" to offset the misery and doldrums of the work itself. These strategies all involve taking people out of their work in order to get them to be able to tolerate it better, instead of deep into their work, so they can appreciate it from the inside out.

Or we keep our "eyes on the prize," working in order to earn money for that new car, the LCD-TV, or our kids' education, thinking that these carrots will manage to elicit better work or more creativity from us. All they succeed in doing is putting "our nose to the grindstone." That's not flow.

Or we pull ourselves out of whatever we're doing by comparing our own achievements with those of others. The fiction is that such comparisons help motivate us to compete more effectively. Were we running a race, perhaps? When we're attempting to get into flow and innovate, all it does is distract us from the possibility of creating something genuinely new from the inside out. Great innovations are not just "better" than someone else's; they are great on their own.

When we approach our work as play, we free ourselves to test new models and ways of thinking without regard for consequences. We're just playing, after all. Yet this simple shift in orientation opens up a re-naissance of new approaches to innovation. We become improvisers, like kids playing a fantasy role-playing game, who make up the story as they go along.

This kind of freedom can be scary because it means we are limited only by our own imaginative capacity. Speculation, after all, is really just the art of expanding one's expertise into an unknown, untried direction. In that context, "faking it" is a crucial component of all innovation. It's the way a child learns the implications of different roles in life—from cops to robbers—and where we adults learn to test out hypotheses and their many implications. Anyone who has sold an untested idea, pitched an advertising account, or attempted to raise money for research knows what faking it is really about.

Once you've taken a speculative leap, you have no choice but to play whatever role you've assumed with bravado. Even if you're just playing devil's advocate, you owe it to yourself and everyone else to play it to the utmost. All modeling and all trials of new ideas demand a certain amount of fakery. It's not lying, but a playful form of self-confidence, and a skill required of the fantasy role-player and business speculator, alike.

Stewart Brand, one of the most playful personalities of the last century, is both. Brand earned his stripes with Ken Kesey as publicist for the "Merry Pranksters."[9] Brand was the one who thought to conduct "acid tests" and hand out diplomas to those who had successfully completed a psychedelic trip with the gang. Brand was later responsible for developing one of the very first, and certainly the most significant, early computer networked communities—The Well—and, soon after, his current organization, the Global Business Network (GBN).

I was among the many people initially dismissive of Brand's reinvention as a business consultant, particularly because he had chosen to associate almost exclusively with libertarians and radical free-market intellectuals. It seemed to many of us who had followed Brand's earlier escapades that the former hippie had, like the rest of the baby boom, sold out.

But the GBN isn't your typical business consultancy. Instead of giving their business and government clients hard advice on what to make or how to market, they take key executives on a little trip. No, they don't give them LSD, but the next best thing: the tools to take a role-playing adventure into several possible futures.

The GBN methodology originated in some work being done for Shell Oil, a company that had come to recognize the fact that shifts in the environment, Arab society, and global stability could influence its business prospects.[10] GBN was founded in 1987 by some of those oil consultants, as well as Brand and a few other terrifically mad thinkers. Their stated goal: encourage companies to question—and change— their mental maps, to embrace uncertainty, and to stop predicting the future based on the past.[11] In other words, to take their clients on something of a psychic journey.

I've been through their methodology a few times, for topics ranging from the future of technology to the future of religion. It consists of building an imaginary landscape across two axes—say, the environment and biotechnology. So you end up with four boxes: bad environment and low development and low biotechnology, bad environment and high biotechnology, healthy environment and low biotechnology, and so on.

Then the group ponders the possible results of each scenario. They imagine a world with a terrible environment but lots of biotechnology. What happened? Was the biotech too late? Did terrorists launch a biotech bomb? What will people's attitudes be like? What might be on *Time* magazine's cover? It's a fantasy role-playing game wherein participants cast themselves as members of fictional futures.

One's success in these activities, I'd argue, has little to do with the results of any particular scenario planning session. Shell Oil was the flagship client of GBN, and barely survived its scenario-planning escapades. Like a college kid recovering from a bad acid trip, Shell got obsessed with its many possible futures. It hired a long string of out-of-the-box consultants, lost track of any core business ethos, and descended into disarray and a bookkeeping scandal.

The value of scenario planning is that it gives people the opportunity to think in new ways and to approach the future with a sense of infinite possibility. While an executive who has been through the scenario process might be better prepared for a future possibility because he has already imagined it, what makes him better off is his experience of playing his way through to solutions.

Real play is the model in-the-box experience, because it means forging discovery from the inside out. Developmental psychologists, chronicled in Pat Kane's illuminating book, *The Play Ethic*,[12] have recently concluded that children's experiences in play actually strengthen and extend the number of neural connections in the brain. This, in turn, allows for a more networked brain, capable of solving problems in more ways.

Achieving this player's mentality, or breaking through to the "flow" state, does not trivialize the matter at hand. If anything, it celebrates it as a source of inspiration and meaning. Smiling at work is not a sin, and won't make your boss or your employees think you're not really working. You're merely *getting into it.*

And why shouldn't the work you do be as exhilarating and spiritually consuming as what a rock 'n' roll musician is doing onstage, or a basketball player on the court? Making one's work a primary source of fun is not a loss of autonomy. It doesn't mean the boss or corporation has beaten you at something or forced you into submission. In fact, those who are capable of immersing themselves completely and playfully in their work are the first to detect when something is wrong with the overall plan—on a business or ethical level—because it inhibits the fun.

The sanitation worker sees the way the poorly designed handles on his truck, as well as his union's policy, inhibit him from doing his job as best he can. They are obstacles to the zenlike fun of his work, so he gets them changed. As for the welder who is capable of doing every job on the factory floor, he fixes machines and even improves them because he "gets into" mechanical problem solving and wants to improve the overall experience of his and everyone else's work flow.

If this violates some unspoken pact that we're all supposed to be suffering under our labors, then let's change that pact and get everybody else into the game.

COLLABORATION: PLAYING TOGETHER

While finding one's flow is essential, a company filled with people all in their own individual joyous trances is not yet suited for our renaissance. Collaboration is the name of the game, and a truly innovative organization is one that plays together.

Why should this be so hard? It may have something to do with 500 years of cultural programming telling us to compete with one another as individuals. Bankruptcy and competition are built into centralized currency systems; alienation is a necessary by-product of literacy and separated disciplines; and one-man-one-vote democracies make it hard for any individual voter to think beyond "what's in it for me?" Enlightened self-interest is self-interest, all the same.

To those living in tight-knit communities or under repressive regimes, it must have seemed as if our roles in the collective would always take care of themselves; one's personal freedom was all that needed fighting for. We didn't take into account how all of this focus on our rights and privileges as individuals, as well as the competitive quality of our free marketplace, could hamper our ability to collaborate freely. Television and marketing compounded these effects, leading to a society of people who think of themselves primarily as individuals.

The greatest opportunity of our new renaissance may be to swing the pendulum of individuality the other way. For an organization to get back in the box of innovation, its many members will have to learn to find the satisfaction and reward in collaborative forms of play.

Learning to play collaboratively, rather than alone, is part of growing up. Psychologists tell us that a child's development hinges on his ability to make play increasingly social. One of the first great play researchers, Mildred Parton, categorized play into five main types, distinguished by their level of social interaction:

ONLOOKER BEHAVIOR: Children play passively by watching or conversing with others who are engaged in play.

SOLITARY INDEPENDENT PLAY: A child plays by himself.

PARALLEL PLAY: A child plays side by side with others in a group, but remains engrossed in his own, solitary activity.

ASSOCIATIVE PLAY: Children share toys and even speak to one another, but their play remains uncoordinated.

COOPERATIVE PLAY: Children play together, organizing into roles with specific goals, like playing teacher, student, or cowboys and Indians.[13]

Our culture and our media can be thought of as passing through these same stages of increasing social interaction. Networks researcher Clay Shirky[14] thinks of the Internet as hovering, currently, in the stage of parallel play. The Web is filled with independent bloggers, sometimes linking to one another, but usually just typing their own thoughts into their own public journals. They exist side by side in the same space, aware of one another's existence, but relatively disconnected. I'd probably argue that these bloggers have reached the associative stage, since they do share resources and programs, and post comments and links to one another's sites.

But the blogger universe, like most of the more playful organizations around today, is still a competitive space. There is playful competition among its various members, but rarely is there the kind of collaboration we see on the technology side of the Internet equation, where open source software and file-sharing networks are the norm.

This is probably because the technologists have some genuine social currency to share. Unlike bloggers and pundits, who are busy wallpapering the Web with opinions that are generally only as valuable to others as they are fashionable, hackers and software engineers are creating viable tools, usable code, and fixes for real problems. They are not hovering above the Internet (like my social theorist friends and me) but getting deep inside, tinkering and altering what's there. They are not changing just content, but the very landscape on which everyone else's interactions will occur. They are not just writing words, but creating whole new alphabets. When people know their contributions have value, they don't have the same impulse to compete for attention.

Howard Rheingold, the leading theorist in virtual community, believes the playful collaborations of these hacker communities portend a more natural and productive way of working for all of us. "Darwin had a blind spot," Rheingold likes to say. "It wasn't that he didn't see the role of cooperation in evolution. He just didn't see how important it is."[15]

Rheingold's Cooperation Project for the Institute of the Future is exploring how, for the past two centuries, science, technology, commerce, and public policy have all attended almost exclusively to the role of competition—survival of the fittest—and utterly forgotten the power of collaboration.[16] Luckily, we are confronting more arguments for this perspective every day:

> . . . [S]cientists are beginning to see how cooperation actually works in biology, sociology, mathematics, psychology, economics, computer science, and political science. And in the last two decades, we've seen a variety of new challenges to business models that stress competition over customers, resources, and ideas. Companies in emerging high-tech industries learned that working with competitors could build markets and help avoid costly standards wars. The open source movement showed that world-class software could be built without corporate oversight or market incentives. Google and Amazon built fortunes by drawing on, even improving, the Internet by facilitating and building on the collective actions of millions of web publishers and reviewers. Thousands of volunteers have created over one million pages of the

free encyclopedia Wikipedia—in over 100 languages. Collective knowledge-gathering, sharing economies, social software, prediction markets—numerous experiments in technology-assisted cooperation are taking place.[17]

The challenge is applying what has been happening online to other enterprises. In the faceless void of the Internet, collaboration is a bit easier than in the trenches of corporate life, where we are confronting the same faces every day. Our coworkers are also our competition for raises and promotions. That's not a reason to give up, but to change the systems underlying our business process to be more supportive of collective behaviors in the real world.

We are further hampered in our efforts by a shift away from long-term employment and associations in favor of short-term consultancies and other more detached styles of engagement. Social theorist Richard Sennett has shown how " 'no long term' is a principle which corrodes trust, loyalty, and mutual commitment. . . . Such social bonds take time to develop, slowly rooting into the cracks and crevices of institutions." Business schools now encourage students to accept consultancies over real jobs, since "detachment and superficial cooperativeness are better armor for dealing with current realities than behavior based on values of loyalty and service."[18]

So far, most examinations of the power of group behavior don't go much further than to assert that teams of people working collaboratively get better results than groups of individuals working in isolation or competition. *The Wisdom of Teams,* by Jon R. Katzenbach and Douglas K. Smith, for example, looked at some of the qualities common to successful groups within larger organizations. Nearly all of the successful teams had self-selecting members, clearly defined goals, and the ability to adjust those goals together.

The Zebra Team at Kodak charged with maintaining the company's black-and-white products, they observed, became a 1,500-member cult dedicated to the evangelism of black and white. The team thought of their mission as a vital, collective mission—and succeeded because of this. "A team's purpose is a joint creation that exists only because of the team's collaborative effort. . . . The better teams often treat their purpose like an offspring in need of constant nurturing and care." It was the common social currency of black-and-white photography—particularly in its battle against the more profitable and utterly dominant color product line—that knit the Zebra Team into a cohesive group. What kept the enterprise alive, however, was the team's freedom to redefine their goals as they went—to make up new rules to the game.

Katzenbach and Smith also describe teams as "social contracts," through which members develop common purposes and decide to which roles they're all best suited. Again, like children staking out the ground for a baseball game or deciding who is going to pitch, the members of a working team need to participate actively in the creation of rules, stakes, and roles. Given this freedom to develop their own priorities and solution spaces, the workers of Garden State Brickface developed a Brickface University, where they could get additional on-the-job training during the slower winter months—eventually earning recognition from Congress for their efforts.[19]

Burlington Northern Railroad's Intermodal team, charged with developing strategies for cooperating with the trucking industry, seemed doomed before it began. Burlington wasn't yet genuinely serious about working with the trucking industry. Made up exclusively of industry misfits, the Intermodal unit was recognized as a dumping ground for poor performers. A self-selected task force within that unit eventually developed proposals that were adopted by Burlington and the entire rail and trucking industry. What Katzenbach and Smith remember about the team is, "None relied on his formal designation or job title. Their roles were a function of their basic skills relative to team needs at the time."

To the authors, this phenomenal dedication to task and interchangeability of roles was only tangentially related to play, and more dependent on a spirit of camaraderie. The team leader at Burlington told them, "There were things we had to do with the rest of the company that were not fun. But it was always fun inside the team. You could really let your guard down. We always really liked being around each other." People working under this team leader recalled, "I never worked *for* him, I worked *with* him." [20]

The authors seem almost surprised that, when interviewing the members of these many successful teams, "All of them described the fun and sense of humor of the team." In another instance, "The team found a lot of fun at work—something we have often observed in real teams and even more in high-performance teams." Or, even more tellingly, "All of them described the fun and sense of humor of the team in contexts that related directly to performance. We should suggest that fun, just like teamwork values, is only real and sustainable if it feeds off the team's purpose and performance aspirations." [21]

It might be just as easy to suggest that a team's purpose and performance aspirations are only real and sustainable if they provide a constant opportunity for group fun! Fun was not merely a happy side effect for these groups, but a sustaining energy and a precondition for all three of the main components of teamwork. Groups only self-select, in the first place, if they sense that there will be joy and satisfaction at doing so. Play is based on the establishment of a mutually accepted goal—a way to "win." And truly advanced collaborative play, just like fantasy role-playing, requires that a group be able to adjust its goals, and even the underlying rules they play by, as they go along. This is what makes it play: it is not bound by the rules of the real world.

That's why getting into one's work as a play experience can yield some of the best so-called out-of-the-box solutions. Everything seems possible, and nothing is too dangerous to try at least provisionally. It's all play, after all. Like David Letterman dropping watermelons off the roof of his show's building, a good enough reason to do something is "to see what happens." This is the same sentiment that leads to the invention of alphabets and steam engines: the childlike wonder implicit in "what if?"

■

As managers or entrepreneurs, how do we instill the organizations we lead with a spirit of collaborative play? Ideally, by giving the people we work with the freedom to do it themselves. But like any culture experiencing itself in new, unfamiliar ways, it helps to have some guidance. At this rather early juncture in the development of a play-based work ethic, a leader's example can count. Until the development of a fully open source, bottom-up corporate culture, some top-down leadership may have to set the tone. Just as a brand can give consumers the framework to develop a culture, a CEO can give employees an environment in which to develop theirs.

Steve Jobs began his Macintosh group this way. It was a self-selected division of Apple, dedicated to developing a friendlier computer. Under its charismatic leader, in a special set of offices, the division flourished as a space for play. In the premiere issue of *MacWorld* magazine in 1984, Jobs explained, "The people who are doing the work are the moving force behind the Macintosh. My job is to create a space for them, to clear out the rest of the organization and keep it at bay . . . Every spare moment I have, I dash back because this is the most fun place in the world . . . they share a quality about the way they look at life, which is that the journey is the reward. They really want to see this product out in the world. It's more important than their personal lives right now. . . . For a very special moment, all of us have come together to make this new product. We feel this may be the best thing we'll ever do with our lives."[22]

The idealistic hackers and former hippies I know who were working on the project shared Jobs's sensibility about really changing the world with their products. It's not just, as Jobs stated, that the Macintosh project was more important than their personal lives at the time. It *was* their personal lives at the time. As such, it required an intensity of engagement that everyone realized could only be maintained for a short while.

The playful spirit has lasted, in some form, for over two decades. It faded, tellingly, only during Jobs's absence from the company in the early 1990s, and quickly returned with his resumption as CEO. Although the Macintosh market share of installed computing platforms is only a small fraction of Microsoft's, Apple is still widely considered one of the best places in the computer business to work. Apple workers still feel they are saving the world. By giving himself and his employees room to play, Jobs also freed them up to redefine their goals as they went along. This way, Apple went from being a software company to a computer company to a digital lifestyles brand with the world's most popular MP3 player and online music store.

Think about it for a minute: Who would you rather be, Bill Gates or Steve Jobs? Sure, Bill Gates is a much richer fellow, but who seems to be having a better time? Who would you rather work for, or with? Jobs was able to create and maintain a fun place to work not by expanding the lunch offerings or gym machinery, but by keeping everyone's experience of Apple at the center of his attention at all times.

That's why Jobs can't be put on the defensive about selling fewer than 4 percent of America's personal computers. "Apple's market share is bigger than BMW's or Mercedes's or Porsche's in the automotive market," he told *MacWorld* just last year. "What's wrong with being BMW or Mercedes? I think we're having fun. I think our customers really like our products. And we're always trying to do better. But I think we're leading the industry and we're having a good time."[23]

Jobs may just as well have said he is leading the industry *in* having a good time. And this is not only a great way to keep people coming into work with a smile on their faces, but also the easiest way to keep them innovating, as well. When people are really at play, the object of the game is no longer to win the game but to keep the game going. James P. Carse's terrific manifesto, *Finite and Infinite Games,* distinguishes between those two types of play. Finite play, like that of a kid playing a video game by the rules, ends when a winner is declared. Rules are fixed, and the "element of surprise" is used only to defeat one's foes. Infinite play, on the other hand, like that of a fantasy role-player or game programmer, is never supposed to end. Its rules and objectives can be continually changed by agreement among the players. The only real object is to keep the game going. Instead of using surprise to vanquish one's opponents, surprise becomes a way to sustain everyone's interest in what's happening. In Carse's words, "Infinite players play in the expectation of being surprised. If surprise is no longer possible, all play ceases."[24]

This is why great playful CEOs like Jobs see innovation as being directly tied to having fun. When you get a group of people together in that zone of infinite play, their shared goal is to surprise themselves with an innovation capable of keeping the game going. Even Jobs's sense that the zone of play is transient and somewhat delicate helps promote this collaborative spirit among the players. The fun will only last as long as they can keep innovating.

THE ART OF PLAY
BEATS THE ART OF WAR

So far, the easiest way to instill an entire workforce with the spirit of playful community is from the top. A truly fun-loving CEO can, by his example, set a tone of playful inquiry and collaboration for his employees. The rash of "CEO porn"—those best sellers by charismatic executives sharing the secrets of their management styles—is just one indication of how desperately most of us still look for cues, for permission from above, to be as confident and uninhibited with our colleagues as we'd like to be.

Whereas CEOs of the past incorporated war metaphors and military methodologies into their competitive battle plans, the renaissance CEO recognizes that battle plans force companies to be defined by their opposition, and opt instead to define themselves and their companies as players. By doing so, they unleash the innovative capacity of their employees, rather than just their rage. The art of war may be simpler to convey and easier to "win," but play is the ultimate strategy for sustainable success.

Compare the leadership styles of two prominent CEOs, who—at their height—were deeply respected, but for very different reasons. Richard Branson, founder of Virgin, and Michael Ovitz, founder of

Creative Artists Agency (CAA). While Branson sought to introduce the spirit of play into a competitive business, Ovitz sought to bring the art of war into what should have remained a playful business. Branson was derided and underestimated; Ovitz was deeply feared, and finally led out by the ear, in disgrace.

I'd been using Ovitz as an example of the warlike executive long before his public hazing in the lawsuit over his ousting as president of Walt Disney Corporation. Luckily for me, he has remained true to form. The son of a middle-class liquor distributor in Chicago, Ovitz rose to fame in 1975 when he led four fellow agents out of the William Morris Agency, where he began in the mailroom, to start CAA. He used his power of persuasion, and his willingness to undercut the industry's standard commission rates by as much as half, to lure Kevin Costner from Morris to his new agency.

Clients ranging from Tom Hanks and Tom Cruise to Steven Spielberg and Prince eventually followed, turning Ovitz's company into what was widely recognized as the most powerful agency in Hollywood. Ovitz seemed determined to project an intimidating presence. As he grew increasingly powerful, most Hollywood observers noticed "an enormous amount of resentment grew up around him [and] toward him. He was not shy in wielding his power, not shy in rewarding his friends and punishing his enemies. And by the middle of the 1990s, he was very much the most powerful man in town, and the most feared, in some ways the most hated."[25] Not an easy feat.

Ovitz worked hard to present himself as an ambitious and dangerous general on the battlefield of Hollywood. CAA's imposing I.M. Pei–designed office building, built in 1988 and described as a "curved, gleaming, fortress,"[26] broadcast Ovitz's business approach, which he hoped would be likened to that of Japanese warfare. An elaborate, public, and well-publicized feng shui ceremony accompanied groundbreaking, and Ovitz was sure to mention how the architectural designs, particularly of his own office, were scrutinized for their capability to manipulate guests and generate more power for Ovitz. A 28-foot specially commissioned Roy Lichtenstein painting loomed in the atrium, guaranteed to intimidate visitors, who had to pass through two huge waiting rooms before at last reaching the chairman in his absurdly long, narrow office.

Ovitz's dedication to Asian fighting techniques took on a legendary significance in Hollywood, bolstered by the agent's frequent references to reading ancient Chinese war texts in translation, or taking Aikido lessons from a master sensei. And if that wasn't enough, he turned this sensei, Steven Seagal, into a movie star, and then made Sun Tzu's *The Art of War* mandatory reading for his employees. He slowly but successfully turned the talent agency from a service business into a mercenary force. According to *Variety,* he "instilled CAA with a certain steely discipline and paramilitary zeal that has endured long beyond his exit."[27]

Ovitz only achieved true notoriety when he revealed himself to Hollywood as a man who cared less about show business than business itself. His near monopoly on major talent allowed him to introduce unprecedented leverage on his "packages"—a take-it-or-leave-it approach to dealmaking that maximized his agency's commission while reducing a studio head's ability to make any choices for himself about who would be in his movies. Refusing an Ovitz deal meant not being offered another one; accepting an Ovitz deal meant paying more for talent than ever before. The skyrocketing costs of making a Hollywood picture are still blamed on Ovitz's deals from the late 1980s.

Ovitz used his Japan-savvy reputation to position himself as the broker for Sony's acquisition of Columbia Pictures, and then Matsushita's MCA/Universal purchase. Both are still considered "bad deals" for the buyers, but earned CAA more than $50 million in commission, and Ovitz even more resentment from an industry that felt that its last vestiges of class and mystery had been surrendered to the ruthlessness of pure, warlike business.

Eventually, Ovitz's warlike demeanor got the best of him. Having won as much power and money as was possible for anyone in Hollywood, he didn't know when to turn off his militarism. It cost him. When Joe Eszterhas, a well-established, but past-his-prime, screenwriter asked to be released from his agency contract so he could go back to being represented by an old friend at another agency, Ovitz broke with standard industry practice and refused. It had always been customary for agents to graciously release unhappy clients, no matter what the short-term cost, because it made future prospective clients less anxious about signing on to an irrevocable term. But Ovitz threatened Eszterhaus, as the writer revealed in a letter to Ovitz: "You told me if I left, 'My foot soldiers who go up and down Wilshire Boulevard each day will blow your brains out.' You said that you would sue me. 'I don't care if I win or lose,' you said, 'but I'm going to tie you up with depositions and court dates so that you won't be able to spend any time at your typewriter.'"[28]

Ovitz wasn't really an agent anymore, anyway. He was a businessman. So he left CAA to accept his old friend Michael Eisner's offer to become president of Walt Disney Company. Senior agents had considered throwing him a goodbye party, but "Ovitz understood the mood at CAA well enough to know that the toasts would ring hollow."[29]

Ovitz was even less liked at Disney, where his aggressive and self-aggrandizing style just didn't mix with the culture of Mickey Mouse. Ovitz arrived late for meetings, berated subordinates, and seemed more preoccupied with the $2 million renovation of his office than joining the team. As Eisner's memo to Ovitz explained, "My biggest problem was that you played the angles too much, exaggerated the truth too far, manipulated me and others too much."[30]

Ovitz blamed Eisner: "He promised me the world and delivered nothing."[31] While Eisner's memos revealed he thought his former pal Ovitz was "a psychopath" who "could not tell the truth."[32] One Disney director said Ovitz was a "cancer."[33] After Ovitz was fired, he blamed what he called Hollywood's "gay Mafia" for engineering his downfall, outing many top executives by name. In interviews across the media, he also accused everyone from Barry Diller and David Geffen to Michael Eisner and his own former colleagues at CAA of conspiring to undo him. He used these excuses as well to explain the disintegration of his most recent effort, a short-lived management group called AMG.

Hollywood sees in Ovitz's failures the shortcomings of a hostile, warlike approach to what should be a friendly, playful business community. NBC's Don Ohlmeyer went so far as to say, "Michael Ovitz is the AntiChrist, and you can quote me on that."[34] Or, as the *Los Angeles Times* explains it, his main flaw was "he was mean to the little people. He broke Hollywood's cardinal rule: 'Be nice to those on the way up because you'll meet them again on the way down.' "[35]

Ovitz's mistake was twofold: First, he was mean and unlikable not just the people he competed against, but to those he worked with. Second, he lost sight of the values intrinsic to the business in which he was working, surrendering them to the generic, short-term goal of profiteering. Both of these errors point to a management style guided by a war ethic, which values only winning, instead of a play ethic, which values staying in the game. War turns the innovation space into a battlefield—and destroys it in the process. Play turns almost any endeavor into a creative act. A war is fought to end itself. A game can go on forever.

Perhaps that explains the longevity of Richard Branson's career, as well as the loyalty of those who work for him and buy from his companies. Branson is a player: he is in business to have fun, and makes no apologies for it.

Sir Richard Branson, the instantly recognizable maverick entrepreneur with the Cheshire cat grin, has led Virgin steadfastly on its climb from a small mail order record company to one of the most identifiable and diverse brands in the world. The company's success is inseparable from Branson, whose outlandish publicity stunts and bold approach to business have both provoked and livened up the corporate world while consistently providing quality products and services. Branson's antics, from pushing fellow billionaires into swimming pools or racing hot air balloons to serving as a flight attendant on his own planes, have not led the company astray. Virgin's has been a measured and sustained ascent, despite criticism from competitors and analysts who cannot yet recognize the space for innovation that Branson's playfulness creates.

Branson's play mentality was forged in childhood. Born into a good home in Surrey, England, in 1950, young Ricky was presented with a series of challenges by his clever and rather eccentric mother, a former dancer and flight attendant. In his autobiography, Branson describes how she sent him off on his bicycle in the morning to places like the seaside town of Bournemouth, over 50 miles away, just to see if he could get all the way there and then find his way back. Branson believes these kinds of challenges are what shaped his playful outlook and his tireless quest for new undertakings.

Branson went into the record business, first, because he thought it would be fun. He picked and promoted bands he liked, and his taste reflected the rebellious, playful spirit of the music industry. Building on his successes with artists including The Sex Pistols, Mike Oldfield, and Culture Club, Branson slowly and quite meticulously diversified into a business that, as of February 2004, had 30,000 employees achieving net sales of $5.2 billion.[36]

To outsiders, Branson's expansion into air travel, mobile telephony, and consumer electronics seems random and unrelated. Each time he ventures into a new area, pundits and industry experts predict his imminent failure. They should have learned by now: Branson's focus on fun and play rather than short-term financial gain does not mean he makes his business decisions whimsically. On the contrary, because he is dedicated to having a great time himself and extending this sense of play and adventure to his employees and customers alike, he only steps in where he thinks he can make a real difference to an undeserved constituency.

As a result, Branson's research is in many ways more complete and painstaking than that of a typical conglomerate branching into a new field. These are not the simple exercises in "due diligence" required of a corporation to satisfy its shareholders. They are extended and expensive inventories of entire industries so as to maintain Virgin's success "in picking the right market and the right opportunity."[37] After all, staking out a field on which to play is an entirely more committed investigation than simply choosing one on which to do battle. The player is invested in growing something there, not just vanquishing everything in his path. Indeed, as Virgin states in its corporate materials, success "is not about having a strong business promise, it is about keeping it." [38]

Branson's reputation and management style are based on a family model and sense of community rather than a strict hierarchy. Clearly, to most people, a family is still a vertically structured organism, and at Virgin Branson gets to play both father and his own favorite prodigal son. But it is decidedly less hierarchical than your average 30,000-person organizational chart, and conducive to a more social work experience.

So Branson rides the crew bus and stays at the same hotel as his flight attendants when he travels—inevitably taking them all out to dinner and a party. As he explained to *Airways* magazine, "How could the chairman send a message to his employees that the hotel his company puts them in is not good enough for him? Besides, I always have eighteen delightful people to go to dinner with this way; that's always fun." [39]

His executives and employees understand that this personal style is meant to be a companywide ethos. David Tait, head of Virgin Atlantic's U.S. operations echoes Branson: "If you aren't having fun doing business, your people aren't going to have fun, and at the end of the line your passengers aren't going to have fun, either." [40] Or as Branson himself explains, "Fun in business, as in life, is most important. Most companies don't have that outlook and they should. I think our customers can tell the difference in our employees by the way they bounce down the aisles." [41] As Branson explained his philosophy to *Forbes*, "Fun is at the core of how I like to do business and it has informed everything I've done from the outset. I am aware that the idea of business being fun and creative goes against the grain of convention, and it's certainly not how they teach it at some of those business schools where business means hard grind and lots of discounted cash flows and net present values." [42]

Whether Ovitz or Branson personally ends up with more cash in the bank is irrelevant (though Branson wins by a long shot). Where

Ovitz took one of the most playful industries known to man and militarized it into a ruthless business, Branson picked serious industries like air travel and reinvented them in the context of fun. Ovitz steamrolled innovation with battle plans, while Branson gave new life to businesses he determined were not yet exploiting the creative power of play.

More importantly, these contrasting styles demonstrate how the player's mentality values sustainable enterprise over the quick win. Playful organizations are not satisfied with victory. The people in them are having so much fun, they want to keep playing.

Branson's devotion to play is in his very nature. It's not that his many successes are accidental, but he exudes a style that was burned into his psyche as a child. It's not nearly as easy to bring the spirit of play into an existing organization. And although many have tried, most fail because they don't yet understand the underlying principles at work, or, rather, at play.

This is because too much of business and enterprise is based in dead metaphors of war and competition. The language of war still permeates business and marketing. We go after "target markets" and conceive "battle plans" in "war rooms," leading to unnecessarily militaristic hierarchies within our organizations and adversarial relationships between management, employees, customers, and shareholders.

It was in the medieval era that competing kingdoms—even when not at war—were first deemed to be "evil," and this myth of competition as a war between epically opposed forces has yet to be revised. It's how coaches motivate their high school football teams to play hard against their rivals from across the tracks, and how companies motivate their employees to "beat" the competition.

Barnes & Noble surely thought it was stimulating a sense of playful competition by setting aside a "Hercules Room" in which its employees were to conceive an online strategy to beat Amazon.com at its own game. Hercules, after all, was the hero strong enough to conquer the Amazons in Greek myth. But Barnes & Noble fell into the trap of letting its opposition define it. It didn't give employees the opportunity to imagine the online book business from the ground up, or even to define the company as an edgy cult brand facing monolithic competition—as Apple did to Windows or Harley-Davidson did to the Japanese motorcycle industry. By keeping its enemy foremost in its mind, rather than the infinite potential for extending its core competency onto a new playing field, B&N had lost before it began. Its future was always limited by the possibilities already exploited by Amazon.

And, according to the rules of "infinite play" described by James Carse, even if B&N had beaten Amazon, it would have nowhere left to go. For, as Carse explains, true play is not about "winning," for once someone wins, the game is over. Barnes & Noble's goal had been so well defined that its play would have to end the minute its sales exceeded Amazon's. The language of war contextualized its business as a zero-sum game. It was working to reach a predetermined finish line. Not that it was in any danger of reaching it. While Amazon kept playing and innovating, expanding into toys, electronics, and garden equipment, Barnes & Noble kept fighting—and competing with last year's Amazon.

Amazingly, even game companies and toy retailers are susceptible to the war mentality, a style that ends up infecting everything from research and development to public relations. In the heyday of the dot-com era, Internet marketer eToys.com seemed poised to establish a niche for itself in toys the way Amazon had in books. Back in 1997, when industry giant Toys 'R' Us was still debating its Internet strategy, eToys had attracted the smart venture funding of Intel, Idealab, and Sequoia Capital, among others, leading to an IPO that immediately shot from its offering price of $20 up to $85. The site—more intelligently designed and easier to navigate than those of its peers—scored 3.4 million visitors for Christmas 1999, three times that of Toys 'R' Us. As a brand, eToys was identified so closely with the power of the Internet that the company won free placement in a popular Visa card commercial.

While its stock price-to-sales-ratio valuations challenged the common sense that later prevailed on Wall Street, the eToys decline came a bit earlier than the NASDAQ crash, and was owed, in part, to the company's inability to play. In a true story that now ranks as

Internet folklore, eToys sought and won an injunction against a group of Swiss artists, called etoy, for using the URL etoy.com, which the toy company claimed was confusing its customers. What irked the Internet community and led to wide-scale protests online and off, was that the small artist collective etoy predated eToys, the toy company, by more than two years. Etoy had an established presence online long before eToys existed, yet was now being bumped from the Internet because it conflicted with big business.

The irony here is that etoy was started as a corporate satire. The collective's art pieces were all in the form of "shares" sold to collectors. Their performance events, such as moving shipping containers around the world, were all meant to mimic the antics of global corporations. To etoy, the attack from eToys was a new chapter in the game. For eToys, it was something it wanted to end quickly.

The more playful etoy got, the more seriously eToys responded. Etoy waged what they called a "toy war," inspiring (but not directly ordering) some of its armies of fans to conduct server attacks[43] against its dot-com "enemy." Etoy members monitored their own site for visits from eToys employees, who may have been monitoring for etoy members' activity, or simply visiting to see what the controversy was all about. Etoy created special messages for them, asking if they were happy at their jobs, and why they wanted to hurt artists. Wouldn't they rather have fun than be mean? According to the etoy artists, many employees defected and began working against their company from within. Meanwhile, smaller, sympathetic hosting companies around the world were so incensed that etoy lost its URL to an American corporation that they began blocking their subscribers from the eToys servers. By this point, eToys stock was down to the low 20s.

EToys eventually offered the artists cash and stock to turn over their URL. But the boys refused on principle. Besides, they were having too much fun. I participated, myself, in an artistic protest at the Museum of Modern Art in New York, along with 50 men in Santa suits and Internet activist John Barlow. EToys survived the year, then filed for bankruptcy in early 2001. In an effort to salvage some value from the disaster, it tried to sell its assets—including a 3-million-customer database with credit card numbers and other consumer information, in spite of a customer agreement that explicitly stated the company would never sell personal information to third parties. Seeing itself as a business and little more to the very end, eToys was capable of engendering ill will and lawsuits, even after it had gone under.

Did a half-dozen Swiss artists and their friends bring down eToys? Not single-handedly. But they exposed a would-be toy company's inability to jibe with the underlying ethos of its business or think and act like players. The dispute tied up valuable resources in a senseless legal battle, put eToys in the headlines for all the worst reasons, and forever equated the name eToys with corporate aggression online.

It has company. Other businesses that should be particularly focused on fun are vying to outdo eToys' reputation for Scrooge behavior. Some disgruntled employees of videogame maker Electronic Arts have been generating headlines on the Internet and off since 2003 for what they claim are oppressive labor practices. That's not a good situation for a company so intimately connected with an interactive culture like gaming. Electronic Arts' customers and employees are all part of the same community. Accused of driving its young workers too hard and failing to pay overtime compensation, the company is now fighting a war on many fronts. One salaried employee has begun a class-action lawsuit, while others are posting accounts on the Internet of their hellish 80-hour workweeks. Those posts have circulated to gamers' boards, where conditions at the company are regularly compared with the factories described in Dickens' novels, endangering the company's reputation forever with its most important young customers.[44]

Hiring young game designers is no crime. As a way of ensuring that its games will be fun for kids in the same age group to play, it's a terrific strategy. Why not turn a game company into a fun factory—an extension of the existing game community you want to serve? Electronic Arts figured its studio would be so much fun to work at, it might as well provide employees with meals, laundry service, ice cream, and anything else they needed so they wouldn't have to go home.

If employees were staying at work voluntarily because they loved the task at hand so very much, supplying them with food or even beds is a great way to support them in their pursuit of fun. But for the employees at Electronic Arts, overtime was not voluntary. One employee told the *New York Times* that these at first seemed like great amenities, but he soon came to feel that "seeing the sun occasionally would have had more of a tonic effect."[45] After two months of 80-hour weeks without a single day off, amenities no longer felt like perks, but symbols of imprisonment. A company spokesman explained to the *Times* that surveys of employees would surely allow any dissention to be expressed. At Electronic Arts, however, such surveys are conducted only once every two years!

Even Trip Hawkins, the company's founder and now-departed CEO, says he is not surprised by recent accusations, comparing Electronic Arts' labor practices to *The Picture of Dorian Gray*. By hiring more young employees, the company hopes to maintain youthful vigor while saving on salary costs, since fresh graduates "are the most suggestible."[46] In other words, young people have no work experience to compare it with. By the time they find out, they're burned out anyway, and can simply be replaced. Of course, this is a terrible strategy for innovation, and Electronic Arts' product line is the proof. The company is great at making deals with brands like the NFL, James Bond, or *Lord of the Rings*, and then banging out games based on these franchises, but they are not nearly as adept as their competitors at creating games or concepts from scratch. People who feel like slaves, however young, just aren't having enough fun to innovate.

If companies purportedly dedicated to selling play can't even get the "play thing" right, it's no wonder everyone is having such a hard time with it.

MOTIVATION AND MEANING

When asked about your job's "benefits," what comes to mind first: your dental plan or the way your work benefits the world?

Making work fun means making work meaningful on a level that goes beyond what we get in *compensation* for working. Even the word "compensation" implies that our pay and benefits package is a form of bribe—money for doing something we'd rather not be doing. Instead of being fueled and supported in our heartfelt commitment to an enterprise, we are being paid for our sacrifice. Even the word "salary" derives from Latin for the salt that Roman soldiers and road builders were paid on schedule to survive in the arid desert conditions. A salary is not even a reward, but a ration to laborers so they don't die on the job. The word "employee" is itself a passive construction. Unlike employ*ers,* who actually do something, employ*ees* are acted upon—passive members of the relationship in which any labor is the extension of another guy's will.

So built into the language of wages and employment is the presumption that work is not supposed to be fun or self-directed. No matter how sincerely enlightened employers attempt to reinvent their workplaces as fun environments, their success will be limited if they are unable to break the compensation paradigm.

The most current thought by motivational consultants is still steeped in the obsolete framework of stoking motivation through pay and perks. In 1998, for example, cable channel operator Discovery Communications began a multiyear overhaul of its compensation policy, switching from a system that rewarded good work with promotions to one that rewarded people with raises and bonuses.[47] Compensation experts now prefer "performance-driven" arrangements like these because their flexibility allows employers to forget about "across-the-board fairness" and reward individuals who do better. What they don't realize, yet, is that moment-to-moment merit bonuses reduce employees to chickens pecking at lighted buttons for pellets. The more frequently you reinforce "good" behavior with cash, the more you disconnect employees from their own experience of the work itself. The focus shifts away from the task and onto the reward.

Though it's nice to reward employees when a company does well—and it's certainly efficient to reduce bonuses when a company does badly—such schemes only make the best workers feel that their pay is being reduced unfairly, while making the worst workers feel they can get by on the hard work of others. That's why some compensation specialists now implement more complex profit-sharing plans, whereby employees' bonuses are calculated by a computer algorithm that reconciles the individual worker's productivity with the entire company's profits to render a more fair result. But even these schemes put workers' focus on the game of extracting more cash from the corporate coffers, rather than doing whatever it is they're supposed to be motivated to do.

Continental Airlines has been named one of *Fortune* magazine's 100 best companies to work for in America for the last six years for implementing policies as compensation-oriented as giving new sport utility vehicles to some (not all) of the employees with perfect attendance for the year. Although business journals interpret this to mean that Continental is an "enjoyable place to work," the raffling off of cars to employees with high attendance records indicates no such thing. The policy has nothing whatsoever to do with fun at work, and everything to do with getting to have fun with that SUV when work is *over*.

A great many employers love to talk about implementing employee incentive programs based on offering something more meaningful than cash, but most often it's just talk. "We're a company that touts its culture as the big draw," the newly appointed "manager of communication and culture" for a warranty administration company told *Entrepreneur* magazine. The company believes it is extending an ethos of autonomy and independence forged during the dot-com era in its pursuit of employees who are not "only focused on the money."[48] But the company's new culture is based solely on cash bonuses! If employees manage to cut costs, they are rewarded with $500 to $5,000. They can also win $250 of "fun money" if they stay with the company for six months. That must be a fun place to work, indeed, if workers need to be bribed to stay on for an entire half-year. If any of these companies really want to find employees who value something other than money, then they'll have to offer them some form of motivation other than money.

In a classic misunderstanding of play culture, a Harvard Business

School Press book about how "the gamer generation is reshaping business forever"[49] contends that kids who grew up with videogames need to be treated differently in the workplace. True enough, but the authors surmise that game play has made young workers more competitive "because the object of all those games is to win." They couldn't be more wrong. Beyond the technology, the main difference between videogames and those that came before them is that many videogames have no winner. Indigenous to our new renaissance culture, they are ongoing adventures, worlds that keep growing, and collaboratively developed stories. That should be a clue: the real difference in creating a work environment for the gamer generation is finding ways to allow them to participate actively and consciously in the evolution of the enterprise itself.

For some insight into how these kids think, take a look at any of the Web sites they've put up about the companies where they work, such as BestBuySux.org, on which electronic retailer Best Buy's young and Internet-savvy employees post their unedited comments about their experiences. From my own count of the five years of comments posted to the site, less than 2 percent of them have anything to do with compensation, insurance, or bonuses. The overwhelming majority of complaints are about not being listened to, not having the ability to make suggestions *that would save the store money,* or being treated more like a criminal than a collaborator. Employees said they feel mistrusted, "disposable," and as if the only things they care about are money or stealing inventory. The saddest part is that many of these young employees are deeply interested in consumer electronics; they love comparing the attributes of different brands and models, and debating the longevity of various home entertainment strategies, given the inevitability of technology upgrades. They care about the differences between LCD and plasma TV screens. At least they care more than their bosses seem to, and certainly more than their bosses give them credit for.

Employers further along the learning curve understand that there's more to the work experience than financial compensation. But, so far, the ancillary rewards they've come up with are still *extrinsic* to the work at hand, or compensatory for its underlying problems.

Twenty percent of employers now have some kind of dedicated stress-reduction program in place, fueling an estimated annual $11.7 billion stress management industry.[50] Employees enjoying such benefits are offered the opportunity to receive free massages and tai chi, yoga, or meditation classes, usually in their spare time or lunch hour. But researchers are finding that the positive effects of these programs are temporary, and eventually employees figure out that these programs are simply ways of preventing workers from realizing how many hours they're spending at work.[51] After all, employees soon reason, a workplace that offers stress reduction must be doing it for a reason.

A few managers do understand that extrinsic rewards, from merit pay to acupuncture, have little to do with making work a collectively engaging enterprise. For most of them, the solution is to turn their companies into more socially rewarding places. They've read the new studies showing that friendlier employees are more productive, since they tend to communicate on a broader bandwidth and thus pass more information to one another than the detached employees in unfriendly work environments.[52] This is true, but friendly work environments cannot be manufactured; they must arise out of mutual mission and mutual trust.

Don't tell that to the latest slew of management consultants, who believe that everything from bedroom slippers to shark tanks can infuse a workplace with social currency.

The CTO at NaviSite, a Web-hosting company in Andover, Massachusetts, got so desperate to create a more relaxed atmosphere for his meetings that he donned a robe and slippers, threw together a fake fireplace, adorned it with candles, and then served hot cocoa. The CEO of Branders.com began holding his staff meetings at a casual restaurant called Redneck Earl's in the hopes that his employees would loosen up and speak more honestly. Monthly meetings at employment firm monster.com are held in the "monster den," a giant room filled with foosball tables and bikes. New employees must introduce themselves by talking about their pets.[53] Juice Solutions, a Palo Alto software firm, installed a giant tank with underfed sharks for employees to swim in at lunch to test their daring. Other companies promote bungee jumping and rock climbing.

For the Clif Bar company, which makes an energy snack (first used by the rock climbers of Colorado), installing an indoor rock climbing wall might make a bit of sense. It is an extension and symbol of the culture for which it is producing its product. But even in this case, a rock-climbing wall has little to do with developing or marketing snacks. The company wasn't using the wall to test the different endurance levels afforded by each bar or to determine how much debilitating bloating one brand of snack produces compared with another.

Like bonuses and raises, employee coddling and entertainment are extrinsic to the work at hand, and in the long run end up communicating the opposite of what they are meant to. A few clever management consultants are closing in on this contradiction and calling for companies to develop "new social contracts" in the workplace. One, outlined in *Challenge* magazine, listed clearly communicated criteria for performance and pay as its first priority, but then went on to suggest that "partnering replace paternalism" and employees be thought of not just as costs to be cut, but "value-adding resources."[54] Being thought of as a resource rather than an unfeeling cog is, at the very least, a start.

But most of these forms of employee encouragement are intangible. Even framed on the wall, lists of abstract slogans are usually perceived as what they are: cynical efforts at "winning the employees' sense of old-fashioned commitment without locking your company into the old-fashioned employment arrangement."[55] In other words, they want employees to be loyal, with no true hope of loyalty in return—especially if that reciprocity is going to cost money.

To this end, companies are attempting to cast themselves as what has become known as "employers of choice." It all comes down to branding, and then treating employees as some new form of customer. In the words of one such strategist: "Position your workplace in the labor market as you have positioned your products in the supermarket.

Know your customers. Convince them you are different. Build brand loyalty."[56] Mostly, this means gimmicks that get remembered, from gifting savings bonds to newborns to running company vehicles on natural gas. Whatever seems to mesh well with employees' value sets at the moment. Of course, these tactics merely distance management further from their employee base, utterly ignoring the prospect that members of a workforce could be treated as partners instead of adversaries to be manipulated.

The inklings of a partnership model are finding their way into best practices not on the factory floor or development lab but in the way profit gets spent. Companies are achieving the greatest success in boosting morale, so far, by giving employees the opportunity to select the charities and causes they want the business to support. The practice has well-tested precedents. The bar associations require attorneys to provide pro bono services—and this is a well-acknowledged part of what bonds the members of their organization to one another. Following suit, corporations are giving individual workers autonomy over how some of the revenue they produce is distributed, often basing the amount donated on their performance metrics. So instead of earning a bonus, the employee earns, say, a new roof for an orphanage. Programs of this sort, instituted at companies including Smuckers and Dynegy, have been credited with reducing employee turnover by up to 50 percent.[57]

This makes sense. Psychologist and researcher Martin Seligman, of the University of Pennsylvania, has concluded that the highest form of happiness is knowing our strengths, and then deploying them in the "service of something you believe is larger than you are." That's why giving employees some say over how corporate giving is conducted produces such a positive impact on morale. But it is still a far cry from actually utilizing a person's strengths to make a difference. Donating corporate profits is once removed. What about the person's actual effort at work? Can't the thing we do be intrinsically rewarding?

Of course it can. Especially if we stop thinking about it as an activity so loathsome that we deserve to compensated for it. As employees, we are afraid to act as if we enjoy our work, lest our bosses not realize how much we are sacrificing on their behalf. As bosses, we can't let on how much fun we think our employees might be having, lest they feel we don't appreciate all their hard work. Even as independents, we feel guilty telling our spouses at the dinner table how much fun we had that day selling houses, trading stocks, or writing books. Whoever had the most fun at work will have to take out the trash.

Experiencing one's work as intrinsically satisfying fun has nothing to do with being employed by one of those corporations that has been successful in branding itself as a "great place to work." All this means is that the company provides adequate compensations for the suffering of work, and community contributions to make everyone feel less awful about whatever damage the company is doing elsewhere. Being a "great place to work" carries with it the sense of a booby prize.

Engendering a productively playful collaboration at work involves acknowledging the flow experience at the heart of each individual's task, as well as the meaning inherent in working together toward common goals. The experience of work must be intrinsically rewarding and, on some level, intrinsically meaningful.

Motivation specialist Alfie Kohn is one of the few who understand this simple new renaissance principle. He's been arguing against extrinsic motivators for years, but made little headway in corporate America:

> The idea that dangling money and other goodies in front of
> people will "motivate" them to work harder is the conventional
> wisdom in our society, and particularly among compensation
> specialists. Those of us who have challenged the Skinnerian
> orthodoxy that grounds this conviction have apparently caused its
> professional apologists to reassert in ever more emphatic and
> defensive language what most of their audience already takes on
> faith. . . . [They] strain to frame the issue as a choice between
> anecdotes and hard science . . . or between utopian fantasy and the
> "real world." [58]

In close to a dozen books on the subject, Kohn has sought to show how competition is poisonous to our working relationships, how incentive plans of any kind tend to undermine quality, and how the pursuit of affluence leads to depression even when it is attained. Most significantly, Kohn has followed a number of studies that demonstrate quite conclusively that people who value "extrinsic" goals such as fame, beauty, and money score lower on measures of vitality and self-actualization—regardless of age or level of income.[59]

Sure, money matters, but mainly to people who are so impoverished as to have none at all, or to those who are using money as a substitute for a more fundamental psychological need, such as nurturing friendships. Since it cannot fill the void, such people end up more depressed. Kohn's work and research demonstrates that rewards are "just one more way of doing things *to* people." They do not motivate spontaneous creative activity *from* people.

Kohn seeks to prove that the removal of incentives plans actually increases output and reduces turnover. In one case study, Marshall Industries, an electronics components distributor, eliminated management incentives, sales commissions, and all pay-for-performance schemes. Employee turnover was reduced by 80 percent, and annual sales rose from $575 million to $1.3 billion.[60] Kohn's main recommendations are to pay people well, pay them fairly, and then do everything possible to take people's minds off money.[61]

Kohn's work, if accepted by mainstream employment and motivation specialists, could revolutionize the way we treat compensation. But this still only gets us halfway. Just because extrinsic incentives don't work doesn't mean there aren't ways to create an atmosphere intentionally more conducive to collaborative play.

It can't be forced. In the 1980s, like many other companies looking to instill themselves with a playful spirit, Chiat/Day designed its entire Los Angeles office on the model of a kindergarten. No one had their own desks, only lockers where they could keep their supplies. People were to find new workplaces at various group tables set up around the office. Everyone quickly learned that they preferred to have their own desks, and that childlike surroundings were not particularly conducive to youthful creativity.

No, productive play requires not less, but more focus on all the competency people have developed through their years of training and experience. For real play involves a willingness to break through obvious, superficial answers to problems and find genuinely novel solutions together.

Douglas Atkin, the developer of the cult brand theories explored earlier, came upon his insights by encouraging heretical thoughts and contributions from his employees. He conducted free-for-all discussions called "dogma heresy sessions," in which his associates examined the standard practices and assumptions in a particular industry, and then imagined what might be their opposites. This is how JetBlue discovered what was wrong with the current airline industry, and what might replace it.

Working as chief strategist for the digital division of an advertising agency, I established a "tiger team" of creatives and programmers who were free to explore any realm of the digital universe they wanted. Membership on the team was temporary—a reward of up to six months, based on having won an account or produced a substantial innovation. It amounted to an in-house incubator for new interactive ideas conceived and developed by workers and based solely on their passion for the project. If a prototype developed in the incubator was deemed by the team to be worthy of further development, the people who conceived it were allowed to spin off into their own tiny division and bring the innovation to market. In this model, the reward for innovation was the opportunity to innovate more. And it led to some spectacular campaigns, and several hundred million dollars of pitches won solely on the passion and innovation in the interactive components the team came up with.

In short, the social currency of an innovative operation is not money, promotions, picnics, or climbing walls, but creativity itself. Real fun is not merely incidental to the work at hand; it *is* the work at hand.

The danger to the status quo is enormous—as it should be for any business that seeks to excel in an ongoing way rather than merely fend off competitors. The business itself and the rules underlying its most fundamental assumptions are all fair game. When playing for real, everything is up for grabs.

But to approach our fields this way, we cannot be outsiders. We must be like hackers, whose willingness to challenge the established rules is exceeded only by our profoundly deep understanding of codes underlying them. We must be willing to get all the way back in the box, and then be open to the source.

chapter five

BACK IN THE BOX

Just because our work is play, doesn't mean our play isn't work. Maintaining a high level of play is not easy. This isn't because play is so highly competitive, but because it stops being fun if it doesn't get more challenging. The "flow" of true engagement can't be maintained without encountering increasingly complexity. Laziness is not an option, and no expert is going to come in and save you when the going gets rough. The only way to play deeper is to *dig* deeper.

That's why, after decades of getting out of the box, it's time we learn how to get back in. This doesn't mean losing perspective or the ability to generate new ideas; it means learning how to innovate by going deep instead of just broad. It's about learning to tinker, to tweak, and to test the most basic, underlying assumptions of one's core business or technology. Besides, you can't go out of the box until you really know what's inside.

Too many of our new business ideas amount to little more than the repackaging of old products and technologies. We treat existing products as the component parts of larger ones—without ever understanding how they work. We line up a series of boxes to create inefficient and unwieldy Rube Goldberg contraptions, rather than getting inside to create products organic to the needs they mean to address.

I've consulted to countless companies where there's no one left on staff who understands quite how the core business works. It often seems to me as if management feel they have been put in charge of an ancient technology that they can only keep running by following the instruction manuals left by their forebears. They dare not pop open the hood or retool anything, lest they break it. On numerous occasions, I've even gone so far as to subcontract specialists to reeducate corporations about what they do![1]

In one case, I showed an Internet-based telephone company how to develop its own voice compression technology instead of buying one off the shelf. In another, I revealed to a computer manufacturer that it had no one on staff who understood LCD-display construction—the most expensive and troublesome component in its assembly. The company simply depended on its Korean subcontractor to provide the necessary parts with instructions on how to run them. And managers wondered why they were having so many problems achieving any competitive advantage in their industry.

The refusal to go into the box—the fear of getting inside and figuring out what's going on—stifles real innovation. Anyone can think outside the box long enough to conceive of putting a VCR in the same chassis as a TV. This is not innovation, but a "kluge," the assembly of existing components into makeshift solution. Contrast that with the development of TiVo digital video recorders or DVDs, which both required a deep understanding of people's television habits as well as the technologies and systems on which video and programming are based. A company that builds the boxes into which already existing TVs and VCRs are stuffed is not a truly fun place to work—at least not for long. TiVo or Phillips, on the other hand, companies built on the marriage of technological innovation and rule breaking, are.

We have come to believe that tasks requiring any modicum of skill—such as programming, product development, or even design— are unworthy of our higher faculties and better sent offshore. These days, computer programming, soil mechanics, agriculture, and hands-on engineering are more central to the curricula of community colleges than those of the Ivy League. That's why management is becoming increasingly disconnected from core competency. By devaluing what goes inside the box we are losing touch with the essence of our industries.

Instead of reinventing our companies and our careers by writing new business plans for what already exists, we need to remember that actually learning how things work is fun. We must come to relish the real tools, tasks, and textures of our professions. There are so many different ways in which our career activity can compel us; we must learn to be open to as many of them as possible.

On the simplest level, we can take a personal interest in whatever project or enterprise on which we are working. Admittedly, as a writer, this is easy for me to say. If I select a topic I'm genuinely fascinated by, then the motivation to explore it is already built in. Picking a subject for a book is really just an excuse to dive deep into a new field and start learning. Great novelists are also great researchers—and, as readers, we can see their love for their subject matter oozing off every page. Herman Melville's adventures, from *Moby-Dick* to *Billy Budd,* are filled with lived and researched experiences of whaling. James Michener's best fictional works are also history and archeology lessons, painstakingly researched over decades spent traveling, researching in libraries, and interviewing archeologists. Even contemporary popular works, from Michael Chabon's *Kavalier and Clay* to Philip Roth's *The Plot Against America,* are tours through worlds as emotionally charged by their atmospheric and historical accuracy as their characters' inner lives. These are authors who love their choices of subject matter, and commit to learning everything there is to know about them—sometimes more than has been known by anyone before.

My own advice to any aspiring writer or journalist has always been to pick an area that interests him and then become its greatest expert and, in the process, advocate. For me, it was the fledgling cyberculture. Back when people would laugh at the prospect that they'd one day have a computer on their desks or ever write an email message, I was writing articles about the crazy young hackers of San Francisco who believed they could launch a new culture around the computers they were programming. To pitch a story on virtual reality or hypertext to

GQ or *Esquire* meant selling this vision to editors. And each piece I published helped put the culture I was selling on the map. By the time experts were needed to explain this stuff to business and the public, I had become one.

Just as important, to connect with the wellspring of creativity innate to any endeavor, we have to love the touch, feel, and smell of what we do. This means the nitty-gritty, moment-to-moment experience of actually setting pen to paper, opening a briefcase, or pushing "speaker" on the phone. Like children playing teacher, doctor, or police officer, we must revel in the details that make up the vast majority of our tasks at hand.

One of my greatest teachers, the filmmaker Alexander Mackendrick (*Sweet Smell of Success, The Man in the White Suit*) insisted that to make films, we had to know everything about them. He studied the anatomy and functioning of the eye, so that he could know how the light reflected on a movie screen interacted with the optic nerve and the brain. He learned the chemistry of emulsion, so that he'd understand the way images burned themselves onto film stock. If one of us turned in 10 pages of a script we were working on, Mackendrick would pre-sent us the next day with 20 pages of notes, showing more appreciation for our work and process than we did ourselves.

Mackendrick also insisted that we relish the physical sensations of making movies. If we didn't appreciate the pencils with which we drew our storyboards, or the texture of the paper, then how could we invest our drawings with the level of passion worthy of the kinds of budgets we hoped to spend on them? I remember him telling one student that her drawings were written too tentatively, as if the colored pencils she used to create them had been borrowed and she was afraid of using them up. He was right: she had borrowed the pencils from her roommate. He told her to work an extra job, if she had to, in order to finance her own pencils, which she could abuse to her heart's content.

What Mackendrick meant to communicate, in so many words, was that if you don't love enough the particulars of the experience of what you do to devour the tangible details, or if you don't care enough about your work to find out everything there is to know, then you'll never be able to *get into it,* and you'll never come up with anything original. Maintaining anything less than total commitment is to be a dilettante.

Great artists and craftspeople of all kinds pay as much attention to their process and their tools as to their final output. On the set of one film, I had the honor of playing a bizarre little game with the famous cinematographer Vilmos Zsigmond, in which someone would shout the size of a lens and then we'd have to guess how wide a portion of the brick wall in front of us that lens would capture. Vilmos always guessed right—within a half-brick. That's because he wasn't guessing.

There's a great story about the Japanese director Kurosawa, in which he told his editor to shorten a scene in his movie *Ran.* "How much shorter do you want it," the editor asked, "two seconds, three?" The director responded by holding his hands about a foot apart, indicating a length of 35mm film. "This much." That's how intimate the great director was with the medium in which he worked.

A friend of mine who works as a chef at a decent New York bistro travels to work on the subway with her knives in a leather pouch on her back. Sure, she could cook or chop with others just as sharp, but her experience of cooking is enhanced by her sense of connection with these tools. It's not superstition, but the delight of experiencing the reality of one's work. Master barbers use their favorite gold-handled scissors, talented gardeners their favorite hedge clippers, surgeons their chosen tools, and great pool players their specially weighted cues, because great professionals savor the hands-on aspects of the jobs they do. My dad, a CPA who eventually came to be president of a major New York hospital, worked with his slide rule long after calculators came into vogue. He didn't do this because he was old-fashioned, but because it helped him stay connected to the numbers with which he was working. As machines and computers came onto the accounting floor, my dad also knew as much about changing the ribbons and replacing the disks as the repairmen.

Sure, you're saying, for artists, craftspeople, or even the lone accountant, such devotion to tools and technique is easy. Hackers love their computer code the same way surfers love the ocean waves, so they have no trouble staying up all night to patch a piece of software, just as they love to sit around telling esoteric stories about coding conflicts to their colleagues. How do we translate this focus on process to an entire business, or even a major corporation?

It's as easy as it is consuming: by discovering what it is about what we do that genuinely fascinates us, and then going as deep into that joy of investigation, commitment, and process as we can stand.

THE UNBEARABLE LIGHTNESS OF WORKING

We can't help but resent that many of the most successful people we encounter are also the happiest. They may not be any more trained or skilled than we are, but they nonetheless coast through their careers from success to success, effortlessly and joyously. And they're so damn happy about it. What we keep forgetting is that it's not their success that made them so happy, but their passionate connection to their work that made them so successful. Likewise, we pity the poor fool who surrenders his vacations in order to work on that new proposal, business plan, or prototype, failing to realize that the object of our pity might be having a whole lot more fun working than he would sitting on a beach in Aruba.

The problem with a business culture based on efficiency is that it frames effort and time as commodities to be hoarded rather than spent. We believe it's preferable to accomplish something in five minutes that could have taken five hours, forgetting that the person who can find five hours of full engagement in a task might just come up with something better in the process. We expect our customers to spend hours, days, even years with our products; why don't we expect the same of ourselves? And without that loving investment, what is our work really worth, anyway?

Businesses today are counting on the power of "community" to keep their products in perpetual circulation. A clever new marketing campaign or a snazzy new package, it is hoped, will stir new word of mouth about the same old product. But the only lasting way to raise the value of a product as social currency is to raise the value of the product itself. While creative marketing is always a plus, it is no substitute for creative development. It's as if businesses are afraid to get involved in their own core strength, preferring to defer to the brand manager or advertising agency for a quick fix.

American Express, for one, has spent millions on innovative marketing campaigns to promote its card in new, nonlinear media. It hired Jerry Seinfeld to star in short, entertaining "webisodes" on the Internet, spent countless dollars installing a breakthrough movie technology on the walls of the New Jersey PATH train tunnels, and even put on a Sheryl Crow concert. Needless to say, all this promotional ingenuity had little impact on its card sales. Amex would have done better to expand the number of airport lounges that Platinum customers can enter for free—a feature of the card I've found myself extolling by word of mouth to my own frequent traveler friends. By spending its time and money on the core enterprise—advocating for its cardholders in retail and travel—Amex would have gone further than any of its unconventional campaigns could toward developing a community of product advocates. I saw my first *Seinfeld* webisode on the very same day I discovered that my American Express Platinum account no longer gave me access to the Delta Skylounge. Membership was supposed to have its privileges. If I want innovative media, I'll go to HBO.

To put it simply, communities naturally build around product lines that overflow with intrinsic value. People may talk about a brilliant advertising campaign, but they will never advocate an ad the way they advocate a product they love. A company's real relationship with a customer is not communicated through the marketing, however compelling it may be. It is communicated through the cup holders in the doors, the easy-to-read LED display in the cell phone cover, the user-friendly menu on the digital video recorder, or the leak-proof absorbency of the baby diaper. Companies speak to us through the details and quality of their products: the feeling of discovering a knob on a dashboard just where your hand happens to reach; finding a copy of the assembly instructions on the company's Web site; getting dropped off right next to your rental car after simply giving the bus driver your name; or coming across an extra pocket in your parka for a cell phone that some dedicated designer has had sewn in there seemingly just for you. The anticipation of one's desires feels awfully close to true love.

This relationship is ongoing and real only when the company seems to innovate and respond to new needs on cue—or, better, to anticipate and respond to them in advance. It's something that can't be achieved through focus groups or market research, but requires that the people making the cars, cell phones, DVRs, and diapers understand these products and their potential roles in our lives better than we do. This is why we customers pay them, why we show them our loyalty, and why we advocate their brands.

A real brand relationship is like a subscription to a path of innovation. The customer is signing on for the trip, as assured of his ongoing surprise and satisfaction as a committed Stephen King reader. A company must stay ahead of its customer the way a mystery writer stays ahead of his reader—the way Steve Jobs doesn't simply anticipate but leads his customers in new directions that turn out to be both unexpected yet right on course. This is the way to sell not just one product to customers, but to engage them in a path of mutual discovery.

To do this, a company must overcome its own fear and trepidation, and accept its role as the true maestro of its field. Evolution begins at home. Yes, as we'll explore in Chapter Seven, customers can often be as contributive as employees to many aspects of research and development. Most of the filters and plug-ins for the wildly successful Adobe Photoshop program wouldn't exist without a base of users toiling away for no expectation of remuneration. But their dedication is *in response* to an even greater demonstration of expertise by the company whose product they're making better. The product, and the work that went into it, sets the tone. The company and its core innovators lead the dance. If we're expecting customers to sign onto a product line as true believers, for life, we ought to have done the same thing, ourselves, from the other side.

That's why any business hoping for its products to rise to the level of social currency must do more than artful advertising; it must engage with its core enterprise as if it were an art. As customers become more educated about the products they're using—even to the point of being willing to tinker with them—businesses must respond by upping the ante, and demonstrating an even greater dedication to the cause. Yes, this means working harder, but it also means doing so with unparalleled joy and gusto. That pleasure of craft is so contagious that it leads customers to buy products, at least in part, for the vicarious experience of getting in the box with you.

LOVE THYSELF: REVENGE OF THE NERDS

For companies to get back in the box and reorient to their core enterprises as ongoing opportunities for innovation, they'll need to reorganize around the premise of intrinsic fun, rather than extrinsic rewards. It's the underlying lesson of *Revenge of the Nerds*—and what made so-called geeks so admired during the early Internet era. Here were some people who enjoyed what they did so much they couldn't help but speak passionately about it. What made the Internet "sexy" was not the computers, but the mere fact that people were willing to work on it for free. Why? Because they had found something worthy of exploration and development, a field so inspiring that they could jump into it with awe, and without an ounce of cynicism, pocket protectors and all.

Companies today are afraid to jump into their own industries, for a few reasons. Some are simply embarrassed of what they do, and like to imagine themselves as part of younger, seemingly more creative industry. I don't know how many times Procter & Gamble executives have asked me whether my breakthrough ideas about innovation could ever apply to a "boring old business" like theirs. Of course they do! P&G might be an old company that makes soap, but it is also a product lab with terrific and consistent legacies in chemistry, distribution, packaging, and marketing. Unlike the marketers and executives I usually speak with, the scientists in Cincinnati have no qualms about dedicating their lives to soap, and P&G's perennially innovative product line shows it.

In an equally self-defeating style, businesses and their advertisers ache to make almost any good or service appealing to the "hip" teen or 20-something demographic. They go so far as to convince themselves that the 18-to-34 age group has the most disposable income (they don't). I remember a meeting in which a brand manager wanted to know how to make the Snuggles bear more hip and Internet-appropriate—seemingly unaware of the product's core constituency or the brand's legacy. Or at least uncomfortable with them.

Businesses and their advertisers like to position their products for teens because it makes *them* feel young. According to one research consultancy, a full 70 percent of brands want to be seen as "younger than they are now perceived."[2] Playing out this midlife crisis on the business landscape can have mixed results, such as GM's "not your father's" Oldsmobile campaign that drove the brand out of existence, Sears' "softer" adventures in fashion, and Maxwell House's efforts to remake itself as a youth brand. Brands can certainly be reinvented or even resuscitated from long naps, but this must be done in a way consistent with the original brand and, more importantly, the actual product and customer who will be using it.

Most important, cycles of innovation and reinvention must be consistent with a company's core proposition and competency. On this score, Gap provides us with a great example of a corporation that has lost its way by avoiding the true nature of its business.

The Gap's biggest problem is that it doesn't make clothes. Although it does have some of the most ethical-sounding outsourcing rules of any American company using Asian labor, the company seems incapable of insourcing almost anything. And the worse things get, the less dependent on its own initiative and insight Gap becomes.

Since its inception in 1969, the Gap has made a business out of providing quality substitutes for name-brand casual wear. As Levi's and other fashion jeans rose in popularity (and price) through the 1970s, the Gap emerged as both an outlet for Levi's products and a place to purchase equivalent styles under the Gap brand, for less money. By the 1980s, the Gap had stopped selling Levi's, or any brand of clothing other than its own. It adopted European counterpart Benetton's style of system selling, training its young employees to engage in a sales routine called GapAct—greet, approach, provide, add-on, close, and thank. As the dot-com boom took off in the late 1990s, so did the Gap's easy, no-nonsense approach to jeans, khakis, and T-shirts that could make everyone look appropriate for pretty much any situation.

Romantic? Maybe not. But at its peak in 2000, the company was a worldwide retail giant, with 4,200 stores selling items made by 4,000 manufacturers in 55 countries. The Gap had also expanded into two other brands, upscale Banana Republic and downscale Old Navy. But then, in 2001, like so many other companies entering midlife crisis, the Gap made a classic blunder: it decided to chase after the trendy teen market being courted so successfully by hip brands such as Diesel and Fubu. This wasn't entirely its own fault. Wall Street analysts with little experiential knowledge of the apparel business were busy condemning the Gap for sticking with its tried-and-true strategy of providing high-quality, low-fuss fashions. "They just don't have the clothes that people lust for," complained Candace Corlett of WSL Strategic Retail. "In their wisdom they have decided that what they do best, traditional Gap khakis, denims, white T-shirts, is their future. I question that."[3]

Eventually, so did the Gap. But trendy fashions are a whole lot more difficult to copy successfully than simple staples—especially with an eight-month lead time between outsourced design and outsourced manufacture—and the Gap was left with clearance racks filled with orange and turquoise rejects. By December 2001, the stock price went down to a four-year low. Meanwhile, the effort to combat trendier competitors had turned off the Gap's mainstream shoppers. Same-store sales figures[4] had undergone a terrible 28-month slide, and the success of upstarts like H&M and Zara made the company even more desperate for a fix.

By 2002, realizing it was in deep trouble, the Gap was finally ready to abandon its failed effort at chasing teens. It announced a new strategy to bring back loyal customers who once loved the chain but had drifted away when the Gap abandoned them for teenagers. Older stars like Willie Nelson and Whoopi Goldberg were hired to pose in ads, and celebrate their "individuality" through their own interpretations of Gap style. The superficial effort at a return to core values didn't help sales or, more importantly to the Gap, the stock price.

Misunderstanding its dilemma as a pure marketing challenge, Gap then hired a new CEO, Paul Pressler, a 15-year veteran of Walt Disney's parks and resorts division. On the news of this hire, Gap stock went up 3.8 percent. But Pressler had no experience in clothes. He was hired for his expertise in international business, customer focus, and marketing. Pressler declared that he would distinguish himself from the former CEO by *not* trying to be an expert merchandiser. In a press conference, he explained quite candidly that he wouldn't be making decisions about "khaki pants." The question that remained hanging, however, was who would?

With core design and manufacturing concerns shelved for the time being, Pressler was free to focus almost entirely on marketing. He went on a focus group crusade, and—in a nod to the new renaissance society of authorship—emerged with a set of campaigns based on the concept "How Do You Wear It?" embodied by *Sex and the City* star Sarah Jessica Parker. In print and TV ads, Parker is shown customizing Gap outfits to fit her own fun and offbeat image. Customers are invited to copy these looks, or invent their own, at special "customization events" and "Show Us How You Wear It" contests. Trend research also inspired the Gap to stage a fashion show in a Chelsea nightclub. The result was so glaringly unsuccessful that even a Gap spokeswoman for the event admitted to the press, "Next year maybe we'll do it differently. It didn't quite work."[5]

Marketing gimmicks like these aren't enough to revitalize a company of the Gap's size and stature. Under Pressler, Gap has successfully trimmed some of its fat by closing underperforming or oversized locations, but same-store sales continue to flag, and the language out of the boardroom is getting increasingly desperate. Pressler's research-driven, efficiency-minded management, coupled with somewhat outlandish public relations events, are symptomatic of a corporation having lost touch with its core competency. The Gap seems a lot more certain of what it is not than what it is. Pressler claims he understands that the company's "midlife crisis" chasing teens was a mistake, but is entertaining the idea of opening entirely separate chains for nearly every target market his focus groups identified: older customers, teens, even the overweight.[6]

What the Gap appears incapable of absorbing is that it is in the business of making clothes. Its core expertise, from the beginning, was stocking its shelves as quickly as humanly possible with great copies of the casual clothes people wanted. Early ads featuring James Dean did not convince consumers that the 1950s movie star actually wore Gap khakis, only that he wore plain khaki pants that the Gap could easily copy. The Gap's core proposition is good copies of classic and stable contemporary styles, in stock and in your size. To meet that challenge and improve upon performance doesn't mean finding better celebrities for the advertising, but focusing instead on the skill set that makes the Gap possible: managing a manufacturing and distribution scheme that spans the globe, and understanding customer needs well enough to keep the right clothes on the shelves at all times.

Would it make as good a movie as one about working behind the scenes at Prada? Maybe not. But there are lots of reasons to see it as more fun, and even more virtuous.

Others seem to think so. For while the Gap has allowed its core capabilities to wither, a spate of European competitors have picked up where the American giant left off, evolving the global distribution and rapid-response inventory model far beyond their predecessor's capabilities. Swedish upstart—now retail behemoth—H&M spends 4 percent of its total budget on marketing; but other than that, it maintains an extraordinarily frugal enterprise. Unlike the Gap, which has floundered because of mismanaged inventory, H&M approaches fashion as a perishable good. "We hate inventory," explains their head of buying,

Karl Gunnar Fagerlin,[7] who has helped develop an innovative stocking system that prevents any accumulation of unwanted goods.

At H&M, all merchandise is designed in-house, by a team of 95 designers in Stockholm. The company then outsources manufacturing to a network of 900 shops in 21 low-wage countries. By accepting responsibility for overseeing the processes through which its clothes are designed and assembled, H&M has compressed lead time from design through manufacture and distribution down to three weeks, and counting, compared with Gap's eight or nine months. H&M's clothes are designed with production in mind.

Remember: inventory supply and reordering *is* the key skill here. The designs are knockoffs, for the most part, and the branding is not an issue—at least not in the logo-on-the-pocket sense. By remembering that the supply chain is the core skill to be honed, H&M spends its time and money not on abstract focus groups, but on monitoring exactly how product gets on and off the shelves in the stores. Every day, Fagerlin and his team tap into the company's database for itemized sales reports by country, store, and piece. Stores are generally restocked daily, but on special occasions, such as store openings, they can be restocked as many as three times daily. Constant restocking allows the company to add and revise inventory essentially on the fly, based on daily sales.

So instead of using focus groups and market research to arrive at a product line and brand image that is then rolled out eight months later, H&M uses the real-time data pouring in from its stores to determine which of its products to manufacture and which of the fashion directions it is emulating happen to be working in a particular region. Just as a product is the best way for a company to communicate to its customers, the product is also the best way for a customer to communicate to a company. By looking at what people really buy rather than what they say they might buy next year, H&M gives itself a tremendous advantage.

H&M's main rival, the Spanish chain Zara, takes these processes and philosophy to their logical extreme. Zara has gotten so far into the box of retail science and technology that it is reinventing the clothing store as a form of fashion media in the process.

Even more focused on "lead time optimization" than H&M, Zara operates on a lead time of just 15 days or less. The hyperefficient chain's 600 stores were developed from the bottom up to serve as nodes in a responsive fashion distribution network. The products themselves are designed as components, allowing for easy sourcing with minimal retooling. For the most part, Zara has brought all these processes in-house, designing, making, and selling its own clothes. The chain has never run an ad campaign;[8] its thousand storefronts *are* its media. The store's ability to reflect hot clothing trends so rapidly has led many Spanish women to stop buying fashion magazines altogether, and simply visit the store to find out what's new.[9] Amazingly, Zara can copy, manufacture, and distribute breaking fashion trends faster than *Vogue* can publish photos of them.

Zara relies heavily on technological innovation, such as point-of-sale terminals, handheld scanners, and wireless PDAs, through which store personnel can easily register what's left on the shelves and automatically order new stock. (The systems were put in place after employees complained about how time-consuming the fax-ordering system had become—particularly because they were sending 50-foot faxes every evening!) Inventories are kept razor-thin, so that about 75 percent of merchandise in the average store changes every three or four weeks. This not only prevents the accumulation of unsold inventory; it guarantees repeat visits by customers interested in the ever-changing fashion landscape in the store.[10] Zara upgrades its technology consistently, allowing, for example, stores to treat one another as members of a Napster-like peer-to-peer network. Instead of ordering inventory from the supply chain, stores can purchase goods from one another automatically so that products unsuccessful in one area can be sold immediately in another before the end of their natural shelf life.

The lesson of the flailing Gap and its focused competitors is that core competencies aren't always the most obviously romantic aspects of a business. The core value of these chain stores is not the branding of their goods, but the responsiveness of their design and manufacturing to consumer needs. The object of the game is not to create fashion trends—that's someone else's job—but to reflect them as they are happening and supply them to the customers who want them. The Gap lost its way by outsourcing design and manufacturing while holding steadfastly to a seasonal inventory schedule, and by utilizing focus groups instead of real-time store sales as its chief form of consumer feedback. The relative success of H&M and Zara stems from their ability to embrace the business they are in, and respond passionately to the challenge of developing the systems for ordering, inventory monitoring, and distribution that turned their shelves into a recognized and cherished form of fashion media.

Businesses that embrace their seemingly unsexy side end up becoming sexy as a result. By getting their egos out of the way, and getting back in the box of replication, distribution, and responsiveness, these discount chains discovered that they could provide customers with one of their most important and valued windows to the world of fashion. Revenge of the nerds.

SIZE MATTERS: THE DEVIL IN THE DETAILS

Other companies lose sight of their core business when they become overly distracted by financials. In a landscape dominated by investor or shareholder concerns, "fundamentals" take on a distorted meaning where growth is often valued over health. By trying to become megabusinesses on scales inappropriate for them, many enterprises lose sight of the market they are serving and dilute the specificity of their product and brand. Size matters, but bigger is not always better. Some businesses work on certain scales, and not on others. That's why the finance department can't run the whole show.

In the worst cases of innovation through accounting, those alien to a company or an entire industry attempt to make important choices about it. For example, the introduction of CD recording technology in the early 1980s led to a huge and unprecedented spike in recorded music sales. This surge attracted the attention of already spreadsheet-driven media conglomerates, which saw in these raw numbers the promise of an expanding industry. They went on a buying spree, snatching up as many independent labels as they could and absorbing them into their corporate infrastructures. Then, as if on cue, sales figures dropped precipitously. What went wrong?

In the first place, small, independent companies don't always adapt well to larger corporate structures. Smaller businesses are often driven by the personal tastes of their workers—whether or not a common philosophy is ever articulated. By being forced to bring their identity into consciousness and then serve, officially, as the "hip-hop" label or "indie rock" label within a corporate portfolio, these formerly creative companies fall into a cycle of imitating their own last successes rather than intuiting their next ones.

Worse than simply mismanaging the companies they had purchased, analysts from the media conglomerates had neglected to examine the components of the sales spike that had attracted them to the music business in the first place. They missed the fact that a great majority of the CDs accounting for the surge were being bought as replacements for vinyl albums that customers already owned. Once those albums were all upgraded, sales went down even lower than before, due to poor pricing, bad packaging, and a reduction in resources deployed to find and develop new talent.

The corporatization of the music industry by outsiders with little understanding of the process by which talent is discovered, nurtured, and then marketed has had disastrous results. Bad pricing and well-publicized exploitation of bands has alienated music buyers, who have turned to illegal music sharing as retaliation. The bottom-up culture through which bar bands developed into club bands and were eventually discovered by "A & R" (artists and recording) scouts and developed into recording artists, has been replaced by the top-down manufacture of prefab bands, which are then pumped out nationally through pre-arrangement with MTV or Clear Channel. Music becomes predictable and indistinguishable as music expertise is removed from the equation. Of course, this only makes room for a new indigenous music culture, currently developing online, to replace the multibillion-dollar fiasco.

Such misunderstandings of the scale and ecology in which a particular business "lives" plague a great many of the firms that buy smaller companies. Seeing their job as growing all concerns into industry giants, those that manage by balance sheet alone view all restaurant chains as potential McDonald's and all technology companies as potential Microsofts—or at least potential Outbacks and Oracles. Size matters, but one size does not fit all.

This was the lesson learned, just in time, by *Details* magazine, which has finally emerged from a devastating slump caused almost entirely by the corporate need to make the niche title fill a bigger role than it was born to.

Scenester journalist Annie Flanders created *Details* in 1982 as a gay-friendly magazine for the club crowd, and quickly earned a loyal base of about 100,000 subscribers.[11] Recognizing an emerging new culture, S.I. Newhouse Jr. picked up the hipster rag for Advance Publications (parent of Condé Nast) in 1988, hoping to turn it into the brand of a new generation. He entrusted the reinvention of *Details* to James Truman, a British unknown who had formerly worked as the pop music editor at *Vogue*. Newhouse gave Truman full license, which he used to kick veteran staffers to the curb and create an exciting, gender-bending rock 'n' roll magazine for young men.[12] As Salon.com put it, "In the twinkle of an eye, *Details* became the hot book for the young, the slacking and the goateed: the antidote to such stuffy adult titles as *Esquire* and *GQ*."[13] Circulation quadrupled and Truman was catapulted to the seat of editorial director at Condé Nast.[14]

But by 1994, the confetti from the *Details* coming-out party had settled. A new editor had to be found to replace Truman; and the reality sank in that in order to support Condé Nast's hefty cost structure, the magazine would have to attain circulation of 750,000 and sell 1,000 ad pages a year,[15] a burdensome load for any magazine, much less a newcomer. And this need to make *Details* function on a scale inappropriate for itself, and suitable only for the place on the balance sheet into which it was slotted, slowly reversed one of the most promising magazine launches of the decade.

Over the subsequent six years, the magazine experienced a veritable revolving door of editors, each with a new vision for bringing the magazine up to the elusive "next level." *Details* went from being a magazine for fashion-forward men to a general-interest men's magazine, and then to a magazine for men whose primary interest was women. None could hit the mark, and readership declined with each successive shift of leadership.

First came James Leland from *Newsweek,* who began by boosting the magazine's journalistic integrity but was booted after just two issues. His successor, the fashionable Joe Dolce from *Vogue,* was a former club doorman who, it was hoped, could help *Details* regain some downtown-club cred.[16] But the rise of the Wall Street style and ethos, as well as upstart money culture magazines like *POV,* spurred Dolce to compete by pursuing stories about money and success—leading many to believe *Details* was turning into another finance magazine for young people.[17] Dolce wouldn't have time to reconcile *Details* image.

The fact that Dolce was openly gay apparently "rubbed some corporate types the wrong way,"[18] particularly in the face of a rash of successful misogynist titles like *Stuff* and *Maxim,* characterized by macho bravado. Responding again to the changing tides, *Details* published "The Sex Issue," featuring Tyra Banks's ample bosom on the cover, as well as a story about "How to Date a Super Model." Condé Nast hired a new editor with an alpha-male reputation, Michael Caruso, to fully hetero-fy the magazine.[19]

Like the Gap paying more attention to its commercials than its product line, *Details* became so obsessed with wooing cool, beer-drinking frat boys that it lost its way. Instead of working on the magazine, it worked on marketing gimmicks such as "Hooked-Up," a 1998 college tour focusing on in-line skating. According to *Details* then-publisher Linda Mason, "It's hard to get young men to come out of the dorms, unless you offer them some irresistible activity, and in-line skating is one of them."[20] So now a magazine whose very soul was forged in the gay-friendly club scene was pandering to college frat boys through in-line skating stunt tours conceived by corporate executives. *Details* also teamed up with companies including Miller Brewing Co. and Sony PlayStation to sponsor a Field Day in Manhattan in order to sell a whole lifestyle of products through the fusion of extreme and traditional sports, music, and fashion. "We're bringing the reader's real life together with the magazine—fusing sports, entertainment, music, and fashion into one experience, just like people do in real life," said Mason.[21] Predictably, these schemes didn't work to boost readership, and Caruso's brief tenure ended.

The cursed quartet of editors ended with Marc Golin, who had been imported directly from *Maxim*. Interestingly, Golin seemed intent on taking *Details* in a new direction—away from cleavage—yet, in the end he, too, would lament not having enough time to realize his vision. "The March issue was starting to get there," he said, "It would have taken another year or two to get it where I wanted it." The March issue included an article by Executive Editor Bill Shapiro on what to do if your girlfriend has been raped—certainly not the typical laddy mag fare.[22] Golin was fired from *Details* in 2000 even though circulation was hovering at a respectable 541,710.[23]

Disgusted with *Details'* performance, S.I. Newhouse Jr. pulled the plug and passed the remains of the magazine to Mary Berner at Fairchild Publications. This was his first bright move. Whereas Condé Nast magazines are expected to sell 800,000 or more, the circulation of Fairchild publications runs only around 400,000 to 500,000.[24] Now *Details* would stand a chance of succeeding as the magazine it was born to be.

Fairchild decided to give unknown 28-year-old Daniel Peres a shot at pulling the sword from the stone. Peres had been working as the Paris bureau chief of *W* in 1998 and leapt to the challenge. He proudly dismissed *GQ* and *Esquire* as "sclerotic," and "*Maxim* and its ilk as moronic."[25] But after a year and a half of "flopping around in search of a formula," Peres learned to bite his tongue. "I've learned that it's not as easy as it looks. The magazine didn't have a voice. I didn't have a voice."[26]

That realization by an editor-in-chief is music to a journalist's ears. I remember working as a writer for *Details* during a few of its many incarnations. No sooner would I complete a feature than the "direction" of the magazine would be changed, or a new editor would be hired who scrapped the entire last batch of assignments. Such behavior doesn't only turn off loyal readers, it frustrates loyal writers, who base their choice of magazines to write for on the probability of their work making it into print. As *Details* floundered, chasing trends and then hoping to incorporate them through new hires, many established writers grew hesitant to invest their time and energy with so little expectation of return.

It's a predicament I've seen more than one magazine fall prey to. The telltale sign is when editorial meetings become less about what the magazine's writers and editors want to tell the world than what the marketing department, through reader surveys and focus groups, has deemed the subscribers want to see on the magazine's pages. Editors too easily lose sight of the fact that readers are paying for the magazine staff's own selection process and point of view. Readers want to be served with useful information, but they also want to be surprised, introduced to new ideas, and led to think in new directions. Magazines are top-down media: someone needs to be in charge. It's that person, and his core group's vision, that subscribers are buying.

Eventually, it was a chronic bad back condition that allowed Peres to get back in the box. Stuck in bed and in bad pain, Peres was finally forced into the kind of stillness where true decisions can be made. He took a good, hard look at his magazine, realized he had been listening to far too many people telling him what to do, and emerged with his own vision. He would remake *Details* in a manner consistent with its original mission. Peres cleaned house, firing both his opinionated executive editor and photo director, and took charge himself. *Details* would return to the "cheeky bisexual content"[27] that put it on the map.

"When Dan quit playing grown-up editor and started just being Dan, things clicked,"[28] publisher Mary Berner said. The result? Under the pose of Peres as the vulgar sophisticate, *Details* has become, according to the *New York Times*, "a gently snobbish fashion and service manual for those young titans who believe anything is possible as long as you look good."[29]

Undeniably luscious if not particularly substantive, the latest incarnation of *Details* has found its rhythm. Nominated for a 2003 National Magazine Award for Excellence, it won the award for design in both 2002 and 2003.[30] A 2002 survey showed that *Details* attracts the youngest, wealthiest readership,[31] and the magazine boasted a 37 percent increase in ad pages for the first half of 2003.[32] Circulation is about 425,000 with a solid subscriber base at 80 percent.[33] And, most importantly, thanks to a renewed focus on defining culture rather than chasing it, *Details* has become a source of its own content and direction. The magazine virtually owns "metrosexual" style, and regularly earns national headlines for irreverent, bisexual-tinged humor that sometimes crosses the line.

By attempting to grow *Details* into something altogether too big for its niche bisexual britches, Condé Nast took a promising property far out of its own box and into a decade-long search for self that ended only when the editor-in-chief was too sick to listen to anyone else, or to look beyond his own intuition.

RIDING THE CURRENT

Too many businesses are addicted to their own growth. It's hard to accept that certain enterprises hover successfully for years at a particular size or even expand and contract regularly over time. While it may not help support high price/earnings[34] ratios for their stocks, companies must learn to accept that most products and all brands have their natural cycles. A down year doesn't mean the end of a business; on the contrary, transient obscurity is what allows for a new season of growth—particularly if the product can still be recognized once the customer base comes out of hibernation. Patience is more than just a virtue in this respect; it's crucial to true longevity.

Duncan yo-yos, for example, have ups and downs as regular and perplexing as cicada season. For no good reason, Duncan's products become wildly popular every 10 years, then retreat into seeming hibernation. The company has learned to ride this ebb and flow, emerging with TV ad campaigns, celebrity spokespeople, and national tournaments just when a new generation of yo-yo fanatics seems to be emerging.

Birkenstock, maker of the sandals known in the United States for their healthy, hippie style, also endures a popularity curve that resembles an ascending sine wave. The company has learned to recognize this pattern much in the way a surfer recognizes the sequence of ocean waves, in order to launch new brands and shops whenever interest is peaking, and then hold tight when it levels off. Using this strategy, Birkenstock has slowly expanded from making just a handful of shoes to a current offering of close to 500 different styles. The trick has been to reach out to whichever demographic is "discovering" Birkenstock for the first time—and then retain them by creating new product lines that appeal to the other aspects of their lifestyles. So, for example, as businesspeople discovered Birkenstocks as a comfortable vacation sandal, the company developed black leather versions for these new customers to extend their Birkenstock wearing to the workplace.

Accepting a company or division's size at a given point in time is as important as knowing how to grow it when the climate is right. Attempting to spur rapid growth in the off-season, however, is like watering seeds in the winter. It's more a symptom of a generic growth obsession than knowing one's business, or even just one's brand image, from the inside out.

One of the saddest examples of drifting out of the box I've studied has to be Levi Strauss & Co. Among the most recognizable brands in the world—the inventor of what we now call blue jeans—is struggling with self-inflicted wounds and facing the possibility of death by acquisition. I don't often have an emotional reaction to assembling a corporate study, but in Levi's case I suppose it's my own sense of connection to the brand as a consumer that makes me wince at the way its value has been squandered over the last decade. Every step of the way, Levi's decisions have shown an ignorance of the strength of its brand, a lack of faith in the endurance of its mission, and a panicky impatience to make things right.

We all know the story by now. Founded in 1853 to suit the clothing needs of gold-rush miners in San Francisco, Levi Strauss & Co. got a patent in 1873 for adding reinforcing rivets to denim trousers. Popularized over the next century by iconic figures such as cowboys and movie stars like Marlon Brando and James Dean, Levi's became the lowbrow costume of choice for many of America's social movements. Rebellious teens of the 1950s, mods of the 1960s, hippies of the 1970s, and even yuppies of the 1980s all wore one version or another of Levi's basic blue jean. Some had flared legs, others were boot-cut, but they were all recognizably and authentically Levi's. They said so on the pocket.

The massive success of Levi's 501 jeans took the company almost by surprise. Yuppies and young baby boomers of the 1980s, facing a difficult job market and economy, became nostalgic for the brands of their youth, and saw in Levi's the authenticity of a simpler era. The 501s were named "the most important fashion of the century" by *Time*. While manufacturers like the Gap were looking at cutting costs and outsourcing production, Levi's had the market share and profit margins to become "a haven of political correctness."[35] It kept design and manufacture in-house, paid its workers well, and sought to embody the progressive consciousness of its home city.

Thanks to the tremendous popularity of the classic 501 style with young professionals in the 1980s, Levi's correctly decided it was a good moment to expand. Leading the charge toward a less formal workplace, Levi's launched the Dockers brand of men's khakis in 1986 (and women's in 1988), bridging the gap between casual and office wear, and inspiring a widespread American practice called "casual Fridays," on which workers are free to wear jeans or khakis to the office. Hitting their "sweet spot," Levi's was both responding to and catalyzing social change. A decade later, Levi's sales began to slow. Peaking in 1996 at $7.1 billion, sales have slowed consistently since then, declining over 40 percent to just $4.09 billion by 2003, which was supposed to have been Levi's celebratory 150th anniversary year.

Most business analysts attribute Levi's downfall to the company's penchant for social responsibility—as if maintaining high standards of fairness were a distraction from doing good business. In Levi's case, it was part of what defined the brand as a San Francisco, left-friendly, countercultural mainstay. No, what pecked away at Levi's market share of the seemingly always-growing demand for denim was a bunch of trendy young competitors, like Diesel, Blue Cult, and Seven. These newcomers were defined less by their styles than by their advertising, and appealed to the fickle population of 14-year-old boys and girls, always on the lookout for the next big thing.

Of course, Levi's had survived, even thrived, through such multi-fronted assaults before. The 1970s saw the sudden rise of the high-profile fashion jeans brands Sassoon and Sergio Valente. With nothing getting between underage model Brooke Shields and her Calvin Kleins, how did an old-school brand like Levi's manage to compete successfully? By creating a few butt-clinging styles and waiting it out. As Levi's seemed to understand at the time, it wasn't really fighting against competitor blue jeans manufacturers. The brands contesting Levi's leadership didn't even make their own products. No, Levi's was in a battle against a short-lived advertising aesthetic. A certain kind of cigarette-legged model, an anorexia fad, and the popularity of disco among high schoolers had combined into a pop phenom. Levi's couldn't chase these brands onto the transient teen landscape, nor should it have. Levi's wasn't dependent on advertising: the jeans were their own form of media, communicating more about a steadfast connection to authenticity than it ever could, or should, about trendsetting. Levi's seemed to understand, at least at that time, that its strength lay in its endurance. When the fashion jeans fell away, Levi's remained on top, stronger than ever.

But the more recent attack of teen fashion brands, no more cunning in their use of media or outsourcing than their predecessors, seems to have pushed Levi's off its center of gravity and into a losing brand war. Diesel Jeans is a media company, after all, defined more by its confusingly cheeky ads than by any particular fashion sensibility. Its ads—featuring, for example, North Korean soldiers cycling past fake

American ice cream billboards (in which the models wear Diesel jeans)—are standard GenX cynicism, made all the more ironic by serving as a form of genuine advertising. Hopping on the quasiretro fashion trend started a decade earlier by thrift-shop buyers and, eventually, Urban Outfitters, brands like Diesel and Blue Cult have clicked with teenagers the way Sassoon did in the 1970s.

Instead of playing it cool, maintaining its aura of authenticity in the face of so much hip cynicism and irony, Levi's made the tragic mistake of chasing it. It was as silly as it would be for Walt Disney World to imitate Chuck E. Cheese's. It's not entirely the company's own fault. Nearly every industry analyst's report on the situation, even now, faults Levi's for failing earlier to take more aggressive action in this direction. Levi's did launch its own competitive hip subbrand, Silvertab, and hired TWBA/Chiat/Day to make ads as strange and cool as everyone else's. The high-concept campaigns sounded as out of the box (read: meaningless) as any of Levi's adversaries. Sean Dee, director of marketing, explained that the ads would be shot in Morocco, because "it's a place where there's little technology. It was a great way to showcase our product and introduce our positioning, which is that Silvertab is equipment for modern living."[36] Multiethnic models were photographed in desert settings using equipment like portable CD players and digital video cameras, in an effort to convey everything from interracial sex and new tribalism to hi-tech materials and a hip media sensibility. In other words, it was utterly confusing, and expensive.

That didn't stop Levi's from plastering the campaign throughout the entire known media universe, from billboards and postcards to TV commercials, cinema teasers, Web site tie-ins, and cross promotions with Sony. According to Competitive Media Reporting, Silvertab's campaign went well over its $5 million budget for 1999. In spite of their high concept, cost, and ubiquity, the ads didn't work. In the words of Irma Zandl, one of the more respectable youth trend analysts, the campaign was "so aloof and unengaging" that she doubted an American youth audience would find a connection.[37] She was right. Levi's sales continued to plummet.

More troubling for the long-term health of the brand, by spending its time and attention on advertising, Levi's became distracted from its core expertise: making jeans and maintaining authenticity in its processes and communications. By the time the company decided to get back in the box, it had forgotten what it was.

In 2002, Robert Hanson, of the European division, was brought in to head Levi's in the Americas—the fourth person to be put at the helm in as many years. In order to "reclaim our future and relentlessly innovate," Hanson would "restore the luster of Red Tab." In what seemed like a promising approach, Hanson explained that "for years Levi's has been doing great stuff, but it has all been outside the Red Tab brand. Why would you put all that great product outside your flagship brand? It doesn't make sense."[38]

It doesn't. But neither does fulfilling that commitment to the flagship brand by changing it. An in-house designer at Levi's had been working on an interpretation of the Red Tab line, in the hopes of creating an interesting, highly stylized Levi's product for a niche market—perhaps in Europe or Japan. It is a conceptual sort of fashion, really, taking the classic logos and pocket design of Levi's Red Tabs, and exaggerating them in the extreme. Called "Type 1," the jeans feature oversized red tabs and rivets, accentuated yellow stitching, and giant stylized arcuate (the trademark stitching on the back pocket). The design amounts to a deconstruction and caricature of the Levi's brand. By accentuating each component of its authentic designs and presenting them out of context, Levi's succeeded in pathologizing whatever mystery was left in the brand. Type 1, predictably, failed to revive Levi's in spite of an exorbitant media campaign, including a Super Bowl spot.

By 2002, industry strategists were still advising Levi's to invent new brands "that move away from the traditional 501 style," and focus "all its energy on understanding the customer."[39] They complained that Levi's began focusing too late on the ever-changing tastes of teens, and should push more work overseas, cut costs, and conduct more focus groups. In other words, they wanted Levi's to become a giant, multibillion-dollar version of its tiny, transient competitors.

In 2003, Levi's brought in "turnaround firm" Alvarez & Marsal to help cut expenses and attend to more than $2 billion in debt. They launched the Signature brand, a low-cost version of Levi's to be sold through mass discounters Wal-Mart and Target. "Fringe fashion products" like Type 1 would be returned to the fringe, saving millions on fruitless advertising. Finally, Levi's entire line of garments would now be produced overseas, mainly in Latin America and Asia. And, thanks to a mediaspace where such facts about brands can no longer be kept under wraps, this outsourcing cost Levi's its "all-American" appeal.

In a desperate scramble for enough cash to remain solvent, Levi's was forced to sell some of its most stable assets. Although most industry analyses showed that khakis were the only products in Levi's arsenal to be increasing in sales, it sold off its Dockers line for a reported $800 million. This, in spite of the fact that Dockers accounted for 24 percent of overall revenue for Levi's in 2003, bringing in $1 billion in sales and $360 million in licensing fees in that year alone.[40]

In spite of being the seventh most recognized brand in the world, Levi's is still losing market share to the less established brands with which it chose to compete. The only real bright spots are the Philippines and Australia, whose markets, though sizable, do not have the cultural or branding power of the United States. By giving up its own ground, and even its home country, Levi's abandoned its core strengths and competencies. As of this writing, the vast majority of Levi's remaining revenue comes through its discount store line, Signature. Many analysts now predict Levi's will be purchased, in its entirety, by a company such as Wal-Mart, and then sold exclusively as an in-house brand.

Levi's went from being a brand in a class of its own to a desperate, struggling chaser of trends. The company was incapable of recognizing its own competitive advantage, and was reluctant to use its ample war chest to ride out a passing fad and then emerge, once again, as the true purveyor of authentic homegrown, countercultural, and all-American values—in the form of denim—to the United States and the world.

And now it's too late for Levi's to go back. Recognizing Levi's abandonment of the throne, cowboy and NASCAR-country legitimized brand Wrangler has capitalized on its own commitment to core values, stepping in as the new "original" American blue jean and riding a new wave of popularity for all its worth, before tacking back and awaiting the next surge.

RETRO AS LOGOS—NECESSITY IS NOT THE MOTHER OF REINVENTION

Perhaps Levi's can survive in semidormancy for decades so that, someday, it will be free to "rediscover" itself. If we're still living in a society characterized by disposable and interchangeable brands, the authenticity of Levi's label, if it is successfully preserved, may just hit a retro nerve.

This was the strategy behind two recent automobile rebirths, the VW Bug and the Mini Cooper. Both were successful initially, but only one of these automobiles was truly developed from the inside out and stands a chance of surviving as more than a fad. Where the Mini Cooper stands out as a feat of engineering, the New Beetle is more a phenomenon of advertising. TV can create great buzz, but in the end, people buy cars, not car commercials.

To be fair, the success of the VW Bug has always been more about marketing than the automobile itself. Originally launched in the United States in 1959, Volkswagen's greatest challenge was to change the public perception of a car conceived, at least in part, by Adolf Hitler as a "people's car." Bill Bernbach, of the DDB agency, developed a strategy that is still studied in first-year advertising courses: VW would attack the conformity and over-the-top selling techniques of the Big Three automakers, "puncturing the mythos of the American automobile in the very year of maximum tailfins on the GM cars."[41] He created minimalist black-and-white print ads that touted the VW's ugliness. In the wake of antiadvertising screeds like Vance Packard's *Hidden*

Persuaders, this new campaign, based on honesty and straightforward-ness, was a hit.

Of course, the campaign was actually more about distancing VW from the Nazis in the minds of American consumers than it was about any sort of honesty. And by focusing on the young, VW found an audience that hadn't been conditioned to make that earlier association of Volkswagen with gas chambers. The new anticonsumerist, antimaterialist image of the VW was communicated to the postwar generation through ads satirizing other car brands' planned obsolescence, dealer shadiness, and disingenuous advertising. VW was not your parents' car.

Not that VW's cheeky ads were any more genuine. In retrospect, slogans such as "Just because we sell cars doesn't put selling at the top of our agenda," says as much about 1960s naiveté as it does about honesty. But DDB had successfully initiated a conversation—a mass society critique that capitalized on the growing antiestablishment sentiment of the time. VW became the "Love Bug"—the anticar, and a symbol of rebellion against the very marketing culture that reinvented it.

Banking on this tradition, VW launched the New Beetle at the 1998 Detroit Motor Show as "a happy combination of the traditional bubble shape and state-of-the-art automotive technology."[42] But the car had little to do with the unadorned, rugged, fix-it-yourself simplicity of the original Beetle. Here was a VW Golf with a larger chassis, expanded so that the shape of the original Beetle could be imitated. Whereas the original VW bubble shape was a result of building the car around the driver, this new profile was nothing more than a design conceit. To create the round shape, the windshield was pushed forward and away from the driver, leaving a huge surface over the dashboard. To imitate the original rounded lights of the earlier Bug, modern headlamps were housed within awkward casings that, from a distance, called the familiar VW Beetle "eyes" to mind.

The New Beetle was not designed from the inside out; it was costumed from the outside in. The only aspect of the car that was truly reinvented was the advertising. Arnold Communications was responsible for generating a bit of sixties nostalgia for the New Beetle. It recast the tempestuous era as a peaceful, loving, and colorful utopia. The catch was that, now, consumers could have all the peace, love, and understanding of the sixties, but get a hi-tech piece of machinery at the same time. In a sense, the ads told the truth: get the superficial thrill of a 1960s icon without the substance or ethos.

Again, Volkswagen's ads were great. They had beautiful music and graphics, clever slogans and concepts. In effect, the advertising campaigns *were* the New Beetle. People who bought the car were supporting the ethos of these commercials much more than any ethos was supporting them. Driving a VW Beetle was like becoming part of the VW marketing effort. A fashion statement. A Golf in a puffy Beetle costume—what became known as "a hairdresser's car." The anticonsumerist Bug had become its opposite. Within two years, sales of the New Beetle were declining. In the absurd belief that aging products were "at the heart of VW's woes," VW began redesigning its cars to make them more like the already obsolete New Beetle.

The Golf—which had remained a Spartan standard-bearer and reliable profit center for VW in the United States since it was born as the Rabbit in 1974—got a new, plush interior that undermined its utilitarian image and design simplicity. Golf sales took a dive that VW observers either called "inexplicable" or blamed on exchange rates. The Jetta and Passat underwent similar makeovers, as VW's classic image and engineering took a backseat to new plastics and trendy color schemes. Having lost the plot of its own story, VW started to chase its competition. It developed two new vehicles in 2003, an SUV called the Touareg, and a luxury sedan, the Phaeton. Not only had the cars lost their definition, now the brand had, as well. VW's core consumers began to look elsewhere for the small, simple, rugged, utilitarian sensibility that defined the car against its competition.

Luckily for Volkswagen, BMW—which has been named as a possible buyer for the ailing Volkswagen of America—rescued this market segment with a revival of its own: the Mini Cooper. In 1994, BMW acquired the Mini from the British Motor Corporation and rebuilt the car from the inside out. Most importantly, BMW worked up from the engineering and driving ethos that had made the Mini a classic for close to 40 years. Yes, the car would have to adhere to modern automotive standards. But the chassis, wheelbase, handling, and controls would be built on the same philosophy as the original Mini: squat, simple, nimble, and fast. Thanks to a design and engineering staff that has achieved cult status for its dedication to technology and design, the Mini Cooper was reborn as a genuine Mini Cooper, only better. It was named Car of the Year in 2003, offering BMW-quality engineering and service, for a sticker price of $16,900.

Now, the only challenge was how to market it. Again, it was back to basics. The original Mini had become a cultural icon thanks to three main factors: association with celebrities like Twiggy, the Beatles, and the Queen; big wins on the racetrack; and the customer's ability to customize the car to his taste. The original Mini became such a popular icon that Mary Quant named her miniskirt after it in 1965. So BMW shunned television ads, opting instead for the kind of bottom-up campaign that fit what was to be America's new "people's car." Highly visible placement in the hit movie *The Italian Job* (2003) certified and demonstrated Mini's speed and handling. Cardboard inserts in magazines like *The New Yorker* allowed readers to assemble their own cars in a wide choice of clever colors and patterns. And, most importantly, Mini found an agenda that matched its ethos: the proliferation of gas-guzzling, road-crowding SUVs. The Mini would position itself against the SUV the way Apple did against the PC—or VW did, originally, against Detroit.

In the fall of 2001, before actual sales began in March 2002, BMW began promoting the valiant little SUV-eliminator by strapping it like a pair skis to the roof of a Chevy Suburban and driving it through 22 cities. The message was clear. According to the creative director of the campaign, the object was to stoke an SUV backlash: "We wanted to communicate that with big SUVs, the act of driving is no longer part of the enjoyment. The sport utility vehicle is to carry the sport with you; the fun always goes on top."[43]

Although these sorts of stunts got the Mini brand some early attention, the car has succeeded because it communicates its quality and ethos directly. Because of its size and turning radius, it's the easiest car to park in America's overcrowded cities, and offers its drivers a less-expensive, higher-quality vehicle than a Volkswagen. Owners discover a Mini's features over a course of months or even years of real use: seats that fold easily, durable cargo straps, BMW cornering technology, special anchors for child safety seats, tires that can be driven on while flat, and JD Power's number-one-rated BMW service department. Mini drivers see themselves as part of a movement away from wasteful consumption of gas as well as space, and members of a community of small-car lovers. While this tiny, subversive antidote to a size-obsessed automotive culture is not for everyone, the reincarnated Mini has achieved what the new Volkswagens could not: to build a business on the belief that bigger isn't better.

GETTING LOST VERSUS FINDING YOURSELF

Getting back in the box should not be a complex process. No guru is required. You'd be better off getting a bad case of the flu than hiring another corporate consultant or renting out a mountain retreat.

Because from what I've seen, the easiest way for a business to get lost is by setting out on a journey to find itself. Many of the mighty have fallen this way. Giant companies like Shell, Intel, and Lucent, under constant scrutiny by Wall Street and its many media arms, sometimes allow a temporary shift in market conditions or the competitive landscape to provoke panic. Then it's off to the woods with a corporate consultant for some outlandish scenario planning, trust exercises, and so-called rediscovery.

Almost invariably, these "off-sites" have the effect of taking the core decision makers even further out of the box than they were to begin with. I should know; I've spoken at dozens of them. But no matter how much I encourage executives to use the off-site as a social opportunity or educational adventure and then make their real decisions back at work in the context of their actual business, they always seem intent on arriving at a new mission statement for their enterprise before they get into the limo heading home.

In most cases, corporate retreats like these are pretty harmless. A bit of time and money wasted for an insight over a campfire having something to do with "creativity," which gets implemented as a new screensaver on the computers of everyone in the company, and maybe a snazzy page in the annual report. No real damage done. But the propensity for decision making through disconnection is symptomatic of an out-of-the-box mentality that can undermine competency and have hugely negative repercussions.

Shell Oil's decade-long descent into field incompetence and accounting scandals has its origin in a few seemingly harmless off-site meetings and funny exercises. Back in the 1970s, Shell's exploration and production unit, or E&P, was considered the best in the business. The team of geologists and mathematicians, beneficiaries of in-house training by more experienced members, had accurately located tremendous oil and gas reserves in the North Sea. This tradition of on-the-job training and advancement was practiced throughout the company. Even young executives were groomed in this fashion, getting sent off to perform challenging tasks in far-off places like Nigeria before being offered cushier decision-making positions at headquarters.[44]

A victim of its own success, Shell's discoveries made oil a bit too plentiful, and prices began to drop by the early 1990s. It seemed like a permanent situation that would require a drastic reconfiguration of Shell's business.[45] In 1993, Shell installed a new CEO—Cor Herkstroeter (not an oilman but a Dutch finance expert)—who brought with him a whole new set of incentive programs and management ideas.

The trial-by-fire system, whereby employees were sent on difficult assignments to test their mettle and gain experience, was scrapped in favor of voluntary applications. Falling prey to what we now know are self-defeating pay-for-performance schemes, he also introduced a system of bonuses based on measurable achievement. Of course, this just shifted employee focus off achievement and onto measuring. It was a system that, according to the *Wall Street Journal*, "several current and former Shell employees believe encouraged short-term maneuvers to boost results."[46]

Meanwhile, Shell continued to devalue what was left of its core expertise. In a push for "unconventional thinking," Shell brought its planners and executives on retreats, where they were asked to perform skits, shake their arms in "energizer" exercises, or stare into the eyes of colleagues and share their innermost thoughts.[47] Great techniques for starting a cult, but not so great for finding and exploiting oil fields.

Such New Age–style exercises, though temporarily thrilling, generate an optimistic, can-do attitude that often betrays reality. While useful for motivating evangelical pyramid scheme distributors to purchase an extra few hundred dollars of merchandise or convert a few more family members to the cause, they can also lead people to make outlandish statements and promises. The object of the game becomes to please the boss or consultant with a more highly committed skit or performance than one's peers. At Shell's meetings, some employees performed nude while others acted out Jerry Springer routines.

At another off-site meeting at a resort in Holland in 2001, Shell managers delivered a few days' worth of motivational speeches to geologists and accountants, broken up only by loud rock music interludes. Eventually, the attendees were subject to "the fishbowl," where anyone who wanted to speak against a particular drilling plan had to sit in an empty chair facing the exercise leader. Consensus was achieved, but at the cost of common sense. Both accounting and geological expertise were ignored, as younger, inexperienced, and enthusiastically agreeable members of the E&P group were promoted. Called "Nintendo hires" by their elders, these unqualified if out-of-the-box thinkers led to the department being dubbed "Excel and PowerPoint."[48] While competitors were replacing their reserves at a rate of over 100 percent per year, Shell was now down to 74 percent—at least according to the numbers it was using as of this writing.

According to the *Wall Street Journal*, "The push for unconventional thinking also undermined discipline in Shell's core business of finding oil and gas. A bonus system prodded some managers to make rosy forecasts that they couldn't necessarily meet. Sound estimation of reserves often went out the window in favor of accounting maneuvers."[49] Management accepted these numbers gleefully, as better reserve figures led to better wages for them, too. More cult exercises and off-site motivational retreats kept the system of "risk taking" alive on adrenaline until, eventually, the SEC caught up with the once unassailable Shell Oil.

Shell's new CEO promises to fix the books, lengthen job tenures, and reduce the company's reliance on consultants. Whether or not he succeeds, Shell's long and costly journey out of the box is a lesson to us all. Indeed, the pages of the *New York Times* Business Section, the *Financial Times,* and the *Wall Street Journal* are filled with articles telling the very same story, just with different company names. Intel makes the wrong decisions for two decades, chasing competitors and target markets before finally returning to core competency and investing more energy in researching the design and manufacture of computer chips. Lucent remembers it provides equipment to phone manufacturers, while Toys 'R' Us conveniently forgets it's a toy store when sales figures go down. Ford's Mustang is reborn as—surprise—a sports car, while Polaroid decides it's not a camera company at all but the provider of "social lubricant," and then goes bankrupt.

Do you see a pattern here?

PATTERN RECOGNITION AND THE PHILOSOPHY OF SEEING FROM THE INSIDE

I've watched dozens of talented consultants win their way into the hearts of CEOs, in pretty much every industry. Many of them formerly psychologists or soft-science purveyors, they seem to hold the key to a boss's or company's true inner essence. As a rule of thumb, the minute you hear an executive talk about a consultant who "understands us better than we know ourselves," you know he's in trouble.

Yet this is exactly what one of the executives in charge of Song Airlines told me about their marketing consultant Andy Spade (husband to Kate Spade and the man half-responsible for her handbag line's success). Sure, Spade understood something about Song's target market—wealthy women—and he had a flair for describing the new airline in seductive terminology. But did he know the airline business at all? Fueling, reservations technologies, scheduling, catering? Of course he didn't. Spade acted certain, made bold proclamations, and recognized enough about the lofty goals to which Song's executives aspired to be able to articulate them.

I've watched another consultant, an eccentric French former psychologist named Clotaire Rapaille, utterly transfix the CEOs of dozens of Fortune 500 companies by claiming to have a system through which he can discern "the code" underlying each of their industries. Through focus groups and hypnosis sessions, Rapaille uncovers people's earliest remembered associations for anything from coffee to jet planes, in order to help clients redesign their products, packaging, and promotions in accordance with the buried archetype or "code."

One Boeing executive I interviewed fully believes that the new Dreamliner aircraft will achieve its success with customers primarily because of Rapaille's input. "It's not enough to make bigger baggage compartments. They have to be 'on code.' " Of course, the executive could not tell me Rapaille's code for the Dreamliner, for if I released it, the competition would be able to redesign its aircraft using the same secret formula.

An interesting feature of Rapaille's work is his insistence on hypnotizing not only random focus groups, but also the key executives involved in making decisions. His combined role of hypnotist, psychologist, and brand guru puts his clients in a particularly passive—what Freud would call "regressed"—position. The net result is to make these executives more dependent on his advice and support. From what I've witnessed going on at his baronial estate in Tuxedo Park, New York, his clients are quite under his spell. They drink his champagne, marvel over his car collection, and listen with rapt attention as he explains that women's experience bearing children makes them more conscious of automobile interiors, or that a luxurious air travel experience is undermined by aggressive search routines at the gates. His insights are either absurd, obvious, or both, but his audience of executives focus on his every inflection with their jaws slack and eyes glazed over.

By hypnotizing his clients, Rapaille also gains insight into their true personal and business aspirations. The information about airplanes he gets from his airplane executives is just as, if not more, important than what he gets from their customers. For those who have forgotten how to get back to the source of their passion and expertise, a hypnotist and psychologist like Rapaille might be useful—at least in the short run—as a form of psychotherapy or internal inquiry. The problem is, of course, that, unlike a course of therapy where the patient learns to solve his or her own problems, here Rapaille ends up receiving credit for the insights gained and retains the exclusive ability to mine for more.

Perhaps it's just an artifact of a consumer society. We're accustomed to purchasing everything, and so we approach even our own creativity as a product to be bought from someone else. It's an exaggerated form of the specialization built into the first Renaissance. Leaders isolated one academic discipline from another in order to enforce the centralization of information and power. After all, if it takes 20 different people to design a ship, none will be able to raise a new navy on his own. Everyone was required to turn to the king's court for the missing pieces.

Today, it appears that we are too ready to turn to the market for our missing pieces, rather than exploring whether the secret codes defining our industries may lie within us. Charismatic consultants with passionate books appear to be having a much better time than people stuck in companies. They seem to be exposed to the real world, and stand a chance of perforating the hermetically sealed boundaries around our businesses.

What they're really doing—and I do this, myself, when I'm called in for a consult—is looking inside you and attempting to figure out what it is you'd say if you felt you had the freedom to say it.

Consultants are using a skill very similar to what I'm advising executives and their research departments to use: pattern recognition. Rapaille's observations are like the musings of Jerry Seinfeld. Rapaille notices details about products—such as the way Americans wrap cheese in plastic, while the French let it breathe in the air—and then comes up with clever metaphors to explain this behavior: "In France, cheese is alive," he says, "while in America, it is dead." Fair enough; Americans want the bacteria in their cheese under some control. But a cheese company should not need to hire an outside psychologist to conduct focus groups in order to determine this. Rather, a great cheese company should be central to—or at least an offspring of—the cheese culture it intends to serve.

Are there codes to cheese, airplanes, insecticide, and coffee? Sure. There are codes, lessons, tendencies—what I prefer to call patterns— underlying all of our activities. The benefit of deep experience in a particular field is gaining the ability to recognize those patterns, see how they might be changing, and then surf or stoke them accordingly. And if you don't like the direction the water is going in, learn about changing the ground underneath, to alter the very course of the stream.

This might be the single biggest difference in approach between the first Renaissance and our own. The original Renaissance was an era of map making. Cartographers (from the word "Cartesian") used grid lines of longitude and latitude to frame geography as a big piece of graph paper. The mathematical grid was superimposed over the globe and then used to identify one's position. This was a terrific system for navigation, and if one knew the longitude and latitude codes—that the equator was at 0 degrees latitude, and so on—it could enable tremendous feats, like circumnavigating the planet. But understanding the maps required that the sailor know the codes—the language through which they were devised.

A surfer, on the other hand, understands the ocean as a series of waves. If a cartographer were to ask a surfer to identify his position in the ocean, the surfer would be unable to offer any help—and the cartographer would assume the young man was hopelessly lost. The surfer orients himself not according to written maps, but the changing surface conditions of the water itself. It's less important to him where he is on the map than where he is in relationship to the wave patterns—data that changes every minute and is reflected nowhere in the cartographer's system. Still, I'd trust the surfer to get me ashore in one piece.

Of course, neither ocean expert—the surfer nor the cartographer—has the complete picture. One is using a metaphor to see the big picture, while the other is using pattern recognition to comprehend what's immediately around him. Pattern recognition is what has allowed Clive Davis to consistently pick rock stars, seemingly magically, from among the thousands of musicians who have sent him their demo tapes over the past 40 years. A metaphor for how the music industry can be modeled and manipulated is what allowed Interscope's Jimmy Iovine to do the same thing: pumping talentless groups through the MTV and Clear Channel promotional systems with equally lucrative, if more temporary, results.

Both perspectives are important, particularly in the increasingly volatile business landscape of today. Most businesspeople seem to have the cartography down, but lack the intuition, passion, and self-trust to do the surfing bit. Consultants shouldn't do this pattern recognition *for* a business, but teach and encourage people in a business to do it for themselves.

Peter F. Drucker, a leadership consultant who bases his work on systems theory, strives to help his corporate and nonprofit clients do pattern recognition on their own. By creating tools like "self-assessment tests," Drucker has his clients ask themselves basic but important questions, such as, "What is our mission? What are our results? What is our plan?"

Neither businesses nor foundations today are as simple as those organized using the top-down structures of the first Renaissance. We can't be "in charge" the same way we were before, but we can still lead from a position of strength by endeavoring to penetrate the conventional wisdom about our industries, and discover the aptitude we gained through our own experience.

There are "codes" underlying the industries and processes in which we are engaged. Once we've learned how they work, we tend to see ourselves on the side of defending them against change, as if our investment in learning how shoes or cars are "supposed to" be made will be squandered if we replace those methods with new ones. Maintaining our authority in a business or organization seems to get tied to maintaining business as usual; innovation itself is a threat. And the longer we cling to this self-defeating posture, the more distanced we become from the reality of our evolving enterprise. We become cartographers only, incapable of surfing at all.

The real advantage of learning the code—as any hacker will tell you—is the freedom it gives you to change it. A corporation can't be a place where rules are enforced, as much as taught, in order for them to be challenged, improved, and changed. The development of a healthy organization should be traced less through quarterly profits than along sustained metrics of learning. If a business is not learning more about its core enterprise over time, then it is not growing in any real way, at all. Simply aspiring to sell more stuff is a much more finite goal than collaborating to learn the fundamental rules through which a system works. Which of the rules we've learned are real, and which are arbitrary? Do things have to be this way, or can they be changed?

Only by learning an industry or enterprise from the inside out can we distinguish between reality and the maps that are being used to describe it. Do phone numbers have 10 digits because they have to or because someone arbitrarily decided it at some point in the past? Why are traffic lights red, yellow, and green? Why do we use the QWERTY keyboard? What is the logic underlying these legacies, and are they based on what's best or on what someone happened to decide?

Engaging a philosophy of going deep means learning the underlying code of your business. You must be determined to distinguish what's real from what isn't, and then fearlessly rewrite the rules from a place of knowledge.

I recently did a short consult for one of the Big Three automakers, where I was surprised to encounter executives who saw themselves as powerless cogs in a system beyond their control. Legacies of gasfueled, crank-and-piston engineering were thwarting the company's efforts to get ahead of, or even catch up with, the push toward hybrid engines, solar power, and alternative public transportation systems. Meanwhile, its sales and service departments were earning some of the worst ratings in the industry, plagued by old-style hard-selling techniques, poor inventory management, and incompetent customer service.

Was one of the originators of what we now know as the American automobile, developer of some of the biggest brands ever, now crying "uncle"? As far as I could tell, the executives with whom I was meeting saw the automotive industry as moving along without them, and the world as a giant set of given circumstances to which they could only respond.

I reminded them of their company's true history. Back when it was just a tiny corporate conglomerate compared with today, it almost single-handedly dismantled the public rail systems in dozens of American cities. A nefarious plot to generate dependency on buses and automobiles? Perhaps. (See *Roger Rabbit* for the details.) But also an indication of how a company was willing to use what muscle it had to change the underlying landscape of our society in order to suit its needs. If this automaker was capable of doing all that for ends that now appear illegitimate, why shouldn't it now—at many times the size and might—be able to rewrite the rules of transportation yet again, and in a way that is actually good for both itself *and* the United States?

When the assembled executives asked if I would come back in a week to share with them my strategies for accomplishing this overhaul of the transportation industry, I realized I had failed in my efforts to bring them back into the box. As automobile industry executives, they were the ones who should have been capable of hacking the transportation business, not me. I'm an author.

Going deep means spending the effort required to learn how something works from the inside out. It's hard, but approached correctly, it's also terrific fun. It's certainly more fun than watching TV, playing golf, or doing whatever it is tired old businesspeople do instead of continuing to learn about and improve the businesses they once loved. Retirement is an option. So is rekindling the passion and innocence with which you first approached your area of expertise, learning even more about it, uncovering more unnecessary presumptions, and then replacing them with presumptions of your own. This process never stops. Even the officially preferred shape of a baby's pacifier changes every year or so. Nothing is written in stone.

And for every enterprise unwilling to learn the codes underlying the industries to which they've purportedly committed themselves, there are many others out there who are already rewriting them. The landscape on which you work is being altered without your permission. Either learn how this happens and how to participate, or make room for those who have already hacked your business wide open.

chapter six

OPEN SOURCE
EVERYTHING

Open source is more than a computer-programming ethos. It's the impetus to an approach toward work and life that makes secrets and protectionism obsolete, and opens the floodgates of innovation on an unprecedented scale. As of yet, however, most people and businesses are still unprepared to confront the challenges to their own sense of competence that go along with it.

If you and your company love what you do, and you're good at it, you have nothing to fear and everything to gain. If you aren't particularly capable in the field or industry you've chosen, then look out: the defenses you've been using to mask your inadequacy are quickly losing their effectiveness.

For those of you who have been out of the technology loop for the last decade (or have been exposed to it exclusively through the well-meaning but misguided business press), open source is—most simply—an alternative to the trade secrecy surrounding the development of computer software. Computer programs are huge projects, often containing thousands or hundreds of thousands of lines of code. Big groups of people, working in coordination, tend to do better at writing these programs than small groups working in isolation.

It's an observation consistent with the evolution of pretty much all the networking software we use today, which was developed by thousands of university students working in loose collaboration with one another. As for-profit companies entered the software space, this freewheeling, collaborative "shareware universe" was replaced by companies working alone and in competition with one another. Microsoft came to typify this more secretive approach to software development, in which the lines of the program—what's known as "source code"—are encrypted before a program is shipped. That way, a competitor can't see how the program actually works. The trade secret is maintained.

Closed source programs make it easier for a software company to make money in the short term. A team of engineers figures out how to solve a problem, and by hiding the solution makes sure no one else can borrow or steal it—unless, of course, they make an equivalent investment of time and energy. Microsoft became equated with this style of development, even though most companies today "lock" their source code. It's akin to putting a mousetrap inside a locked box with a little doorway, so that no one will ever know why mice go in but don't come out again—least of all one's competitors.

While locking up source code prevents anyone else from borrowing it, it also prevents anyone else from improving upon it. That's the rationale behind open source, first implemented by Linus Torvalds as a development strategy for the operating system called Linux. By maintaining an open and accessible record of all the code, open source development enables anyone to analyze a program, test it, and improve upon it. So now, instead of having just your own team of paid software engineers working on a problem, you get the whole world working on it with you. The catch? Anyone can publish it, too. They're even allowed to charge for it or give it away. All because the common goal of better software is seen as a higher one than the individual goal of profit.

Open source developers do what they do, chiefly, because they are passionate about their work. It's fun. In the words of Eric Raymond, who wrote a collection of essays about open source called *The Cathedral and the Bazaar*, "Our creative play has been racking up technical, market-share and mind-share success at an astounding rate. We're proving not only that we can do better software, but that *joy is an asset*." [1]

Not that people can't make a whole lot of money off open source software. Redhat, a company that distributes the Linux operating system along with a carefully selected suite of open source programs, earned $125 million revenue in 2004, and currently has a market capitalization of over *$2 billion*. People and businesses are willing to pay for Redhat's skill in choosing which programs to include with the system and for their easy-to-follow installation instructions.

Meanwhile, Firefox, a Web browser based on Netscape but developed by a community of open source programmers, is now challenging Internet Explorer for dominance on the World Wide Web. Universally acclaimed as a superior, faster, and more efficient program than Microsoft's, Firefox helps call into question the belief that proprietary products developed in competition are necessarily better than what the collaborative nonprofit community can offer. Most persuasively, as a result of being tested and "banged on" by thousands of developers, Firefox and other open source programs are much more secure against viruses and other attacks. Their development process is like an extended inoculation. Microsoft programs, by virtue of the much more limited hours spent on their development, don't get truly tested until they are in the marketplace. Once vulnerabilities are discovered, all Microsoft can do is announce the problem and offer a "patch."

Proprietary programs are also plagued by market considerations that often don't correspond to technological common sense. Microsoft was at pains to integrate its browser into Windows as a way of leveraging its operating system monopoly on the Internet. (That's what the lawsuit was about.) Microsoft also writes "back doors" into its programs, in order to allow for marketing and monitoring. Both of these business considerations make the entire operating system more vulnerable to attack. Open source developers, on the other hand, have no allegiance to anything but the code—the quality of the programs, themselves, and their ability to interoperate with the rest of the networking ecology. Their work ends up being leaner, friendlier to other programs, and more resistant to attack. That's why it's starting to sell so well.

Open source may be a new business model but it's also a well-tested, even ancient, approach to innovation. While lawyers busy themselves arguing about implications for intellectual property and copyright (or what open source advocates have adapted into an opposite appellation, copy*left*), creative people in all walks of life have been inspired to consider just how much of the code in their endeavors is still open for discussion.

These curious people include your customers and your employees.

It's the underlying sensibility of the *Matrix* movies: the world we are living in has been coded by others, and the path to power and awareness involves learning that code from the bottom up. The enlightened character can see through the illusion to the computer code, in the same way a hacker can see beyond the windows of his computer software to the command lines underneath. Once people achieve this awareness—usually by having an experience of one open source technology or another—they tend not to look at the rest of the world the same way. Things that they took for granted, from urban planning to gender definitions, begin to seem more arbitrary. Indeed, someone decided these things.

It's the same sensibility that people often come to after a spiritual or psychedelic experience: they become more aware of the conventions and unspoken agreements by which we live. They tend to see laws as creations of people, rather than some preordained authority, and much of what society values as a construction rather than having intrinsic worth. From then on, a whole lot of stuff that used to seem like hardware seems instead like programmable and changeable software. That's probably part of the reason why San Francisco psychedelic culture was so closely related to Silicon Valley computer culture. These were the people who were ready to accept the deeper implications of being a coder.

Already we are seeing extraordinary examples of this new willingness of people to be their own coders, to embrace the open source ethos and become self-made authorities. Wikipedia, a completely user-generated online encyclopedia, has already surpassed the *Encyclopaedia Britannica* in range, depth, and, by many accounts, accuracy. It's set up like a giant, hypertext encyclopedia. The catch—and best feature—is that anyone can correct or add to the existing entries. The entire encyclopedia (at www.wikipedia.org) was written in a Web language called "wiki"—Hawaiian for "quick"—that lets any visitor to a page add to or change the content. So far, the project lives entirely off donations.

America also saw how a presidential primary was almost determined by a swell of enthusiasm by the Internet community for a candidate who did little more than recognize their existence. Thousands of people around the country gathered in support of Howard Dean, self-organized through an online tool called Meet-up that allows large groups of people to select a time and place to meet. The campaign also raised millions of dollars in record time by exploiting the convenience and ethos of the Internet, soliciting small contributions from millions of people rather than large ones from just a few corporations. For a while, thanks to campaign manager Joe Trippi, it seemed as if Dean was an "open source candidate," through whom a growing population that wanted to engage more directly in democracy would be empowered to do so.[2]

Slashdot, a set of online discussion boards inhabited mostly by the programmer community, also played a part in keeping the democratic process open source. Before conducting the Slashdot interviews with various candidates, they solicited questions from their users, who then voted on which ones they most wanted to hear answered.

These efforts do impact the public at large. It's as if everyone feels more capable of taking matters into their own hands. It has led to a do-it-yourself culture, where the most compelling television shows and advertisements are less about ways to be and things to buy than *how* to do something and which *tools* to get. The cable dial has opened up a new universe of instructional shows. Nigella Lawson teaches us how to cook; *What Not to Wear* teaches us how to dress; Martha Stewart teaches us the intricacies of anything from needlepoint to stone masonry; *Trading Places*, *This Old House*, and the entire Home & Garden network teach us how to fix, remodel, or even sell our houses. It's a world of makeovers and fixups, where the object is not simply to get the job done, but to understand how it happens and get empowered to do it for oneself.

The market for products enabling the do-it-yourselfer is still growing. Home Depot and Lowe's equip the consumer with professional grade tools, while Vitamin Warehouse and herb shops supply the self-healer. Amateurs are now more responsible for formerly expert-only aspects of their own lives, and they're comfortable with it. The "no user serviceable parts" warning on the back of a radio or TV set has become a challenge.

It's pure renaissance. Like gamers learning to play, then cheat, and finally program for themselves, people feel they can be trusted with the code. And they are willing to go ahead and do the hard work of learning it if they feel they can improve upon what already exists.

This renaissance ethos of authorship isn't limited to some isolated group of "cultural creatives" in New York, San Francisco, and Cambridge. No, it's a mainstream "red state" American trend, as well, emerging as crafts fairs, a NASCAR culture of car modification, gun kits, backyard farming, and even home schooling. For every Northeasterner musing on how he would have drawn up the plans for New York's street grid to include bike lanes (and then working through the city council to create some) there's a Midwesterner challenging the curriculum of the local school system, and rewriting his own version based on the facts and values he thinks are more important to teach a young person.

This is the spirit of authorship presaged by the Internet and now extending to every area of our lives. The hacker mentality is all around us, evidenced in everything from the hubris to learn the entire genetic code and attempt human cloning to a growing stack of new translations of the Bible. Meanwhile, our unintentional impact on the environment, from melting polar icecaps to mercury-toxic oceans, only underscores how much influence we wield.

This is the real legacy of the open source movement—misunderstood even by many of its participants as solely a way to develop computer operating systems, and underestimated in its potential impact by even its staunchest opponents. As I've analyzed it, the movement is based on three far-reaching assumptions:

1. The systems by which we live are inventions and
    conventions.
2. The codes underlying those systems can be learned and
    rewritten.
3. This process best takes place collaboratively.

It's those same three stages of renaissance we've been looking at all along: moving from passivity to gaining a perspective and then to attaining the power of authorship. Finally, the desire to acquire and spend social currency fuels a spirit of collaboration. We play the game by the rules, we learn enough codes to cheat, and ultimately rewrite the game and share our creations with others.

Approaching work this way offers us a path not only to greater innovation, but also to a more cooperative and less painfully competitive style of doing business. Still, it requires that we relearn both our own areas of expertise from the inside out, as well as the way we think of how to share them with others. Luckily, the two go hand in hand.

Law professor Larry Lessig's Creative Commons project is a nonprofit effort meant to support those looking to move beyond traditional patent and copyright laws and adopt a more flexible approach to protecting their work. He offers a few different licensing options for creators to consider: "Attribution" allows anyone to copy or distribute work, as long as they give credit; "Noncommercial" grants permission for copying and adaptation for noncommercial purposes; "No Derivative Works" requires works not be changed; and "Share Alike" applies original licensing terms to any copies or derivatives.

Lessig may not have thought of everything, yet, but his reconsideration of copyright restrictions to allow for more open source and collaborative creativity is itself an example of the open source willingness to rewrite laws that previously seemed sacred. In other words, it's not a question of how to make open source developments conform to existing copyright law. From a new renaissance perspective, we might just as well rewrite existing copyright laws to conform to the new reality of collaborative work and shared ownership.

Early successes of the Creative Commons approach—such as authors and musicians giving away their work through peer-to-peer services only to see their sales in stores go up—pose a challenge to the dog-eat-dog model of business. The competitive landscape, like the corporate structures and monetary policies that have grown on it, may itself be an artifact of an earlier age, and ripe for reappraisal.

IT'S ONLY PAPER

My friends and students are often compelled to ask me how I can justify talking "to corporations." In my best Groucho imitation, I tell them I've never met a corporation I didn't like. In fact, I've never met a corporation at all. How could I? They don't have eyes or ears or hands. They don't even really exist.

Corporations are simply sets of rules, written down on paper. Like computer programs, national constitutions or board games, they are just lists of commands designed to achieve a particular purpose. And they can all be amended. Money is a similar invention. It isn't even real; it's an agreement. A game. A medium, not a message. Here in America, it is lent into existence by the Federal Reserve to those of us who believe we can pay it back, with interest, by competing for more of it with everyone else.

From an open source perspective, both corporations and the money they were created to earn are simple software. They were designed by people, for specific reasons, and with particular biases. To the new renaissance participant, both are up for reconsideration, and a good number of successful enterprises have been built on this very premise.

Corporations, conceived during the Renaissance, were fully developed by the early 1600s in order to allow for the colonization of the New World. The monarchs of expanding empires like England, Holland, and Spain officially chartered these early corporations as a way for investors to pool their resources and undertake tremendous colonial ventures that none of them could have accomplished alone. The resulting colonies, in turn, provided crucial natural resources for the monarchies and new markets for their exports.

Originally, corporations were to be provisional in nature. They were temporary agreements granting "entity" status to a giant project so that it could get off the ground. Occasionally, however, the entities seemed to take on a life of their own, choking the ability of others to conduct fair trade. The American Revolution was fought, in part, against corporations such as the British East India Trading Company, whose overwhelming and mandated monopoly inspired the Boston Tea Party. Free-market advocate Adam Smith, himself, spoke out decidedly against what he saw as the unnatural influence of corporations in the monetary ecosystem. In *Wealth of Nations*, he wrote, "The pretense that corporations are necessary to the better government of the trade is without foundation."[3]

It was an effective enough convention over the next few decades, however, when a cash-strapped U.S. government needed to charter tremendous efforts like railroads, bridges, and roads. Still later, when an embargo cut off America from the manufactured goods of Europe, a new kind of corporation was invented to allow entrepreneurs to amass the capital they required to build their own factories. Laws needed to be adapted to a new situation in which corporations were no longer temporary in status, nor created simply to serve an immediately pressing public need.

A series of Supreme Court decisions eventually defined corporations as "persons," and granted them the same rights granted to African Americans under the Fourteenth Amendment, such as the right not to be deprived of life, liberty, or property without due process. As the slaves were emancipated, so was the corporation.

The problem with this arrangement is that it tends to make corporations seem more real than they are—as if they were, as the U.S. Constitution declares on behalf of America's human citizens, "en dowed by the Creator with inalienable rights." The modern corporation's many enemies, such as antiglobalists, argue that if the corporation were a person, that person would have to be a psychopath.

They've got a point: the corporation is certainly single-minded to a fault, focused solely on its own growth, and guiltless in making money for its shareholders by any means necessary.

More importantly, a corporation's seemingly psychopathic single-mindedness allows the individual participants to surrender their own ethical considerations to the perceived will of the entity in which they work. I know an advertising executive who targets commercials to kids, while preventing his own children from watching TV. I was once offered a job by a liquor marketer who orders print campaigns that purposefully appeal to the urges of alcoholics. Working as a lawyer for an industrial polluter, an old college friend of mine delayed a hearing on an environmental liability case so that river contaminants would be irretrievably buried under silt, rendering moot the hearing on a corporate-sponsored cleanup. In his other life, this lawyer is a member of the ACLU, and does pro bono work for victims of spousal abuse.

Corporations are not, in themselves, evil entities. It's just that, like any bureaucracy, they can turn the people within them into cogs who feel pressured to surrender their individual wills and sensibilities to the motions and needs of the greater machine. By granting corporations personhood, however, we exacerbate this tendency—the same way nationalism can lead patriots to conduct foul acts in the name of manifest destiny, or fundamentalism can lead zealots to commit bloody crusades in the name of their God. Must corporatism suffer the same fate? Is it, as Mussolini suggested, the definitive form of fascism?

Only if we allow it to happen. The beauty of corporations is that they are truly man-made. While any of us might fall prey to nationalism or religious idealism, those of us involved in business owe it to ourselves to remember that the corporations we think we're serving were put in place to serve *us*. They are inventions: projects coded entirely on paper and completely open to our intervention. They are not violated by redesign; they are improved.

The strength of a corporation should be its flexibility, not its intransigence. Railroads and coal mines are hard to move; corporations dedicated to providing transportation or energy resources, on the other hand, are entirely more nimble—if they are allowed to adapt to changing circumstances. And they can only adapt when the people participating in them choose to make an adjustment. This means challenging the sanctity of corporations as they are now understood, and revisiting them in an open source context. We must see them not as preexisting entities, but as the result of our collective imagination.

When the corporation was first born, remember, so, too, was the entire notion of the individual. It was only natural to model the corporation on the newly individuated human being. Likewise, new oceans had just been discovered, making the formerly limited map seem unlimited by comparison. Accordingly, corporations were designed to grow to fill these limitless new expanses. The promise of a "sustainable" level of corporate activity would have seemed ludicrous in an era when the object of the game was to fill the greatest amount of space in the shortest amount of time.

Moreover, the United Kingdom was not the only colonial empire on the block. With at least three major seafaring empires claiming turf at any time, chartered corporations were encouraged to compete as ruthlessly as necessary with other nations' corporations for the spoils of these new territories.

Corporations carry this legacy with them to this day. Some have been able to leverage this obsolete code to their advantage, but the net effect of their operations is increasingly being called into question, not just by environmentalists and labor advocates, but by smarter businesspeople with the courage to bend their corporations to their own vision of how things should be.

DISCOUNTING HUMANS

Any business book worth its pulp would be hard-pressed to call Wal-Mart a corporate failure. Yet in spite of its tremendous financial success, the number-two employer in America (behind only the federal government), has become the poster child for the way corporate practices can work against the interests of the people they might best be serving and, ultimately, against its own sustainability.

Wal-Mart's more competitive maneuvers seem ripped from the playbooks of those early, chartered corporations. The British East India Trading Company infiltrated new territories, built dependencies on new technologies, and then exploited its monopolies. Wal-Mart colonizes new territory by pricing items below cost and rendering local merchants incapable of competing. Once the competition goes out of business and the community is dependent on Wal-Mart, the corporation raises prices to more profitable levels.[4]

Although Wal-Mart enters new regions promising gainful employment and an expanded local tax base, the reality more often than not has been the opposite. A Congressional Research Service report found that for every two jobs created by a Wal-Mart store, the local community ends up losing three.[5] Further, the jobs created are at lower wages (an average of under $250 a week), fewer hours, and reduced benefits. In fact, a majority of Wal-Mart employees with children live below the poverty line, qualifying for public welfare benefits such as free lunch at school. Some studies have shown that, as a result of the increase in social services spent on the families of Wal-Mart employees, the net effect of a new store is to place a *greater* financial burden on the taxpaying community.

In spite of a huge "buy American" campaign, Wal-Mart purchases 85 percent of its merchandise from overseas, and is consistently associated with sweatshop scandals from Kathie Lee Gifford's clothing line and Disney's Haitian-made pajamas to child-produced clothing from Bangladesh and Wal-Mart brand apparel manufactured by underage Chinese workers in New York City sweatshops.

Seventy percent of Wal-Mart employees leave within the first year of employment, and do so—according to a survey that Wal-Mart itself conducted—because of inadequate pay and lack of recognition for their work.

My point is not to attack Wal-Mart for poor corporate citizenship—there are plenty of organized protests and lawsuits under way, already—but to demonstrate how the company's allegiance to a stiff set of competitive business practices has led it into a self-defeating cycle of corporate insensitivity and shortsightedness.

It's as if Wal-Mart functions not by decision, but by equation. It is mathematically efficient to open two stores too close to one another if it succeeds in putting local merchants out of business. The less profitable of the two can be closed once all outside competition has been eliminated. As of 2000, by utilizing this competitive strategy, Wal-Mart had already left behind 25 million square feet of space. In one Kentucky town, the abandoned Wal-Mart was eventually torn down at taxpayers' expense. As of 2004, Wal-Mart was still opening one new store per day.[6]

Empty stores, ravaged competition, poverty wages, child labor, and increased taxes don't sound like a recipe for corporate longevity. Even Wal-Mart's suppliers have been turned into its enemies. By demanding that wholesalers and manufacturers conform to and pay for everything from RFID tags for inventory management to language guidelines for music and magazines, the retailer has forced many of them to choose between servicing Wal-Mart and servicing everyone else. The larger Wal-Mart gets, the fewer alternatives the suppliers have.

The biggest kids on the block don't take these sorts of practices lying down. Tired of being bullied by the Wal-Mart machine, Procter & Gamble purchased Gillette for $5.7 billion in shares. Its hope, analysts have surmised, is to take back pricing power from Wal-Mart by consolidating and then leveraging its new relative size.[7]

This is not a position that Wal-Mart, or any company, should seek to be in with its customers, employees, and suppliers. But by blindly following the logic of colonial corporatism, Wal-Mart management seems destined to continue down this road until they have either been successfully subdued or they have ravaged the very landscape on which they hoped to build their business.

Wall Street, still mired in ancient indicators of corporate health, continues to reward Wal-Mart for some of its most self-destructive behaviors. Superstore competitor Costco is punished at the trading desk every time its 2.9 percent operating margins are compared with Wal-Mart's, which are roughly double that. But, even from a shareholder's perspective, the wrong company is being punished.

Costco's famous, industry-leading pay package (including 92 percent of health insurance costs compared with Wal-Mart's 66 percent) still allows the company to produce more dollars of profit per employee than Wal-Mart. Yet shareholders "lower their heads every time living wages are discussed,"[8] as if offering a decent salary and benefits package were something for a corporation to be embarrassed about. "From the perspective of investors, Costco's benefits are overly generous," Bill Dreher, retailing analyst with Deutsche Bank Securities, plainly told the *Wall Street Journal*. "Public companies need to care for shareholders first. Costco runs its business like it is a private company."[9]

Costco's president does not agree. "The last thing I want people to believe is that I don't care about the shareholder," explains Jim Sinegal, who owns about 3.2 million Costco shares valued at $118 million. "But I happen to believe that in order to reward the shareholder in the long term, you have to please your customers and workers."[10]

There's a logic, too, behind keeping your annual employee turnover rate down to 24 percent, compared with Wal-Mart's whopping 50 percent. By virtue of being happier and staying on with the company longer, Costco employees are more familiar with their jobs, friendlier with customers, and more likely to speak well of the store when they're away from work. Plus, the more permanent the workforce, the less a company has to spend on new employee training and exit costs. Moreover, when a company has better-skilled employees, fewer are required to do the same amount of work.

Costco is also in a more sound position financially than its much larger rival, with net cash on hand of $.9 billion as of May 2004, compared with Wal-Mart's net debt of $25.6 billion. Were interest rates to go up or the job market to improve, Wal-Mart's highly leveraged, take-no-prisoners, expansionist business practices could undo it quite rapidly. Same-store sales increases for Costco in 2004 were roughly double those of Wal-Mart. Yet even though Costco practices business as if it were in it for the long run, the company's P/E ratio hovers at around 20, compared with Wal-Mart's 25. Costco opens fewer stores, but it closes far fewer, by all measures, as well; it doesn't open locations as a short-term competitive strategy, but as a long-term investment in the store, and the business itself.

So, Costco's workers make more money and the company has more cash on hand, lower turnover, better public relations, higher employee expertise, and better sales growth from its existing stores. It achieves this by staring down Wall Street's conventional understanding of what makes a company valuable, and being willing to redefine what makes a good corporation based on its real circumstances on the ground. Wal-Mart, on the other hand, seems to be run not by living people but by a crew with blinders on, committed to a rather orthodox mandate to grow larger at all costs, thrill the stock exchange, and deal with the consequences only if and when they come up. And at that point, by addressing worker, supplier, and community disgruntlement with PR campaigns instead of substantive change to core processes, Wal-Mart may put itself on a collision course with a Boston Tea Party of a whole new kind.

REINVENTING CORPORATISM: GOOGLE

C ostco might not be consciously reinventing corporate code from the inside out, but neither is the company enslaved by the legacy of obsolete code. By trusting his own instinct for doing good business over the business school obsession for maximizing every efficiency and colonizing every open space, CEO Jim Sinegal prevents himself and his company from becoming victims of the directives of the corporate balance sheet. He ends up with happier, more responsive employees and a business that isn't seen to be treating its territories as if they were mere resources to be exploited.

Is Costco the best example of an open source approach to corporate governance? Perhaps not, but even the most innovative and un-orthodox reinventions of what it means to be a corporation follow this same basic logic of doing what's best for everyone involved, rather than what's best for the abstract concept known as the corporation.

In this light, even the extreme lengths to which Silicon Valley pioneer Google has gone to maintain a corporate philosophy of "do no evil" seem like simple common sense. Though less than a decade old, the company's story is now legend: Two Stanford doctoral students, Sergey Brin and Larry Page, take an interest in making information on the Internet easier to find. They develop a couple of algorithms through which their new search engine can rank the importance of sites (based on criteria such as how many other pages link to them) and end up with a much more effective utility than anything out there.

Patiently, they continue to develop their search engine, letting people discover its advantages through word of mouth and direct experience. As Google grows from a school project into a common verb ("did you Google that?"), the company grows from two guys in a garage into a campus of more than 3,000 employees. And while, as I've mentioned earlier, the self-contained "Googleplex" may appropriate more of its employees' lives than is ideal, the company has earned this tremendous commitment from its workers not just by providing free lunch, but by embracing an open source approach to corporate rules.

Most famously, Google set Wall Street on its head by conducting its IPO in the fashion of an eBay auction, cutting out many investment brokerage middlemen, and making its stock available to the general public, instead of favoring institutions and brokerage-house-favored clients. In spite of numerous attempts by brokerages, regulators, and competitors to undermine the effort, Google's unconventional offering went through. And widespread expert predictions of disaster notwith-standing,[11] the offering price of $85 had more than doubled within weeks, and remained there long after employees' options threatened to dilute share value.

All the while, Google continues to do business as its founders choose to, rather than as Wall Street told them to. Helping forge a new trend, the company refuses to give "guidance," and says as much in its offering prospectus. It doesn't want to be distracted by fluctuations in share value; investors should proceed at their own risk. The company refuses to advertise to consumers; cluttering the information space with marketing would be a form of "doing evil." And the only ads on the Google site are in the form of clearly delineated "sponsored links" that are contextualized to individual searches. And, true to Google's egalitarian ethos, it's a form of advertising that any size company can afford since it's paid for in increments of 5 to 50 cents, based on whether someone clicks on the link.

The only people to whom Google elects to publicize itself are the nerds it wants to hire. In an effort to find back-in-the-box thinkers, Google pays engineering magazines to carry tear-out inserts of a painfully difficult nerds-only exam nicknamed the GLAT, for Google Labs Aptitude Test. The exam, required of all prospective employees, functions less as a way of weeding out the incompetent than of enticing the truly dedicated. Questions include bizarre math problems, sequence analysis, and brainteasers. The founders are looking for the kind of employees who find such challenges *fun*. And—contrary to conventional wisdom about how executives should delegate responsibilities—Brin and Page still interview nearly every prospective employee themselves.

Most interestingly, Google's founders refuse to submit to those notions of competition born in the Renaissance. Just as they didn't like what they saw in the Web search engine universe before they built a new one from scratch using a new set of priorities, Brin and Page didn't like what they saw in the corporate universe, and refused to enter it unless it was on their own terms. They delayed becoming a public company for several years longer than any of their investors wanted, because they did not see the value in submitting to the demands of an artificially competitive development space.

Innovation at Google—of which there is plenty—is not a result of fear or competition, but passion. The company mandates that all employees spend a certain number of hours each week working on their own pet projects. Again, for fun. Out of this work have come ideas for a new kind of Web-based mail, book searching, scholarly document archives, a utility that lets people search the surface of the Earth using images culled from orbiting satellites, and even searchable television.

Google sees itself as an enabler of transactions and communication between smaller businesses that may not have been able to find one another previously. But it doesn't see itself as being in competition with anyone. While Bill Gates conceded "Google kicked our butt in Internet search," and then launched a prototype of his own designed to overtake it, Google doesn't see Web search as a zero-sum game. Unlike the "browser wars" and "operating system wars" that Microsoft fought against its rivals Netscape and Apple, the search engine environment can accommodate many complementary models. "It's perfectly possible that the current competitors can all compete and coexist actually quite well," Google CEO Eric Schmidt told *60 Minutes*. "I disagree with people who say that this is a zero-sum game. We believe that this space will have many players, in which we'll be one significant one."[12]

Many players? Peaceful coexistence is not part of the standard corporate code! Corporations were originally chartered to conquer territory in the face of competition from the other colonial empires. When control of a territory was contested, it meant full-blown war.

What most corporate chieftains can't yet see—the gigantic, simple fact staring them in the face—is that the *territorial model of corporate behavior only makes sense in the absence of innovation*. The territories of the New World, though plentiful, were still bounded. There was a fixed quantity of land, resources, and labor to be exploited. Each parcel claimed by someone else was a parcel lost forever, barring sale or war.

In an atmosphere characterized by innovation, resources are as plentiful as the combined imaginative capacity of everyone involved. Collaboration, even between supposed rivals, yields more possible combinations of fertile ideas than the secrecy of competition.

But most corporations still seem incapable of making the leap from a model of resource scarcity to one of creative abundance. Trapped in a mind-set forged in the era of the Conquistadors, they are ruled by corporate code that assumes a fixed amount of territory and an obligation to defend the turf already claimed as if it were irreplaceable. This assumption of scarcity expresses itself today in an obsession with corporate secrets, patents, and intellectual property. As if innovation were something that defined a person or company at some moment in the past and now all that can be done is to protect these "competitive advantages" as long as possible.

The earliest chartered corporations that left us this legacy can't be blamed for their territorial model—they were, after all, in the business of conquering and colonizing a limited universe of unclaimed territories. But other than a fear of challenging these 400-year-old practices, what's the excuse of today's corporations? Their closed source mind-set comes from working with and for the ultimate closed source, Renaissance-era invention: money.

MONOPOLY MONEY

All money is monopoly money.

By definition, money is an agreement to use something as a medium of exchange. That something might have intrinsic value, like the cigarettes convicts use to conduct transactions; or that something might have no intrinsic value, at all, like the dollars we use today.

It's easy to forget that modern currency has no real value. The stuff we think of as money is a relatively new invention, conceived during the Renaissance to be a different sort of currency than had been used for centuries before. Fourteenth-century bankers and the monarchs they served understood that the way money is created and managed has a lot to do with its effect on the society in which it is used. Fiscal management can influence everything from the class system to spiritual beliefs. And the less people are aware of the rather arbitrary nature of money's many underlying codes, the less likely they'll be to question them.

But if we are really ready to approach business in an open source manner, we have to be able to reckon with the way closed source currency fuels, and in some ways distorts, so many of our priorities and activities. Whether or not we're in a position to revise the operating system through which money is created, we can at least be more willful in our reaction to its underlying agendas.

Of course, even such a statement sounds positively communist by today's standards. We like to think of money as "value-neutral"—as if the dollar were a measurement, like a liter or an angstrom. As Adam Smith argued, money is devoid of bias, because all people can use it in exactly the same way. True enough, and consistent with the best Enlightenment ideals, a dollar in my hand has the same value as a dollar in yours, no matter what our religion or race. And this property of money dovetails quite nicely with the beginning of the Industrial Age, during which all human beings came to be understood as interchangeable parts of bigger machines and systems.

Like most Industrial Age thinking, however, this egalitarianism doesn't account for the way money's particular formulation influences the character of an entire economy. Different kinds of money, over time, change the dynamics of the group using that money. Historically, this has meant a shift from a system of multiple currencies to one of single currencies, and an economic framework of abundance to one of scarcity.

From biblical times all the way through the Middle Ages, centralized currencies usually existed right alongside local ones. Ancient Egypt, for example, used centralized currency for long-distance trade with other kingdoms. But for exchange between people and businesses within the realm, currency took the form of grain storage receipts. If a person brought 100 pounds of grain to the store, the attendant would give him a receipt representing that quantity. Often, parts of the receipt could be broken off to make transactions for fractions of the total value of grain stored. This way, a person wouldn't have to sell all his grain at once, but could trade small portions for various items and services.

The interesting thing about these local currencies is that most of them had *negative* interest. Money's value decreased over time, since the grain storage facility had to charge for its services and some grain was always lost to moisture or vermin. Every year or so, a "demurrage" would be assessed on the money, decreasing its value by a certain percentage.

As a result, money was not something one held on to or, least of all, hoarded. It was advantageous to trade it sooner, while it still had higher value. So the best "savings vehicles" were not money, but productive assets. By the late Middle Ages, 10 percent of all gross revenue was immediately reinvested in equipment, land improvements, windmills, and even cathedrals,[13] all of which were capable of generating further income. Many times more assets went into preventative maintenance of equipment and facilities than today because they represented almost the entirety of an individual's or business's savings. This, in turn, led to an emphasis on long-term thinking and models for sustainability.

Advocates of alternative or complementary currencies today like to point out that money's most important function is not to store value over time, but to serve as a medium of exchange. When money is developed in a way that favors its exchange over its accumulation, it tends to be spent more readily and distributed more widely. As economists Bernard Lietaer and Stephen Belgin demonstrate in their radical treatise, *On Human Wealth*,[14] regions utilizing local currencies in the Middle Ages were extraordinarily prosperous. The working class ate four courses at lunch and dinner, worked six-hour days, took Mondays off and an average of 170 other holidays. As a measure of health, the average height of women was taller than at any time in British history; men only caught up with their Middle Age ancestors in 1998.

Not surprisingly, in societies with local, bottom-up currencies, bottom-up culture and production dominated as well. Small landowners yielded far more crop than seigneurial holdings (those owned by lords and worked by serfs); France, alone, had 20,000 privately owned water mills; women, who enjoyed relatively great professional freedom, were employed in 172 occupations and accounted for 15 percent of financially independent people; arts, in particular poetry, originated less from the court than from the vernacular.[15]

Meanwhile, kings and other elites capable of international trade used centralized currencies such as gold coins and silver bullion. In order to be worth anything to foreign kingdoms, these currencies needed to be able to maintain their value over time. This is why they were kept scarce: they served as a way not only to exchange value, but to store it. Where grain receipts could be as abundant as the season's crop, centralized currencies maintained their value through engineered scarcity. That's why the values they engendered had less to do with investment than accumulation. As competition between the empires grew more fierce, monarchs were motivated to consolidate their power and garner more financial resources. By the thirteenth century, most local currencies were made illegal.[16] Now that people were forced to use interest-bearing currency, they could no longer make ends meet by achieving what were previously "sustainable" rates of production.

Along with local currency went a whole way of life. Just as the Renaissance reinvented classic Greek values of citizenship and equality in a new context, it repressed the bottom-up values engendered by a society and an economy based more on perceptions of abundance than scarcity. Pagan faiths were outlawed, esoteric creativity was quelled, widespread killing of women for witchcraft began, and archetypes of fertility and abundance were replaced with those of top-down authority and fear of scarcity. Most significantly for our purposes, open source, local economies were replaced by the closed source, centralized monopolies we still live with today. While we enjoy the use of currencies that are respected globally, the biases of these currencies also dictate more than we may suspect about our relationship to transaction, prosperity, and, most of all, innovation.

Money today is issued by "fiat"—like God's creation of the Earth, out of nothing. A central bank, like the Fed, loans a certain amount of money into existence under the condition that the debtor pays this money back, with interest. So if a business borrows $100,000 at 6 percent per annum to get started, it will have to pay back $179,000 in 10 years. Where does the extra $79,000 come from? From other businesses fighting for the very same money to pay back their own debts. Competition is built into the rules. It's a zero-sum game of musical chairs against a world filled with debtors. No, it doesn't work out right; bankruptcy and ruin are built into the system.

When money is borrowed into existence by a central authority, the laws of scarcity will rule: economics will be characterized by competition, hoarding of cash, a requirement for perpetual growth, and the concentration of wealth. In such an environment, conflicts are bound to arise between the short-term needs of the shareholder to raise or accumulate cash and the long-term interests of a company for sustainability.

Intensifying this dynamic, in 1971, President Richard Nixon disconnected the dollar from any relationship to precious metals. This made the global currency marketplace even more furiously speculative than it already was. By the 1990s, currency speculation had become a bigger business than business, itself: today, 96 percent of all currency transactions are speculative, unrelated to the exchange of goods or services, and dangerously vulnerable to mood and rumor.[17] That's why over 85 percent of Fortune 500 companies spend valuable cash and resources on derivative hedging strategies to reduce their exposure to sudden, often irrational shifts in exchange rates.

No matter how ethereal money's relationship to reality, most of us still treat currency as if it were sacred and inviolable. We surrender unconditionally to the psychology of scarcity implicit in the underlying biases of our money. When we think of money having a value all its own, we tend to relate to our savings more as a battery for our energy than a means to an end. Psychologist Ernest Becker[18] suggested that our faith in money was a direct result of our newfound sense of "individuation" and the loss of belief in our own immortality. Money becomes a symbol of something that lasts forever and, thanks to interest, accumulates value over time even while our bodies deteriorate. Of course, as numerous studies have shown, the more money we accumulate, the sadder we get.[19] We commonly chalk this up to worrying about how to invest it; the more you have, the more you can lose. But, if Becker is right, then it might have more to do with the futile struggle against death. The bigger the mound of cash we have accumulated, the more we are reminded of our race against mortality. And the less likely we are to challenge the underlying integrity of money's foundational code.

FALSE SCARCITY

Whatever the reasons, by accepting the premise of scarcity implicit in our monetary system, we end up depriving ourselves and our businesses of valuable experience, creativity, and opportunity. When we stop seeing money as a tool and begin relating to it as the goal, we have actually embraced our business's innovative death.

Last year, I agreed to do a talk for a giant but failing church in Denver. The organizers were concerned about attendance, and whether the publicity they had done for my engagement would fill their 300-person hall. Only about 100 people from their membership usually came to speaking events; the rest would have to come from the greater community. Problem was, while members were allowed to come for free, nonmembers were required to pay a $15 admission charge.

It's not that the church needed the money to pay for my talk; I had agreed to appear for free if I would be allowed to sign some books afterward. The other meager expenses for the event were covered by the annual membership budget. No, the reason "outsiders" were charged admission was so that those who paid their annual dues could see what they were getting for their money! If the public were allowed in for free, then members would no longer enjoy the exclusive privileges of membership. Actually, they'd enjoy the privileges, just not the exclusivity.

So the church charged $15 a head to the public, and only a couple of dozen came. Dozens of pews remained empty, the event felt small, and no revenue was earned; but the church made its members feel special by creating a sense of artificial scarcity for its product.

Of course, if they could have reoriented themselves to money, church leaders could have transformed the entire event into an opportunity for more fun, more community involvement, and greater long-term revenue. I made my talk to the group about this very principle. They needed to see money not as the key to exclusive privileges, but as the tool through which they could seed the growth of a new community. Instead of seeing their membership dollars as a fee for service, they should see them as an investment in a project they were building together.

Wouldn't it have been more rewarding to welcome hundreds of people to a free talk sponsored by the church rather than keep them out? They turned away students at the door. Mightn't a packed event, made possible by the goodwill of the existing community, have served as a better way to grow membership? Wouldn't the prospective members in attendance have been more likely to join a congregation with strong ties to the greater community, better turnout at its events, and a spirit of giving? Wouldn't the whole event have been more fun, and more in keeping with the values the church was purportedly espousing?

This Denver church, like so many fiscally confused businesses I've encountered, was incapable of relating to its resources other than through the model of scarcity. Seats for my talk were in abundance. The church was attempting to create a market for a commodity where no need for a market existed. In the process, it ignored the markets that did exist for community and belonging.

Make no mistake: though in abundance, those seats were valuable. Each one represented an investment made by the church in the past that could be reaped now in the opportunity to reach new potential members. When a model of scarcity overwhelms us, we lose the ability to value the things in abundance, even though they might be crucial to our survival, such as air, water, conversation, and other people.

Markets need only arise when supply cannot meet demand. When supply is ample, however, the scarcity model piggybacking on our monetary scheme no longer applies. And by creating false scarcity for markets that shouldn't exist, we end up ignoring those areas where genuine needs are being unmet.

OTHER MONEYS,
OTHER VALUES

Because the money we use is based on the economics of scarcity, prosperity often seems to depend on markets even where none exist. Instead of looking to the well of inspiration for new ideas, we dry up the well in order to sell water at higher prices. This often backfires. Eventually, customers discover that scarcity has been artificially generated—like a red velvet rope in front of an empty nightclub—and then they turn against us.

The Nestlé Corporation is still recovering from the 1970s public relations fiasco surrounding its generation of a market for baby formula in Africa. The company used aggressive marketing tactics to convince mothers of the superiority of formula, going so far as to give free samples that, if used for more than a week, threatened the mother's natural supply of milk. That's one way to create a market for a product where abundant alternatives already exist. In the Nestlé case, it also led to the most extensive and prolonged nonunion boycott in history.[20]

DeBeers, which controls 60 percent of the world's diamond business, depends on the scarcity of its gems in order to make an effective market. This has required the firm to price-fix[21] and hoard inventory. According to *The Economist*, "A huge stockpile helped it to maintain high prices while it successfully peddled the myth that supply was scarce."[22] Now that several African companies have managed to overturn some of DeBeers' more repressive trade strategies and emerge as independently functioning diamond mines, the former industry leader will be hard-pressed to maintain its market dominance. Meanwhile, the entire diamond industry has been tainted with DeBeers' manufactured scarcity, and many customers are looking toward alternative gemstones.

No, all this isn't money's fault. But our inability to work with abundance is inextricably tied with the operating principles of closed source currency and our predisposition for relating to them as if they were the laws of nature rather than the rules of a man-made game.

The many alternative models of currency developing around the globe serve less as threats to the Fed or World Bank than as positive examples of collaborative prosperity and a new renaissance willingness to rewrite the codes of money from the inside out.

In the spirit of authorship, people are storming one of the last bastions of top-down authority and are making their own money. Using computers and creativity, many local communities are developing currencies that serve certain needs better than centralized money. Most local currencies are not created by lending, but by doing. A certain amount of labor—say, restoring a local park—creates money in one's account, which can then be traded with others. The more labor that happens, the more money exists.

As Japan was hit with a devastating recession through the 1990s, alternative currencies systems were established in order for people to get healthcare for their elderly relatives. There was more than enough labor to go around; unemployment was quite high. There simply wasn't enough centralized currency getting into circulation for people to pay for their parents' healthcare. Dozens of complementary currency schemes have emerged to address the demand for services, which are abundant, in a closed fiscal system that otherwise can't tolerate such abundance. In the new complementary currency scheme, Japanese can earn Fureai Kippu—"elderly care units"—by caring for an elderly person in their area. This labor is credited to that person's "healthcare time savings account," which they can draw upon in order to care for their own parents in a distant province. At last count, the alternative currency was accepted at 372 centers throughout Japan; and patients surveyed said they like the care they get through the Fureai Kippu system better than what they got before.[23]

Local Exchange Trading Systems (LETS) are nonprofit exchange networks that utilize computers to help communities develop more cooperative strategies of wealth creation. This is not some isolated hippie commune phenomenon, but an approach to money that is reaching wider acceptance every year. *Forbes* magazine recently declared that there are too many electronic currencies emerging for central banks to maintain their monopoly over money, and that "complementary currency is out of the bag."[24]

Citizens of Ithaca, New York, use Ithaca Hours in local shops and even service stations. While a mechanic may need to charge in U.S. dollars for the auto parts he has purchased from a distant distributor, he is free to charge for his labor in Ithaca Hours, which he can then spend at the more than 1,500 local businesses that accept them. Why bother? By creating currency, the Ithaca community also creates jobs, puts money into circulation without interest, and keeps that currency from draining out of their region.

Complementary currencies are being accepted by groups ranging from Brooklyn New York Elderplan to public school teachers as a way of supporting the value of goods and services that are in abundance, in regions where centralized currency is scarce.

These radically innovative approaches to local economics can be adapted to the way any business confronts the fiscal landscape and its own internal billing policies. Does a business need to create its own money? No. Still, you may want to think twice about charging and recharging your own departments in borrowed dollars across the spreadsheet.

But that's not the most important reason to reconsider the role of money in our business affairs. By learning to think about the dollar and its built-in agendas in new ways, we can liberate ourselves and our enterprises from the bias of scarcity, and smash the last sacred cow standing in the way of our innovative capacity. For those who have faith in their own ability to innovate, nothing is sacred. Everything can be questioned, and anything can be explored down to the source code.

CREATIVE ABUNDANCE

The companies most threatened by this prospect are the ones that see their greatest innovations as behind them. If you've already invented your best cell phone, mop, marketing methodology, or catcher's mitt, you will spend more time guarding your secrets than coming up with new ones. Even if you enjoy a competitive advantage today, you carry on with the lingering knowledge that it's only a matter of time before someone else figures out a better way to do what you do. To stave off this inevitability, you lock down your advantage and processes as much as possible and maintain a closed source enterprise—even to yourself.

This bespeaks a sad exhaustion, and an unwillingness to dig deep, challenge dogma, invite heresy, and unleash new innovative possibility. It's what motivates the "anticompetitive" practices of a Microsoft, which links its browser to its operating system as a defensive measure, only to realize it makes both more vulnerable to viral attack. Locking down its source code as a way of slowing down competition only denies Microsoft the creative contributions of its many users.

Companies that engage in anticompetitive (or, more accurately, anticollaborative) practices are usually so heavily steeped in a scarcity model that they put more effort in protecting the past than building the future. Companies that see themselves as having nothing to lose find it a lot easier to take the steps necessary to confront well-entrenched processes, penetrate their faulty logic, and then reinvent them from the inside out. They don't fear the participation of consumers or other companies in this development process, because they have confidence in their own ongoing ability to generate new ideas and add value to any collaboration. There will be enough value to go around.

In fact, in the emerging new renaissance culture, ownership is itself something of a burden. Who wants to worry about maintaining a bookshelf filled with CDs or a hard-drive's worth of MP3s when having *access* to that data is just as good? Accumulation of stuff is giving way to the right to use stuff—the misunderstood principle at the heart of every Internet phenomenon from user-to-user trading sites such as eBay to file-sharing applications such as Bittorrents.[25] That's why they call it *sharing*.

With new models of ownership come new models of currency and new ways of creating value for all players. PayPal, the most popular form of alternative cash on the Internet, rose in popularity as a way for eBay customers to conduct secure transactions with one another. Originally, the service was free to use. The company's business plan revolved around holding funds for two days and skimming profit off the interest earned—the "float." But the established banking industry didn't approve; earning interest in this fashion is a closed industry. If PayPal wanted to keep on acting like a real bank, it would have to become one. So PayPal changed its plan and started charging users directly to use the service.

But PayPal remains a great example of a business willing to step in and reinvent currency transaction from the bottom up, creating something of an alternative economy—albeit in dollars—through which people can send money to one another via email without involving the standard credit-issuing institutions. And it was a successful strategy. In 2002, just four years after its founding, and at the very nadir of the dot-com bust, PayPal was purchased by eBay for $1.5 billion. PayPal had no secret formula. In fact, eBay had its own imitation of PayPal called Billpoint that was arguably more convenient. But—at the time, anyway—PayPal had engendered so much goodwill from people who might otherwise never have been able to get into business, and ubiquity, that it was a force to be reckoned with.

PayPal's open-source-inspired relationship to cash and banking is emblematic of the way new renaissance businesses large and small, established and brand new, must challenge the rules. Reinvention is not just for the young at heart. A spirit of creative abundance could have saved titans like AT&T, AOL, and TWA, which, sorrowfully, put more faith in their preexisting market leverage than in their sustainable competency to develop new technologies or business models.

Why mess with a good thing? Because if you don't, someone else will come along and do it instead of you. Just because you don't want to treat the rules of your industry as open source conventions doesn't mean a new competitor won't. It should not take a JetBlue to wake up a Delta, or an Amazon to stir a Barnes & Noble. And once awakened, venerable business institutions must do a whole lot more than ape their young upstart competitors. The veterans should already understand their own industries from the inside out, and like expert mechanics, know how to retool any part of the engine.

Instead, too many established companies have drifted from their own areas of expertise, and are forced to confront every new idea—whether it emerges from a customer or a competitor—as a threat to the all-important status quo. Rather than clinging to existing circumstances, successful innovators see every established convention as an opportunity for reappraisal and every customer as a potential asset in that process. Examples abound. And in nearly every case, these companies and the entrepreneurs behind them were told it couldn't be done.

Atlanta television veteran Ted Turner almost single-handedly reinvented the rules of journalism by creating his own 24-hour always-on cable news channel. The major networks scrambled to keep up with his scrappy young network that always seemed to be in the right place at the right time. As a cable channel, CNN was free to use lower-quality video than normally permitted on broadcast networks. This gave it access not only to its own bureaus' footage, but to the camcorder tapes of amateur videographers who just happened to catch the latest earthquake, uprising, or instance of police brutality. CNN was widely criticized for its fast-and-loose editorial policy, particularly during the first Gulf War. Its reporters took pretty much whatever they had and threw it on TV. But this same Gulf War footage put CNN on the international map, and made it a major player in television news.

Once absorbed by Time Warner, which immediately ousted Turner from CNN, the network lost its sense of purpose. CNN buckled under pressure from upstart rival Fox to become more about debate than information. CNN strayed so far from its core competency that it took a comic, Jon Stewart, to remind two commentators on the air during *Crossfire* that the channel's responsibility was not to air entertaining debates, but to deliver news. The network's new president, Jonathan Klein, agreed. In a classic example of reinventing from the inside out, he canceled *Crossfire* and steered the network away from what he called "head-butting debate shows" in favor of all-news television. To hell with the conventional wisdom that heated red-state/blue-state debate is better business. "CNN is a different animal," said Klein, grounded confidently in the box. "We report the news. Fox talks about the news. They're very good at what they do and we're very good at what we do."[26]

CNN's path to innovation—its true box—is not to turn itself into one of its competitors but to revisit its core values: 24-hour news from unconventional sources, distributed widely, and using new technologies. It might innovate from the inside out by continuing to develop new formats for reports from remote regions of the world via video cell phone and other new technologies. Or it might shake things up all over again by developing business models that allow it to stream 24/7 news programming through the Web—even though it upsets cable companies that now carry the network with some degree of exclusivity. If CNN could innovate a new national television network, it can certainly handle a new kind of Web site. CNN's original renegade model created value for myriad companies where none existed before. That's how the network has to think about the future, as well.

Look around at the businesses that have caused the greatest consternation in established industries and chances are you'll find the companies willing to take an open source approach, ready to welcome their customers into core processes, and able to create new value for the businesses with which they collaborate.

Voice over Internet Protocol (VoIP) technology allows consumers and businesses alike to ditch expensive landline service and replace it with a low-cost, Internet-based alternative. Landline companies attempted to fight the competition in court, arguing for more regulation of these new communications companies, but to no avail. By year-end 2004, 20 percent of U.S. businesses had made the switch,[27] and over a million U.S. consumers had been seduced by low monthly fees and a wide array of user-programmable features. Furthermore,

VoIP companies tend to leave themselves open to the innovations of their consumers. Because they are Internet-based, new features are easy to implement and customize. The ones that consumers themselves hack—like advanced call-forwarding or software-based calls that require no modem—are quickly made part of the standard package of offerings. Like CNN, which created tremendous value for the cable industry, airport lounges, hotels, and satellite services, VoIP has given businesses from Cisco to Earthlink new life. It has become the single greatest excuse for consumers to upgrade to broadband service, and—along with cellular—is a leading growth area in many equipment manufacturers' annual reports.

Or consider Exchange Traded Funds (ETFs). In 1992, the American Stock Exchange, a smaller and less revered institution than New York's "Big Board," was facing competition from the upstart NASDAQ exchange. NASDAQ, itself a technologically enabled reinvention of the trading floor as a distributed network of brokered exchange desks, had become the favored place for all those young technology, fashion, and dot-com companies to launch their IPOs. Hip new companies went to the NASDAQ, while more established companies went to the NYSE. Many went from one to the other as they "grew up." But almost none went to the AMEX. For a while, it looked like the AMEX might even be overrun, or even absorbed altogether, by NASDAQ.

But getting back inside the box of exchange-based investing, the American Stock Exchange[28] took advantage of a failed SEC order allowing for a new kind of hedge fund. It created and launched the first ETF, basically a mutual fund but with much greater flexibility.

The ETF reinvents what it means to be an exchange from the inside out. Marrying the real needs of investors for vehicles to bet their hunches with the capability of an exchange to allow for all-day trading, the ETF gives people the chance to invest in whole categories and indexes rather than single stocks. It amounts to a stock market hack that adds value for brokers and exchanges by increasing volume and commissions, as well as for the companies and regions that receive new investment they wouldn't have seen otherwise.

The first "Spider," or SPDR, tracked the S&P 500 just like an index fund—except it could be traded throughout the day like a regular stock and with much lower management fees. The SPDR was a tremendous success, and soon financial institutions from Morgan Stanley to Barclays were developing ETFs for everything under the sun, from single-country and regional funds to ones that focused on specific industries. AMEX had innovated its way back into the box, and out of a hole. It wasn't until April 2, 2004, that the NYSE, realizing it had missed the boat on ETFs, finally launched its own.

Don't worry, not every open source innovation has its roots in some newfangled computer or communications technology. Stately soap maker Procter & Gamble has made a goal of having 50 percent of its ideas come from outside the internal research and development organization, according to CTO G. Gil Cloyd.[29] This doesn't mean P&G is going outside the box for innovation, but that it trusts its own expertise enough to see the value of collaboration. Procter & Gamble has faith in its ability to add value to almost anything that comes its way.

While P&G isn't exactly putting the formula for Crest online, it does listen to consumers, inventors, and fellow companies for ideas. The Crest Spinbrush, a battery-powered disposable, came from an outside entrepreneur, and is now the biggest-selling brush in the United States. The Mr. Clean Magic Eraser, one of the biggest home-care product launches of the decade, was first seen in Japan and then adapted to this country. Adopting what has become known as the "open innovation" strategy,[30] P&G hires firms that specialize in facilitating connections between itself and other companies.

There's no shame in opening up innovation to others, or even to one's customers. Accepting ideas from the bottom up is not an indication of weakness, but a sign of strength. It can even engender the kind of participatory ethos that builds a brand in today's open source environment. That's why shoemaker John Fluevog offers an "open source footwear" forum on his Web site through which his fans can create and post their own footwear designs. Fluevog picks finalists from among the hundreds of entries and then invites the online community vote for their favorite one. The reward? He goes ahead and builds the winning shoe as part of his next collection. He names the shoe after the designer, who receives no compensation beyond satisfaction and social currency. Fifty pages of entries and a former fringe brand racing toward broad global penetration attest to this strategy's success. Fluevog's willingness to accept the ideas of his customers doesn't compromise his authority or reputation in the least; it only enhances them.

In any industry, a truly accomplished hacker understands the code so well that he knows what he doesn't know, and is willing to accept help in reinvention. To run an open source business means to be so completely committed to innovation that you accept help when you need it, confident that you can bring something to the table yourself. You are unthreatened by the contributions of others, because you know how very much you are capable of contributing yourself.

Fields like genetic engineering, cold fusion, and energy research—among the most promising new business opportunities of this century—all depend on such an open source approach to innovation. These are collaborative efforts, orchestrated by consortia of researchers, corporations, and even laypeople. Nanotechnology does not come into being without engineers willing to get back in the box and then share their results with others. Value created for one is value created for all.

That's the abundance that comes from being open to the source—and to one another.

chapter seven

CALL AND RESPONSE: ANSWERING REAL NEEDS

At last, our renaissance brings us to a place of almost absolute simplicity. Having exhausted the alternatives, we come to realize that the easiest path to both satisfaction and profitability is to do something well, and to do it with and for other people.

No, even though we've arrived at the last chapter, this is not the part where we hold hands and sing "Kumbaya." But by learning to replace an adversarial stance toward both customers and competitors with a more collaborative one, we'll end up in a much better position to solve real problems, answer real needs, and, in the process, make real profits. Just as an open source approach requires us to go deep, it also demands we open wide.

Of course, the challenge of running a business with an open source ethos is that at some point we can't help but wonder, "Where does it stop?" Who is included among our company's many partners and beneficiaries, and why exclude anyone? Where does "our team" end and the "other team" begin? What is to motivate us, if not competition? With all this openness, how do we draw a line between management and employee, company and customer, or "us" and "them"? Is nothing sacred?

Ultimately, the answer is no. The first Renaissance brought us division of the realms, clearly delineated disciplines and a rat race of parallel but never-meeting competitive tracks. These many distinctions are held sacred because were they put up to scrutiny or discussion they would be exposed as meaningless. And destructive. When we are defined exclusively by our distinctions, we end up in a world that values division over unity and passivity over action. Knowing who you "are" feels more important than knowing what you do. And once you've accepted your externally derived identity, you've tacitly accepted the way in which you've been pitted against everyone else for artificially limited resources. Employers exploit workers, and salespeople scam customers, while customers and employees steal whatever they can in return. (In fact, American businesses lose over $200 billion annually to cash and merchandise thefts by their own employees, accounting for 60 percent of all small business failures.[1])

Our new renaissance reintroduces all of these artificially separated groups of people to one another. The networked organization, like a networked society, must be painstakingly transparent if it is going to pretend to promote rather than suppress the growing urge for authentic engagement with the processes organizing our lives. The days of the locked wooden suggestion box are over. Anonymity and intermediaries simply reinforce estrangement. You must engage with your employees, shareholders, and even your clients, as partners in the open source enterprise. Your business must be structured so that the more they know, the better you look, and the better you really are.

TARGET MARKETS

An "us and them" mentality defines the relationship between most businesses and their customers today. The business is the hunter, forever stalking the consumer, his prey. As in any cat-and-mouse dynamic, new stalking techniques lead to new defense mechanisms that in turn lead to new countermeasures. It's an arms race. Consumers are experienced as bacteria, growing ever more resistant to new marketing attacks. Businesspeople are experienced as ruthless mercenaries, willing to do whatever is necessary to capture consumers' attention, hearts, and wallets.

No one comes out a winner. Consumers don't get whatever it is they might really want, and the businesses that mean to create loyal customers end up generating ill will instead. Marketers begin seeing customers as the enemy, and employ increasingly aggressive tactics to keep up with the growing consumer cynicism. The cycle feeds on itself until consumers have no more idea what they're shopping for than businesses do about what they're selling.

Offering insight into this mess of their own creation are the market researchers. Using focus groups, statistical modeling, and sheer guesswork, these psychologists, sociologists, and ethnographers seek to get inside the heads of consumers, predict their behaviors, and lead them toward certain decisions.

The first of the three main techniques, focus groups, usually pits one researcher against a group of consumers who are being paid for their opinions. The focus group almost never yields an accurate picture of whatever is being sought. In the vast majority of the dozens of groups I've observed or led, the purpose was less to glean new insights than to confirm the insights already held. This is no crime in itself. Advertising is almost never based on research. More often than not, the research departments of agencies are called in to support whatever conclusions the creative or strategy divisions have already reached.

I remember consulting to an agency working on a pitch for a boy's deodorant. Its strategy department had decided that the target consumer—the teenage boy—was very concerned with fashion. So the agency commissioned a series of videotaped focus groups for which the leaders were instructed to get teenagers to talk about their fashion concerns. The agency then selected the clips that demonstrated this point. When a new account executive took over the pitch, he decided that the strategy should be reversed: boys resent fashion. New clips were chosen from the *very same focus group footage*, showing the boys espousing the corrected stance. When their words weren't enough, lines from Susan Faludi's book *Stiffed*[2] were superimposed over the boys' angry faces.

Even when focus groups are conducted without preconceived conclusions, they hit only about as often as they miss. As a result of the classroomlike setup, subjects are rendered quite impressionable and become eager to please the leader. Other times, participants use the focus group as an opportunity to vent, engage in psychodrama, or demonstrate their own marketing prowess. After all, these are people who agreed to participate in a long evening of questioning for about 50 bucks. They usually have their own agendas. Also, in spite of careful screening to prevent it, a large number of focus group participants go to groups as a kind of hobby, participating in dozens of different ones each year. While shooting a documentary about teens and marketing, I realized that—unbeknownst to the researcher—several boys had managed to get into more than one group for the same research project simply by changing their T-shirts. This is hardly scientific research.

Of course, for every failed series of focus groups there's another army of researchers offering new and improved techniques. Clotaire Rapaille, the psychologist who discovers the "codes" for different products, claims he can hypnotize his subjects so that they deliver information directly from the "reptile brain." Market researcher and Republican pollster Frank Luntz gives his subjects handheld dials through which they can measure their moment-to-moment responses to products, pitches, and politicians.

But no matter what the newfangled technique justifying their existence, focus groups don't look at all for what a person might want or need. Rather, they look at how to position what a business already has to sell. When one teen fashion focus group revealed that what teenage boys really want is a zero-cost, low-fashion atmosphere in which to enjoy one another's company, this finding was not acted upon. There are most certainly several great business opportunities in this insight—if you've read this far, I'm sure you are capable of rat-tling off a few right now—but not one that this particular designer jeans company could discern. Instead, it looked at what advertising imagery could do to stimulate the necessary fear and panic to make teenagers desire something more related to status, like overpriced jeans. Then it conducted follow-up groups where short videos were shown to boys to see which worked best at changing their expressed desires.

While these techniques might work on some level in the short run, they have also been responsible for many of marketing's greatest mistakes: Coke2, Burger King's Veal Parmesan, Cadillac Cimmaron, and, perhaps most comically, Clairol's "Touch of Yogurt" shampoo, which tested off the charts in focus groups, yet couldn't find any cus-tomers in the real world.

Meanwhile, true entrepreneurs have almost no need for focus groups. The high-end Dyson vacuum cleaner has sold more than 12 million units worldwide[3] thanks to the determination and clarity of focus of its inventor, James Dyson. Focus groups suggested that the vacuum's transparent collection bin disgusted consumers. People said they did not like finding out their carpets were so dirty. Dyson trusted his instincts more than his focus groups, convinced that a display of disgusting grime "would give people a certain sense of satisfaction after they had vacuumed."[4] This sensation has proved a great selling point— and a new household maintenance addiction. Instead of being embar-rassed by all this dirt, owners of the Dyson regularly demonstrate the product for visiting friends. Sixty percent of buyers have had the vac-uum recommended to them by a friend.[5]

The problem with focus groups is not just that consumers can't be trusted to tell the truth; it's that the technique itself, like so much of market research, takes the human beings we should be serving and re-duces them to lowest-common-denominator consumer appetites and impulses. Seeing dirt may not please the reptile brain, but it was a vital part of the equation for innovating the home carpet cleaning industry, which Dyson has done seemingly overnight. Conducting a focus group about people's interest in personal computers wouldn't have predicted their success in the marketplace, either. That's because focus groups can't tell a lot about what does not already exist.

Neither can any market research technique, because they all treat real, whole people as consumers—as if they could be defined entirely by their roles as customers of products. And because you can only research the market's past, not its future, consumer research doesn't ever lead to true innovation. It only helps companies to sort out some of last year's trends in order to create an illusion of sales predictability.

This holy grail of being able to predict and guide consumer behavior has alienated most of American industry, retail, and even government from their own constituencies and their own capacity for creative renewal. Of all these techniques, the one that makes marketers feel most secure—and the one that seems to be based in the pure cold reason of numbers—is market segmentation.

Segmentation was originally developed by the direct mail industry as a way of saving postage and increasing response rates. The earliest research firms dedicated to segmentation amounted to little more than shelves of shoeboxes filled with index cards, each card representing a household in their region. With the advent of computers, the industry took off and direct mailings grew exponentially. As stacks of junk mail filled consumers' mailboxes, the job of research firms became to figure out which messages could penetrate the clutter and avoid the dustbin at any particular household.

Companies like Acxiom and Claritas arose, competing to collect consumer, census and any other data on every person in America, and sometimes beyond. By striking deals with some of the merchants they were serving, these two firms grew to behemoth proportions, taking in as much data from their clients as they were providing to them. That's when things got more interesting. Using a range of statistical models, they began grouping people into segments based not just on demographic information like region and age, but on past behavior. Researchers attempted to compile their files into "clusters" for which behavior of one person or household could predict the behavior of all the others in that segment.

Let's be clear: consumer profiles have nothing to do with people or their desires. These profiles are mere data sets of information rang-ing from which TV shows the target consumers watch or which books they read to how many doors are on their cars and whether they like dogs or cats. The research firms then use statistical modeling to infer other sets of facts from the ones they have. In the 2004 U.S. presiden-tial campaign, for example, it was discovered that undecided voters in Ohio were much more likely to have call waiting on their phones, and cats instead of dogs. Why? No one really knows. All that matters is that this statistical truth gave campaign managers the ability to target cer-tain households, and not waste their time, energy, and money on oth-ers. (That said, it was the Kerry campaign using Acxiom data in this way, and look where it got them.)

Statistical modeling depends on the predictability of consumer behavior. The unintended consequence of this technique is that a targeted communication also carries with it the subtler message that a recipient can be counted on to act in certain ways—as if to say, "we've got your number." Segmented marketing is intended, after all, to ex-ploit what a marketer knows about a consumer in order to make him *more* like his profile. A person who has clicked on a few banner ads about dieting, or purchased a book on carbohydrates, is an ideal target for an onslaught of diet product ads. The consumer experiences seg-mentation and targeted messaging as having been "found out" and is then pushed further toward a static identity. The intent and, when it works, the effect is to make consumers more predictable or even stereo-typical.

Businesses that already recognize this phenomenon, however, shouldn't be surprised that market research can make their *own* behav-ior entirely more predictable, too. The predatory cat's movements are just as predictable as those of the mouse! For businesses, it amounts to a reactionary strategy, trapping them in analysis of the past and deter-ring true innovation or speculation.

Not every facet of the human personality has something to do with shopping. The work of the market research firm, while delivering on its promise of predicting consumer responses to certain stimuli, un-necessarily limits itself in its approach. It understands people and their behavior exclusively through the lens of what they might buy or what ad they might respond to. It has no way of knowing or predicting what they might need or want that doesn't yet exist. In other words, it has no real connection to innovation.

Worse, segmentation is divisive. We are not a nation, we are a collection of separate households. Under the market researcher's scalpel, society is sliced into ever more precise consumer tribes. Mac users versus Microsoft users. Ford drivers versus Chevy drivers. Nike wearers versus Reebok wearers. These divisions are alienating; they define people by what they want as consumers, rather than what they can do or contribute as community members or, dare we mention it, citizens. Contrary to the laws of social currency, a customer model is steeped in aggrandizement of the individual: the customer is always right. The marketer tells consumers they matter, and the consumer is to believe that buying himself something will make him happy.

Consumers who are trained to think in this way are dangerous. They are selfish and self-centered. They are the ones who think of stores as targets and salespeople as swindlers. They don't like being dependent on you for identity; they resent you for patronizing them; and they feel no loyalty to you at all. These are people who have no qualms about getting a commission-based salesperson at an electronics store to spend half an hour teaching them about DVD players before going online to purchase one for just $3 less (plus postage).

The company that treats its customers as consumers to be stimulated, prodded, and behaviorally controlled will be treated in kind. Us versus them is a divisive trap that works both ways.

THERE'S A FLY IN MY SOUP

There's nothing like a crisis to expose the fiber of a relationship. If you were in trouble—real trouble—would your customers turn on you or rush to your defense?

It all depends on whether you have held them off as the consumers you hope to manipulate or embraced them as part of what you do. The latter seems harder—or a strategy limited to the new media companies like Adobe we looked at earlier, which invite users of their programs to create and share their own "plug-ins." But the lessons learned by an Adobe or an Apple, whose tremendous bases of consumer producers fuel cash flow, innovation, and, most important, enduring loyalty, are fully applicable to brick-and-mortar businesses, as well. Maybe more so.

A few summers ago, there was a tremendous blackout in the northeast United States. I was living in New York's East Village at the time, a neighborhood populated by wealthy artists, homeless addicts, and pretty much everything in between. People who lived on our block had few choices of where to buy groceries: the Koreans on the corner, the Puerto Rican bodega, or a new supermarket. When the blackout hit, the three competitors sealed their fates.

Under orders from corporate headquarters, the supermarket shut its doors. It even posted a couple of guards—presumably to prevent looting.

The corner store, on the other hand, realizing the power was not coming back on anytime soon, implemented something akin to a favored customers policy. The owner stood in the doorway, pretending the store was closed. But when he saw a person he recognized, he permitted the customer to enter the store and rummage through the dark for the things the customer wanted. A flashlight and battery-powered calculator were used in lieu of the cash register; tax was duly collected.

The bodega around the block, however, decided to turn the whole crisis into an opportunity for a celebration. A battery-powered boom box blasted music down the street, which was thick with families. A fire hydrant sprayed water on overheated children, and people waited on line to get into the store. Lit with votive candles, the bodega took on the quality of a tiny, if dirty, chapel. The distinction between patron and storekeeper was nonexistent. People found the items they needed on the shelves and passed money toward the counter where it was put into a cigar box. They called to each other, in English and Spanish, to get change passed back to them.

Needless to say, the chain store didn't make many friends during the three days it remained under self-imposed siege. Their policy made the residents of our little neighborhood feel like we were being colonized by an enemy. The store had only been open for a few weeks. We had endured months of construction, closed streets, even the eviction of people in the apartments above what became the supermarket. This crisis was the store's chance to prove that it could serve the community whose turf it had claimed.

Instead, by looking at its clientele as a threat rather than a constituency, it squandered a tremendous opportunity—the only one it would have, it turns out, before burnishing its reputation in the neighborhood as an exploitative company not to be trusted. The irony here is that after being closed three days, the store needed to stay closed an additional several days in order to clear out and replace the spoiled inventory! It lost thousands of dollars of meats and dairy that could have been sold or even given away—and either option would have been rewarded by the neighborhood with enduring loyalty. To this day, the only people I know who shop there do so begrudgingly or when they don't have time to go up the street to the next grocery store.

The corner store gained a reputation for snootiness and selectivity. Perhaps it was their long-range goal, but they've retained a small customer base of mostly wealthy, white people, and have raised their prices accordingly. Most community members know to go around the block to the bodega, which has established itself as a center of neighborhood activity, expanding its clientele to include all of us who experienced their three-day fiesta and all of our friends.

From tainted Tylenol to Kathie Lee Gifford's sweatshop scandal, there's nothing better than a crisis to test the existing dynamic between a corporation and its customers. For while a company's response to crisis is a key factor in whether it will survive the episode, the relationship already established between a company and its customers, employees, and even shareholders will have a lot more to do with determining what happens. Companies entrenched in us-and-them behaviors will discover just how quickly the tables can turn, putting them at the mercy of those they have intimidated, shunned, or exploited in one way or another.

The classic case study in inevitable retribution is Perrier. In 1989, coasting on the lifestyle aspirations of the yuppie set, Perrier established itself as the "champagne" of waters. In America, there was as yet no perceived reason for people to buy expensive French fizzy water other than status. Perrier turned its water into a "badge" and reached sales of 1.2 billion bottles by 1989.[6] Then, in 1990, traces of benzene were discovered in some bottles, forcing Perrier to pull 280 million bottles off the shelves.[7]

Perrier kicked and screamed all along the way, claiming that benzene did not pose a health hazard (it does) and eventually blaming the problem on a blocked filter at the bottling plant. This did little to reassure customers. The unacknowledged question it raised was, if benzene had to be filtered out of Perrier, then why use water from that spring in the first place? Sales dropped by half, and never recovered.

Nestlé—another famous crisis victim—bought Perrier two years later, but has been unable to turn the brand around. Launched in 1899, and a hit with British military officers and once a favorite on the Queen's table, Perrier is now the worst-performing water among all of Nestlé's international brands, with zero percent operating margins on about $245 million in annual sales.[8] As a result, the company has committed to cutting jobs and benefits, leading to labor disputes with French Perrier employees who believe they are the ones defending "a Perrier spirit that transcends any multinational corporation."[9] This, in turn, has put Perrier in a public, ugly, and extended war against France's most powerful trade union, the communist-backed Confédération Générale du Travail.

Perrier's problems—probably unsolvable at this late juncture—stem from the company's entrenchment in an us-and-them mentality. By basing its brand in frivolous exclusivity, Perrier could never hope to maintain a truly loyal customer base once a genuine issue like health came into play. Admittedly, Perrier was attempting to establish a market for a product—water—that seemed to be in great abundance. But rather than educating the public on the benefits of spring water, Perrier focused on the brand attributes that its market research determined could get people to spend money on something that didn't have inherent value for them. Perrier distanced Americans from the reality of Perrier production—a rich history—and sold status instead. Paul Tarling, senior market analyst at Zenith International, explained it this way: "In the '80s, it added a touch of French sophistication to the . . . dinner party. . . . Today consumers are more discerning. They are no longer so preoccupied with projecting an image of sophistication and are more concerned about associating with a product that embodies health and natural purity." [10]

By focusing on brand image rather than product attributes, Perrier ultimately communicated that its customers were patsies. By refusing to communicate anything about the product's actual attributes, Perrier left itself vulnerable. The first real fact most people learned about this water was that it contained benzene! Finally, by responding to the century-old company's problems primarily with employee cuts at its landmark home branch, parent Nestlé alienated what was left of its employee base. Rightly, the employees feel they understand Perrier better than its owners. Maybe the next owners will choose to see its customers and employees as integral parts of the same community, rather than as "others" to be manipulated or quelled.

As a counterexample, consider South African grocery store chain Pick 'n Pay. By establishing itself as a true consumer, employee, and shareholder advocate, the company not only survived an extortion threat, it thrived during it. In 2003, medical tests indicated that customers had been poisoned by eating Pick 'n Pay products. The company was being blackmailed; if it didn't pay out, the extortionist claimed, more people would be poisoned.

Pick 'n Pay responded well to the crisis. It expanded its existing customer care phone lines to 24-hour service, increased operator shifts, and managed to take 20,000 calls in the first week alone. [11] It implemented a policy whereby customers were free to return any product they had purchased at the store, for a full refund. Almost no one chose to do so.

These appropriate responses to crisis don't fully explain the way customers, employees, and shareholders rallied around the company.

Amazingly, Pick 'n Pay's sales *increased* during the crisis. It seems customers "were going out of their way to shop at the company's stores in a public show of support."[12] Employees, for their part, generated unprovoked word of mouth about their dismay that a company as caring as Pick 'n Pay would be attacked in such an awful way. This is South Africa, remember: Pick 'n Pay is a white-owned company with mostly black employees that established itself during the apartheid era. Share price remained unchanged by the scandal (imagine that happening on Wall Street), as if speculators were afraid to seize on Pick 'n Pay's misfortunes, or knew better than to bet against it. They were right: the company's market capitalization increased by more than 41 percent over the next year.

How does a grocery store transcend race, politics, and economics in order to engender such customer, employee, and shareholder loyalty while simultaneously earning double-digit annual profit increases? By getting back into the box and remembering the corporation exists to serve its community, rather than the other way around.

Most of Pick 'n Pay's growth took place under the tenure of Raymond Ackerman, son of the chain's founder. Thanks to his father's obsession with customer relations, Raymond's first job was to serve for six months at the door as a greeter. After that, to ensure that he would take a hands-on approach to the store's products, the younger Ackerman was made to spend the next six months sorting women's underwear.

Between that and an enlightenment-inspired education, Raymond Ackerman ended up a strident free-market capitalist *and* consumer advocate. Ackerman says he was taught that "consumer sovereignty is an enlightened form of self-interest: fight for the consumer and she will fight for you."[13] In his biography, Ackerman explains that he was often challenged on the motivation behind operating from a perspective of consumer sovereignty. "The cynical observation," he writes, "is that such philosophies in business are little more than window-dressing disguising the real motive for trading—making bigger and better profits. On the contrary, I've always said that following the principles of consumer sovereignty and caring for people is precisely the way to make money and to be successful. It is an absolute fact that the more we ploughed into staff benefits, the more we gave to charity, the more profits rose. . . . The division between caring and making profits does not exist."[14]

To Ackerman, apartheid was not just an abhorrent system, but an economically unsound one. "You could not build an economy based on apartheid because the system worked against releasing economic energies."[15] He was one of the few wealthy white capitalists in South Africa to work openly and fiercely against the status quo, bending and even breaking apartheid policies on occasion, on behalf of his employees.

Ackerman's grandest act of civil disobedience, it turns out, was on behalf of his customers. Demonstrating his axiom of customer sovereignty, Ackerman protested a nationwide government-enacted price-fixing policy on cigarettes by buying up every carton he could find before the price hike went into effect. He filled an entire warehouse with so much inventory that no one would insure it, and then ended up guarding it himself, with a gun. When the price fix was initiated, Pick 'n Pay continued to sell cigarettes at normal prices, and paid more in fines than it made in profits. And even though it's cigarettes we're talking about, here, not antibiotics, Ackerman established Pick 'n Pay as a staunch defender of the consumer—and people—against restrictions on their economic and personal freedom.

As a result of their focus on supporting communities by creating good jobs, selling at fair prices, supporting local suppliers, and improving both environmental quality and educational opportunities, Pick 'n Pays are welcome additions to pretty much every town in which they build a store. An *Ask Africa/Business Day* survey rated it the "most trustworthy company in South Africa" just months after the crisis. Growth, in terms of new stores and same-store increases over the following year, remained as robust as ever through the crisis, and accelerated shortly afterward.

Whether or not Pick 'n Pay is worthy of a medal for good corporate citizenship is beside the point. What matters is that it broke down the distinction between consumer, employee, and shareholder, treating all of them as human beings who can benefit through the operations of a company rather than as resources to exploit. That's why a crisis like the one it experienced, rather than stoking the built-up rage of its consumers, employees and vendors, offered an opportunity for that community of beneficiaries to reciprocate.

I AM YOUR FATHER, LUKE

Turning customers, employees, management, and shareholders into a community of people with complementary rather than competing interests is no small feat. It's especially difficult in an environment where so many companies are working on developing the illusion of a fully integrated corporate ethos, while doing little to actually implement it.

For most companies, integration still means brand integration. Through a combination of "knowing the customer" (market research) and "lifestyle branding" (target marketing), companies hope to create the sense of a seamless transition between their customers' lives and their product universes.

This strategy takes on a myriad of forms. A new breed of marketers hopes to marry the advertising know-how of Madison Avenue with the entertainment experience of Hollywood's Vine Street. Dubbed Madison/Vine, these firms seek to bury product placement within the content of television shows and movies. The lifestyle branding of companies from Nike to Song airlines strives to integrate a brand's values with a person's so completely that the two become indistinguishable. Other businesses, such as phone and credit card companies, use computer-generated telemarketing scripts customized for each consumer called, as if to create a perfect marriage between an individual's needs and the stated offer. Still others, like music, media, and fashion companies, sponsor existing subcultures in order to absorb them whole. When the subcultures resist, corporations adopt a "who me?" or ironic "wink wink" stance. Yes, we're Sprite; yes, we're a soft drink; and yes, we want your money; so reward us for our cynical honesty and buy Sprite!

These kinds of tactics work against the spirit of trust and connection they mean, or pretend, to engender. And they work no better on employees or shareholders. Misguided, patronizing incentive programs often have the reverse of their intended effect. Others simply come too late. When a hospital in New York decided to provide remedial education for its employees, workers were convinced that the math and English tests administered were going to be used to identify low scorers and terminate them. "They're gonna weed us out," one panicked worker told a television news reporter. Likewise, CEOs who get bonuses while share prices decline, insiders who sell stock at the mysteriously divined top, and drastic restatements of earnings at every change of the helm don't make public shareholders feel like members of the company family. Every minute irregularity becomes an opportunity for another class action suit, winning just pennies per share for the plaintiffs, if that, but earning huge sums for the lawyers who have learned to exploit this animosity, and costing the company a tremendous amount of time, money, and goodwill.

Questionable corporate behavior eventually costs us all. The scandals, class action suits, and sentencing hearings taking up what seems to be a majority of the business section every day make it hard for people to accept the premise that any corporation might have their best interests at heart. Not when the cash value of their pension plans appears to end up in the pockets of the executives who cost them their jobs in the first place. When we're not being fleeced as employees, we're being fleeced as consumers—observed, prodded, and fooled into acquiring more debt. Big business has replaced government's big brother as the ultimate "they," forcing people and companies into unnecessarily adversarial positions. Instead of considering what we can offer each other, we want to know what we can get from each other—or, better, *get away with*.

We are unable to see that the divide between people and business, the counterculture and overculture, "us" and "them," is entirely artificial and, in the context of making people's lives better or more meaningful, absolutely useless. The inability to find common ground—to embrace the other—is costing everyone, from venture capitalist to vegan counterculturalist, far too much.

We must all cross the great chasms of animosity and mistrust between management, shareholders, employees, customers, and the greater community. We are, in most cases, the very same people. The most important lesson of the new renaissance is that *there is no divide*. Our competitors are our collaborators; we are as much in the service of our employees as they are of us; our customers are not our targets but our bosses; as shareholders, we're not investors in someone else's company but ultimately responsible for our own. The old dualities no longer function. High and low culture have merged, along with culture and counterculture, progressive and reactionary, capitalist and philanthropist, or even writer and reader. We're in this together.

The very same people I'm addressing at an environmentalists' rally on a Sunday afternoon might be in the audience at the advertising agency I speak to on Monday morning. The students attending a university lecture aren't just the civil libertarians of tomorrow; they're also tomorrow's marketers and CEOs. The broker must invest his clients' money in the stocks that will earn the most money, or he's not doing the job with which he's been entrusted. As a result, however, the university teacher's pension plan ends up holding stock in the very same companies he may be criticizing for their crimes against humanity. As far as I've been able to tell, none of these people intend to do evil. Sure, some act out of fear or panic, but they are as much victims of the system in which they have found themselves as they are the perpetrators. And while unconsciously conducted business can be blamed for many of

America's ills, I've met more selfishly corrupt operators in the so-called nonprofit and foundation worlds than in big business.

It's time for the business and socially progressive sectors to realize they are on the same side—or, better, that there are really no sides at all. But thanks to fiscal and corporate legacies long overdue for revision, we are operating on a battlefield that does not support rapprochement. While most business people are too fearful or ignorant to challenge these legacies, most people in the antibusiness camp are too mistrustful of commerce, altogether, to see the seeds of societal renewal in any business proposition.

Participating in the new renaissance means learning to see customers, shareholders, employees, and managers as the same people, engaged in complementary enterprises.

There's no need to hire consultants to figure out how to manipulate your target market, seduce your desired constituency, or vanquish your unwitting competitors. Instead of trying to convince people you have what they want, look around yourself to discover what people actually need, and then figure out how to provide it. That's innovation from the inside out. There's no shortage of unanswered needs in this world, just of innovative solutions.

The key to business ethics and guilt-free profits is so much simpler than it looks. Answer real needs.

SOLVING REAL PROBLEMS

In an era offering true opportunities for reintegration, it's not enough to try to compensate for one behavior with another. Too many companies today are so addicted to one business process or another that they'd rather spend their effort creating a market for something unnecessary or even destructive than developing a solution for a real problem. The best of them understand on some level that they're doing more harm than good, and work to compensate for their impact on society or the environment through charitable giving.

It's hard to fault any company for donating some portion of its revenues to charitable causes or its labor to serving a community. Whether earnestly or cynically conceived, efforts such as corporate-initiated social outreach and environmental rehabilitation are positive forces. But when a company is doing community work to rehabilitate the same neighborhood it has decimated with layoffs, environmental cleanups to mitigate the effects of whatever might be spewing from its smokestacks, or drug rehabilitation for people living in areas militarized by its assault rifles, something is amiss.

The separation of business practices from people's genuine needs only works against both. It tends to let firms drift toward more questionable actions in their real work, as they attempt to compensate for this behavior in their public relations and charitable giving. Some form of cognitive dissonance—an awareness of being at cross-purposes—will emerge both within and beyond the company, making it impossible to achieve a sense of purpose.

Companies such as cigarette manufacturer Altria (formerly Philip Morris) epitomize this style of philanthropy: its revenue derives from selling tobacco, yet it attempts to manufacture goodwill among its detractors through lavish spending in unrelated fields, such as the arts, fighting hunger, preventing domestic violence, or supporting environmental protection. These efforts are not insignificant in themselves: between 1990 and 2004, Altria has contributed more than $450 million to hunger relief organizations, and since 1998, given $28 million in grants to organizations that help victims of domestic violence. In all, Altria donated over $1 billion over the past decade to some of the nation's worst social problems.

Of course, highlighting the most dramatic of public health crises—spousal abuse and hunger—makes cigarette consumption appear to be a nuisance issue in comparison. Is that too cynical an analysis of Altria's best intentions? It's only natural given the company's long record of irresponsible marketing and denial of nicotine's addictive qualities. What are the company's real intentions for us? It's hard to determine. While Altria is quite public about its charitable donations, it keeps quiet about its political donations; shareholders overwhelmingly rejected a proposal to disclose detailed lists of recipients of political donations in 2004.[16]

You don't need to be a business theorist to see that a company like Altria is at cross-purposes. While submitting to the We Card program designed to prevent U.S. teens from buying cigarettes, Altria still promotes the Marlboro Man, one of the most popular and recognized brand icons among teenagers in the world. While backing a proposal for the FDA to regulate tobacco,[17] Altria has refused to bow to the World Health Organization's tobacco control treaty—well, only to the provisions that it not advertise in certain countries, or that it submit to increases in cigarette taxes.[18] If it's hard to wrap one's brain around the idea of a company spending money to make and promote a product while simultaneously undermining its salability to teens, imagine what it's like to work *inside* a company like that.

Many can't. In an effort to become less dependent on selling cigarettes, Philip Morris bought Kraft and, later, Nabisco; but many of the food industry's best people couldn't bring themselves to work for an antinutritious industry. "Don't underestimate the issue of working for a tobacco company," explained one recruitment firm after a raft of resignations. "Some Kraft executives can't get their heads around the idea of a transfer to Philip Morris tobacco or corporate."[19] The combined loss of brainpower included CEO stars Bob Eckert (who ended up running Mattel), Jim Kilts (Gillette), Alan Lacy (Sears), and Bob Morrison (Quaker).

The greater public didn't take the acquisition any better. Thanks to its association with Philip Morris, Kraft's own practices are now coming under increasing scrutiny. Activist shareholders, as part of a campaign called Infact, charge that "Big Food" is mirroring the tactics of Big Tobacco. At a recent shareholders meeting, they contended, "Kraft, in lockstep with parent corporation Philip Morris/Altria, is looking to fatten its profits at the expense of global health. . . . As countries come together to address an epidemic of malnutrition that is being driven by the food industry, Kraft and its allies are taking a page directly from Big Tobacco's playbook on aggressive influence-peddling."[20] With shareholders like these, who needs enemies? Still, with 400,000 Americans dying each year from smoking-related illnesses, it's hard for a cigarette company to make friends, no matter how many ballet companies it sponsors.

Of course, tobacco is an easy target. No one is going to associate cigarettes with altruism, even under the Altria brand name. But what of companies that claim to be conceived with a socially conscious agenda in mind?

Again, it depends on what that company actually makes or does. The business you're in is the main business you are in. No matter what the processes surrounding or benefiting from your core enterprise, if what you actually do doesn't answer a real need in a positive way, you're going to have a hard time feeling good about it or convincing anyone you're working with or for to do the same for very long.

Questioning the ethical commitment of a company such as Ben and Jerry's Homemade Ice Cream may be as outlandish as questioning the long-term profitability of a Wal-Mart. The company was started with end-to-end social responsibility foremost in mind. It is committed to using organic ingredients, grown in a sustainable manner, from local farmers wherever possible, and with continuous monitoring of environmental impact. The company's "social mission coordinator" oversees an employee-led grant-making program, and the human resources department is one of the most caring and lauded in any industry.[21]

But when push comes to shove, Ben and Jerry's makes ice cream in a nation where 64.5 percent of the population 20 or older is overweight, 30.5 percent are obese, and type II diabetes is at an all-time high.[22] According to the World Health Organization, obesity-related illnesses claim more than 500,000 lives each year.[23] Ben and Jerry's chocolate-dipped waffle cones each pack 320 calories and 10 grams of fat before any ice cream is added. Its homespun ads showing cows on clean pastures make ice cream look positively healthy. Does encouraging charitable giving, environmental responsibility, and fair labor standards compensate for the obesity encouraged by its products and marketing campaigns?

The contradiction just doesn't stand; and neither could Ben and Jerry's. With a sagging stock price and exhausted executives, the company agreed to be acquired by Unilever in 2000. Voicing a widespread sentiment, Governor Howard Dean told Reuters, "It would be a shame if it were sucked into the corporate homogenization that's taking over the planet."[24] Ben and Jerry attempted to reassure their remaining fans, explaining that theirs would remain a separate company with its own governing board. Of course, the truly radical move would have been to infect Unilever with a bit of Ben and Jerry's ethos from the inside out. By agreeing to be sectioned off, behemoth Unilever's standard operating procedures could remain unchallenged. Meanwhile, Ben and Jerry's adds yet another layer of contradiction to its already ambiguous mission: a socially conscious company selling sugar and fat to Americans, in the service of a Big Food conglomerate whose own practices Ben and Jerry's was originally born to contest.

This division between social responsibility and revenue generation costs companies in two ways. First, it disconnects their core businesses from the real needs of real people. So they lose track of the long-term benefits they mean to bring to their customers or constituents. Second, it turns their donations and charitable work into a drain on resources, rather than a way of growing new ones.

When I see the names of some of the corporations underwriting public television or AIDS charities, sometimes I can't help but laugh. Big Oil paying for a documentary about ecology? A weapons manufacturer paying for a show criticizing the Pentagon? This kind of behavior reminds me of the opening scene in *Godfather II,* in which a dozen "hits" ordered by Michael Corleone are intercut with a scene of the mobster in church for his son's baptism.

Corporations aren't the only ones with such glaringly contradictory behaviors. I'm often more surprised by the extent to which nonprofit organizations with no other stated intention than to do good end up working against their own efforts. They seem unaware that the things they actually do are as important as the issues they talk about.

Just last year, I was invited by a Nobel laureate, a New Age guru, and a Central American president to speak at a conference convened to launch a new organization dedicated to making the world more peaceful and environmentally conscious. By the time I got to the Caribbean resort where paying attendees munched on endangered Chilean seabass and drank spring water from tiny plastic bottles, I realized the conference's good intentions were not backed up by correspondingly well-thought-out actions. Making matters worse, they were publicizing their meeting using a questionable media tactic called "video news reports," or VNRs. These prepackaged stories are shot and edited by public relations companies and then distributed to budget-strapped local news channels to broadcast as if they were their own reported segments. In their effort to create some buzz for their fledgling civilization, my well-meaning hosts decided to utilize a form of media that seems destined to be remembered as one of the more egregious violations of television news standards.

These would-be messengers of peace ignore their inconsistencies at their own peril. For just like adding plastic to ground fill while complaining of global warming, it is internally incongruent to preach peace and understanding via corrupted messaging. In fact, if this conference really did want to make the headlines, the organizers would have stood a better chance at raising attention by forcing the hotel in which they stayed to adopt environmentally responsible policies (and then shown them the financial savings), demanding fair labor practices for hotel labor for just one weekend, serving organic vegetarian meals, or bringing speakers to the event via that blasted satellite instead of wasting so very many tons of jet fuel.

Like companies that engage in destructive business practices, then donate money to fix some portion of the mess they've made, nonprofit organizations, too, can only be judged on the basis of what they actually do. What services do they provide? Who are they helping? And how are they going about it?

Clearly, nonprofit enterprises can be just as internally inconsistent as any business. Even major religions, when they begin to view their constituencies as markets to be manipulated or maintained, rather than people to be served, end up getting in their own way.

The most profitable businesses and productive organizations in the twenty-first century, just like those of every century, will be the ones that help people create meaning, communicate better with one another, travel more efficiently, find new energy sources, achieve better health, or do better whatever it is they're trying to get done. Alternatives to oil, cures for AIDS, desalination of ocean water, replenishment of topsoil are among the great business opportunities of tomorrow, just as rail transportation, telephone communication, scientific agriculture, and patent medicines were the opportunities of yesterday.

Most bigger businesses today are too busy defending the particular solutions they came up with last century to continue developing new answers. They would do better to remember that they are the great experts in their areas, and the most capable of devising new approaches and then putting them into practice. Instead of hiring marketers to reposition the same old goods and services as something new, companies must come to accept innovation as the most stable and certain path to sustained success. Instead of hiring scenario planners to help strategize how to maintain the status quo by repressing change, competition, and alternative solutions, leading companies should see themselves as best positioned to manifest and thrive off the very changes they are resisting. The truest continuity for any enterprise is to address the real needs of whatever communities can benefit from its core competencies.

For individuals and corporations alike that solve problems and address real needs, there's no separation between profitable business and public service, and there's no need to compensate for one behavior with another. It's all good.

THE REAL STUFF

When a company is answering real needs, its role as a for-profit enterprise ends up married to its role as one of society's bene-factors. This doesn't mean just giving everyone what they want. If a company is going to undertake to provide the goods or services that fulfill people, it is going to have to take some fiduciary responsibility, as well. That's part of what people are paying for.

So it's not enough for a food manufacturer to put more sugar in its products, using increased sales to justify that it's giving people "what they want." People want good taste, but they don't want to be obese or sick—even if that's not foremost in their minds. A company like Odwalla, maker of naturally produced energy bars, is in the business of selling tasty snacks that are actually good for you. As a result, its marketing is at once a sales pitch and nutritional advocacy.

Or take the story of Seth Goldman, graduate of Yale School of Management who quit his high-paying job as a fund manager because it lacked meaning. Deciding his next project would be more connected to real needs, he came upon his idea for a new business while standing in a convenience store looking at the available beverages. Every drink—even the ones that claimed to be healthy—were filled with sugar. He didn't want any of them, and said to himself, "I want to do something about this."

Goldman shared his desire to make a new kind of drink with a former professor of his Barry Nalebuff, who, coincidentally, had just been to India for a case study on the tea industry. Among other things, he learned that most of the tea purchased for bottling by American companies was the lower-quality dust and fannings left after quality tea had been produced. He had gotten a first-hand look at a nation with labor, resources, and economic need. Together, Goldman and Nalebuff decided to create a low-sugar, completely organic beverage line called Honest Tea. A brand name like this, they concluded, would create "an obligation to do something socially responsible."

By starting with the premise to not just be a socially responsible company, but to make a socially responsible product as well, Goldman ended up discovering and addressing needs that many people didn't know existed. For instance, he learned that Americans might not really have as much of a sweet tooth as the supermarket shelves suggest. New research has shown that in market tests comparing beverages, people always choose the sweeter taste, even if they wouldn't have preferred that drink in a real-world context. The resulting sweetness inflation has nothing to do with answering real needs; it's about distorted market data. And along with artificially low prices of corn syrup due to government subsidies of corn, it has made soft drinks the number-one source of sugar in the American diet.

A portion of Honest Tea sales go back to the Indian and Native American communities that raise the herbs, as investments in health and education. But the real impact of the company is in its everyday trade practices, such as banning pesticides (other brands wash them off), ensuring fair labor standards, and maintaining environmental responsibility throughout the entire distribution scheme. Although books like David Brooks's *Bobos in Paradise* criticize such "crunchy" exercise as vain, ego-driven, boomer-fulfillment escapades, this one has turned out to be good business. In 2004, Honest Tea was on *Inc.* magazine's list of fastest-growing companies, with revenues of $6.5 million. When people are addressing real needs, the distinction between social action and business tends to disappear.

The unlikely career of transportation activist Aaron Naparstek takes the same shape as Goldman's. Naparstek was serving as a consultant for various new media companies, and had lived through the promise and perils of the dot-com boom. One morning, while working at his computer from his Brooklyn, New York, apartment, the interminable honking noise from the street got the better of him. He decided that if that one blue sedan that wouldn't stop honking was still there and making noise by the time he could go to the kitchen, get an egg, and return to the window, he would throw it at the car. Which he did.

"I realized that I had snapped. I had crossed a line. I had soaked up so much honking and road rage that I had become the honking."[25]

Instead of seeking therapy, Naparstek decided to let off a little steam more creatively than lobbing eggs, and wrote his first "honku":

> *You from New Jersey*
> *honking in front of my house*
> *in your SUV.*

He went out late at night and posted his little poem on telephone poles and signposts on his block. Each night, he came up with another honku. Then, he noticed something strange. Other people were writing and posting honkus, as well!

The honku phenomenon was picked up by *The New Yorker* magazine, and in turn became a successful book for Naparstek. But Aaron's encounter with the madness of Brooklyn urban planning, street signals, and road rage inspired him to learn more about these problems and their possible solutions. He became an authority on traffic issues in New York, an active leader of the bicycle and pedestrian advocate group Transportation Alternatives, and a *New York Press* columnist on transportation and energy issues. While Naparstek's work has led to bike lanes in Brooklyn, the cancellation of a drive-through Commerce Bank, and myriad crosswalk and traffic signal changes, it has also created an entirely new and profitable career path for him.

The lesson in Naparstek's experience is that addressing needs can start small. In a variation on the theme of Fidelity fund manager Peter Lynch's famous advice to invest in the companies making products you know and use yourself, Naparstek's activist and career paths emerged quite naturally from his pursuit of a single car horn outside his own window. In what we might even call "fractal activism," responding to the tiniest of perceived needs eventually forces us to address systemwide problems. And doing this yields enduring prosperity as a matter of course. Naparstek is currently at work on a documentary about traffic in America, a series of commissioned studies on oil capacity and energy alternatives, and a business plan for a new "green" taxi service in New York City. Stay tuned.

Not every effort at responding to real needs has to be so politically progressive in its sentiment. Whether designing a Mr. Clean Magic Eraser or a Swiffer, companies dedicated to answering real needs find enduring success by directing their innovative potential toward practical solutions. As a New Yorker, one of my favorites—but one that also reveals a flaw in our current understanding of sustainable profits—is the roach killer, Combat.

Most of us grew up in the era of synthetic insecticides and "crack-and-crevice" aerosol roach killers. Not only were these sprays toxic, but they were hard to contain. Spraying the kitchen meant poisoning the counter. Spraying the baseboards of the cabinets meant creating a hazard to pets. Besides, the formulations never seemed to work. Every few years, roaches would develop resistance to the ingredients, requiring the addition of new ones more toxic than the last. Like fighting bacteria with antibiotics, it seemed a losing battle.

Then, in 1979, some researchers at American Cyanamid in New Jersey happened upon a new solution to a 3,000-year-old problem. They were looking for new applications for an odorless, tasteless agricultural insecticide called hydramethylnon. It was a great poison, and environmentally much safer than spray insecticides. But there was a catch in applying it to our urban arthropods: like the agricultural pests that attacked plants sprayed with hydramethylnon, roaches would have to eat the stuff. And that's when the researchers came up with the idea of baited traps. They tested the concept by dipping communion wafers in hydramethylnon and waiting for roaches to come eat it. It worked. (They even toyed with the idea of selling wafers under the brand name "Last Supper."[26])

A few modifications later, they ended up with the plastic pucks we know today as Combat. Combat proved safer and more convenient than traditional sprays. Its active ingredient is quite toxic to cockroaches but much less so to mammals. It has a half-life in soil or water of less than two weeks, meaning it breaks down before reaching groundwater, and does not accumulate in crop plants.[27] Better still, the small plastic pucks in which the bait is delivered allow homeowners to control placement and limit pet and child access.

The unexpected consequence of Combat was its level of effectiveness. It turns out that not only did 10 to 20 percent of the roaches in a given area take the bait, but the poison was so mild that roaches that ate it had time to go home to their nests before they died. Other roaches would then eat the carcasses and suffer the same fate. Entire roach populations were wiped out.

Combat was so successful at killing roaches that, by the end of 2000, *Pest Control* magazine ran the headline "Are Cockroach Baits Simply Too Effective?"[28] After peaking at $80 million in 1995, the market for consumer-grade roach products had begun to shrink. It has gone down by 3 to 5 percent every year since then. Combat has killed its market along with all those roaches. Combat parent Clorox's marketing VP Derek Gordon put on a happy face, saying, "If we actually manage to drive ourselves out of business completely, frankly we'd feel like we did the world a service." Clorox execs seemed less impressed by Combat's service record, and sold off the brand to Henkel, of Germany, as part of a larger deal.[29]

Instead of selling off its winning Combat unit, Clorox might better have returned its scientists to the lab to exploit their growing expertise. They were the ones who figured out a new use for hydramethylnon after the agricultural market for it had leveled off. Perhaps this team could develop a version of the insecticide to kill the ants that, in many regions, took the place of the roaches.

In any case, businesses that succeed at solving problems should not be punished. Like a town refusing to pay the piper after he had rid it of rats, we abandon our most successful enterprises at our own peril. By quietly and safely addressing the great roach problem, Combat's scientists did us all a service. They also established themselves and their brand as the leader in a field, with applications far beyond urban roach control. Although we probably haven't heard the last from the roaches, in a world still fighting a scourge of insects from disease-carrying mosquitoes to tree-threatening caterpillars, we certainly haven't heard the last from the people behind Combat.

Finally, there are companies that set out both to solve a social ill and to make money while doing it. The World Resources Institute holds international conferences dedicated to "Eradicating Poverty through Profit" that have shown many Fortune 500 firms how to build vast markets by focusing on the 4 billion people who have been largely ignored as potential beneficiaries of corporate activity. Other companies have been conceived from the get-go with this aim in mind, and are quickly learning that providing solutions rather than palliative care for the most pressing global problems is not a drain on revenue but a tremendous business opportunity.

Paul Meyer, a former Clinton speechwriter and a friend of mine from the end of the dot-com days, was actually surprised the first time he realized his nonprofit work for humanitarian agencies could actually become sustainable businesses. A few weeks after the 1999 war in Kosovo, Meyer figured that the easiest way for family members to find one another would be to have access to the Internet. So he went over, set up a satellite dish, and started IPKO, the first Internet provider in Kosovo—and still the largest. It was hailed by the U.N. Secretary General as "a model for future humanitarian emergencies." And it became, for Meyer, a new way to think about his work: solving real problems can and should be good business.

He went on to found a company called Voxiva, dedicated to leveraging existing telephone technology in less developed nations to allow for the rapid dissemination of vital information. It's a simple but innovative concept: provide small cards with telephone numbers and two-digit codes that can be used to access special services on the Internet—without a computer. Voxiva's simple touchtone programs allow emergency workers and ordinary people to use special Internet databases through which to share and receive information about any number of urgent concerns, such as the outbreak or spread of diseases, and the locations and residents of refugee camps. "New identified case of Diptheria? Press 369." The market for these services? About 70 percent of the planet.

Of course, Voxiva has also proven a valuable utility to the distributors of everything from medicine to canned food. Voxiva can be used by local merchants to access ordering systems previously only available online, or by traveling distributors to report back inventories. The Department of Defense engaged Voxiva to deploy a national disease surveillance system in postwar Iraq. Meanwhile, Meyer was named a Global Leader for Tomorrow by the World Economic Forum in Davos, and Humanitarian of the Year by MIT's *Technology Review*. Operating on five continents and more than doubling his revenues every year since inception, Meyer's company earned $2.7 million in 2004, and over $6 million in 2005.

Now *that's* what I call laughing all the way to the bank.

THE NEED FOR MEANING

Responding to a genuine, practical need is the most direct way of developing a business that is necessarily aligned with the greater good. But not all needs are so very practical. What about businesses whose products may not cause any harm but neither do they serve an obvious essential need? Aren't there times when addressing real needs can take the form of addressing people's need for meaning?

It's dangerous territory, in which it's easy to fool ourselves that a new commercial or snazzy package is really a gift to society just because it's clever or pretty. Still, in a world driven largely by its markets and media, people depend on brands and products to represent and communicate their otherwise unarticulated values.

For example, Animal Planet is a successful national retail brand that helps people identify with environmentalism and wildlife preservation, while Nick at Nite acknowledges the social currency gathered in childhoods spent in front of the TV set. Brands like these can be value statements, but they only work in the long run when they are genuinely invested with those values by the people on the selling side of the equation. Just as the people working for Nick at Nite must genuinely value the cultural contributions of *The Dick Van Dyke Show* and *The Brady Bunch,* the managers of Animal Planet must source their products in a humane and ecological fashion.

It's easy to lament the fact that our children use the combination of labels in their wardrobe as a way of expressing who they are to their peers. For unlike religious or artistic iconography, most brand icons are not invested with values other than those calculated to best promote the product itself. The McDonald's double arches and Nike swoosh are imprinted indelibly into the minds of most of the world's children by the time they are 18 months old.[30] But are these symbols invested with the same intentions as those of our religious systems? Do they transmit ethics, respect for life, or human dignity?

A few of them do, and point toward an approach to communications that can actually allow a brand to impact people's lives in a positive way. All business is ethical if it's addressing the human need for well-being, meaning, and connection. For to do so, the business must bring itself into alignment with the values it is espousing with its brand. The core proposition of the brand must be congruent with the core proposition of the product.

Do consumers really demand such integrity? More than most businesses suspect. It is not coincidental that investment by individuals in socially responsible funds tends to go up during economic downturns. Following the dot-com crash and accounting scandals at Enron and Worldcom, mutual funds experienced their first net outflows in many years. The only sector spared was the social investment category, which has proven for the past five years to be a better filter for investments than most.

More than demonstrating the economic sense of investing in a socially responsible fashion (fewer lawsuits, scandals, and opportunities for ill will), the sustained interest in ethical ways of investing money shows that people are looking for more than returns. They want to feel good about how their money is working. Social responsibility funds, like the Calvert Index, are brand propositions. They give their customers the opportunity to speak with pride when they share their investment strategies with others. Many of these socially responsible fund brands are good products, but they are also good social currency. The better they align their dual proposition of generating returns while providing capital to worthy causes, the more they invest their brands with the kind of meaning system their customers are looking for.

Almost any company can be in the business of making meaning, but whatever the medium or product you're using to express those values simply must be consistent with the meaning system it's providing people.

Back in 1997, responding to the growing environmental concern among his employees, British Petroluem CEO Lord John Browne became the first major oil company executive to acknowledge global warming. In his speeches, he began to refer specifically to the contribution of fossil fuels to the problem. After resoundingly positive reception, Browne approached his adman, John Seifert of Ogilvy and Mather, for ways to spread this message further. As Seifert recalls, "Lord Browne came to me with a dream proposal. He said, 'I want this company to be a force for good in this world. Build that image and I will hold the company accountable to it.' "[31] Seifert did what he was told, launching the now-famous Beyond Petroleum campaign, and landing BP in a heap of trouble.

Any company deriving 99.5 percent of its revenues selling oil and gas would face mighty challenges representing itself to the public as moving beyond fossil fuels. But Browne saw himself beginning a long process that would start with a single conversation—a simple call and response. He'd declare BP's intent to move beyond petroleum, and consumers would respond by holding his company accountable over time.

Unfortunately, Lord Browne didn't get the results he expected. Environmental activists labeled the marketing effort "greenwashing," a public relations scheme to project an environmental image even though nothing was really being done. They were unsatisfied with BP's $200 million investment in solar energy, since it represented only a tiny fraction of the $26.5 billion it spent to buy ARCO in order to increase its production capacity for oil.[32] If BP were serious, Greenpeace and others argued, it would give up on drilling in Alaska and invest more seriously in solar power. Others pointed out that BP was spending not even 1 percent of its annual budget on renewable energy sources, representing several orders of magnitude less than they spend on advertising and public relations. In short, the Beyond Petroleum marketing campaign cost more than all the actual efforts to move beyond petroleum.

This wasn't the worst of it. City of London and other stock market analysts downgraded BP's stock, unconvinced that a company so large could transform itself so radically or ever compete with newcomers in renewable energy.[33] BP's shareholders responded in kind, and the stock price began to tank. BP shelved its Beyond Petroleum campaign temporarily, even though a culture of environmentalism persisted within the company.

Between undying employee commitment to the new BP and a spate of energy corporation scandals, BP began testing the waters, again. This time the company had a bit more success. Shareholders had learned the hard way that they would rather stick with a company that, at the very least, talked about the long-term impact of its actions. And BP had learned to temper its stridency with a bit of modesty. With each ad announcing another BP initiative, such as promising to grow its solar businesses to $1 billion by 2007, it added the caveat, "It's a start."

Leading energy policy journalists, such as Amanda Griscom, started warming to BP, realizing that starting a good conversation through brand values was as important as the initiatives being discussed: "I'd argue that BP's greatest contribution to the clean energy movement hasn't been its 20 percent marketshare in the solar industry, or even its 25 percent reduction of greenhouse gasses," she says, "but rather its flair for publicity. Hopefully, whatever greenwashing BP perpetrates to capture the public's attention and encourage debate will, in the long run, only force the company to become all the more accountable to its claims."[34]

Beyond Petroleum is a call-and-response campaign that puts BP on public trial and, as Seifert put it, "bridges the us/them barrier, that brings the consumer into the debate so that we can address the problem together."[35] When a brand is turned into a true meaning system, the company will eventually have to follow.

Breaking the commitment to a company's stated value system can prove disastrous. Royal Caribbean Cruise Lines declared itself a "green" company adhering to "Save the Waves" principles, yet was still forced to plead guilty to 21 felony counts for intentionally dumping waste oil and hazardous chemicals at sea rather than disposing of them properly (and more expensively) at port. Royal Caribbean also admitted to lying to the Coast Guard about its activities through falsification of logbooks and disposal of the bypass pipes used for dumping.[36] The company replaced any rhetoric about protecting the environment with ads built around an old Iggy Pop song. Although older travelers still patronize the cruise line, it will take more than the chorus of "Lust for Life" to rebuild a brand image with those who equate Royal Caribbean with raw sewage.

Nike, a brand based on the ancient Greek goddess of victory, never quite restored its meaning system after activists and, eventually, the mainstream media took the company to task for its treatment of underage sweatshop workers in developing nations. And Wal-Mart's promise of bringing prosperity and jobs to towns where its superstores land has been undermined by a reality of low wages and drains on local social services. Wal-Mart must fight widespread local insurrections whenever it applies for a building permit.

Even Apple could face serious challenges to the validity of its core premise of serving the creative community. Against its own ethos, the company decided to sue the authors of independent Web sites that leak news of Apple products before they are released. That Apple doesn't realize it's a bad idea to sue its most ardent fans and best publicists is one thing. That the company can't recognize how this corporate behavior contradicts its brand proposition could mark a tragic tide shift.

It's not just any nefarious practice that can undercut brand value systems in this way. As long as the meaning system people are paying for remains intact, companies can err in other, unrelated ways. Just as Bill Clinton remained popular despite his extramarital affairs, Martha Stewart's brand was only temporarily and superficially damaged by her illegal exploits on Wall Street. That's because insider trading has nothing specifically to do with a meaning system based on quality, craft, and elegance. Would we invest with her? No. But we would still buy her bath mats. Customers will overlook a lot in order to get what they want—except failings in the articles of faith specific to a given brand meaning system.

Congruence is the name of the game in any quest to make meaning for people. Brand is the beginning, but the products or services must follow through. Sometimes the best way to communicate a brand proposition is to lead with the product, and then let marketing follow through. An ad or marketing plan doesn't have to be directed entirely at new customers; it can just as easily educate existing consumers about the brand values they happened to buy into.

Most people buying Patagonia outerwear for the first time have little awareness of the company's rather extraordinary mission to save the planet. They just want some warm, well-made gear for some up-coming outdoor adventure. Patagonia provides the adventurer with more than high-quality fleece. The company gives its customers a meaning system consistent with the values of today's global travelers, and a corporate policy that allows buyers to improve the health of the environment with each purchase.

Patagonia is noteworthy for the sheer magnitude of its impact, such as donating a 155,000-acre estate to Argentina's National Parks system, restoring a significant portion of Oregon's woods, or giving grants to independent environmentalists. But what makes the company exemplary for our purposes is the congruence between corporate behavior, product attributes, and brand culture. Unlike Ben and Jerry's or BP, these elements combine to make a meaning system that is both ideologically and practically consistent.

Patagonia's meaning system emerges pretty organically from its culture: "We prefer the human scale to the corporate, vagabonding to tourism, the quirky and lively to the toned down and flattened out." [37] Patagonia sees itself as a culture dedicated to "dirtbags"—people who have temp jobs so that they can take long breaks; people who do "tribal travel," following the seasons, even foraging for meals between surfing, climbing, or exploring. And though most of Patagonia's customers have grown up and gotten real jobs and lives, the brand allows them to reconnect with the meaning system to which they still feel committed.

Patagonia follows through on the dirtbag ethos in both its product line and its corporate giving. One doesn't compensate for the other. Patagonia uses organic cotton and recycled fleece and shell materials, so that its manufacturing takes as little toll as possible on the environment. The products themselves are designed to be versatile rather than particular, so that consumers don't have to purchase an entire product line in order to be equipped, and so that hikers can get by with the fewest items in their packs. Patagonia is an acknowledged leader in the innovation of new fabrics and processes, such as stitch-free seams and "base-layer" wicked insulation that keeps the body warm from the inside out.

Finally, as we've seen, Patagonia has demonstrated a corporate commitment to protecting the very landscapes and lifestyles its customers cherish the most. It gives its own employees a vacation schedule that accommodates the vagabond lifestyle, and requires them to adhere to the Patagonia value system. Even people applying for jobs are asked to be "environmentally responsible in the presentation" of their information.

People purchasing Patagonia clothing may not know about the company's meaning system until afterward, or ever. But the more they use the products, the more opportunities the company will have to share its values—through literature on tags, the Web site, and the quality of its workmanship. A modern garment that lasts for a decade or more makes a communication all its own.

Unlike most corporations adopting an environmental culture, operation, and brand image, Patagonia is at little risk of being "found out." This is because, luckily, the owners' and employees' passion originates from this core ethos. Congruent behavior of this magnitude requires faith in the central premise. If you don't have that faith, you won't commit unconditionally to your own cause, and the gaps between your enterprise's mission and actions will become more pronounced.

This can happen to any institution dedicated to selling a meaning system rather than exemplifying it.

Not even religions are free from this sin. In a desperate attempt to remain relevant to young people, proselytizers of failing faiths fund rock concerts, publish cynically "hip" magazines, and even offer cash scholarships to girls who submit to a medical exam proving they are virgins on entering college. Instead of simply offering what they have to people who might need it, these religions are communicating by association, repackaging, or offering extrinsic rewards. As in any enterprise with such a self-negating strategy, the core proposition is devalued and the core competency withers.

I've been summoned by more than one religious foundation looking to "rebrand" its faith for the twenty-first century. To Lutherans, Methodists, and Jews alike, I suggested that the best way to jumpstart a religion is to restore the core processes from whence it came. If Judaism and Christianity are really inquiries into the nature of existence, quests for meaning, or paths toward greater compassion, then why not invite young people to engage in those activities and see what, if any, needs emerge? I crafted invitations for daylong events at which participants were welcome to discuss their faiths—or lack of them—in any way they chose, or even to rebuild their creed from the ground up. Open-source religion.

The results surprised my clients. Invariably, the chief complaint was that churches and synagogues seemed to be obsessed with religious fidelity, intermarriage, conservative politics, and self-preservation rather than offering any invitation to a spiritual path. Simply letting these kids talk about their real relationship to religion made them want to explore further on their own. They went home and started Bible and Torah study groups! They didn't want to be religion's consumers, but its new stewards. You'd think this would count as a success.

Unfortunately, these religious foundations were obsessed with promoting the very objectives their target markets despised: preventing intermarriage and premarital sex, increasing official membership counts, and maintaining steadfast and automatic support for conservative causes or Israeli policy. Selling these priorities to people who rejected them would call for some heavy public relations guns. So in came scores of consultants who were supposedly knowledgeable about this generation and how to market to them: scenario planners, trend watchers, and even Republican pollster Frank Luntz were recruited by some of the same foundations that had called on me. Predictably, these experts decided that for religions to be more relevant to young people, they would have to be made more compatible with the lifestyles depicted on MTV.[38] If young people aspired to being hip, then religion would have to become as trendy as *The Real World* and as tawdry as an MTV *Spring Break* special. Each religion would become a new brand identity—its icons the next "bling."

What the rebranders of these religions didn't realize was that their methodology and, as it turns out, their motivations went against the core value propositions of their faiths: connecting with people regardless of social status, doing unto others, and getting beyond pretense. By adopting a positioning so inconsistent with the core values of their religions, these well-meaning foundations merely exposed their lack of faith in their own offerings, and further alienated their would-be members. If they cared as much about serving their constituencies as they did about extending their brands, they would have had much better luck in their efforts.

The offering of any business or consumer proposition should be undertaken with no less consideration for congruence in message and action. In fact, more businesses should approach both their products and meaning systems with the sense of integrated purpose with which we approach a sacred undertaking.

By abandoning the us-and-them mentality, and instead engaging with our customers, employees, shareholders, and even the uninvolved as potential beneficiaries of our enterprises, we stand a chance of serving real people through everything we do. This requires we achieve true congruence between our intentions, our cultural values, our products, and the impact of our operations. Our target markets instead become the communities we aim to serve, and our prosperity is not merely a personal gain but the fuel for a virtuous circle.

I didn't fully get this principle, myself, until I finally set out to write this book. I made a valiant pitch to a number of literary agents, to see how they thought publishers would react to the idea. Most of them were excited by the breadth of research and the clever insights I had unearthed. But one young woman, by reputation and deed one of the most astute literary minds on the block, called me on my own sense of purpose.

"Who are you writing this book for?" she asked.

"People should know this," I responded. "We're in the midst of a new renaissance."

"Yes, but what need are you addressing?"

"I don't get you."

She smiled, closed my folder, and handed the proposal back to me.

"When you figure out how all this great stuff you learned can answer a real need that other people have, then you'll have a book to sell."

She was right. I knew why *I* wanted to write the book, but I didn't know whom I meant to serve with it. That's when I came to understand the biggest lesson any one of us can take from this new renaissance: it's not about *me*.

epilogue

THE NEW RENAISSANCE PERSON

The story up to now: Those of us smart or lucky enough to get back in the box are free to develop a framework of playful abundance that fuels unending inquiry and innovation. Discovering this bounty of creative potential takes our attention off of selling to people and puts it onto serving them.

But then what? And what happens when everyone else learns these principles? Do those of us who already "get it" lose our competitive edge? And if we've dispensed with competition, altogether, in favor of collaborating, what's left to motivate us?

These are the kinds of questions I hear every day. They usually come from people who are on the verge of adopting a new approach to life and work, but haven't quite made the leap. They're still doing the new renaissance by the numbers, mindfully subduing patterns of thought and behavior that they know to be obsolete or even destructive to their work and lives. Eventually, however, the wealth of positive experiences that result from living this way outweigh the fear and paranoia about doing so. The evidence just becomes too overwhelming. That's when a person can let go of the reasoning behind adopting a renaissance approach and start living that way spontaneously.

A whole new set of interests and aspirations then come into play.

A person starts doing things not for any particular gain, but *for their own sake*. We've all met people like this. They move through life with a confidence and assuredness so profound that they seem more interested in helping or encouraging *us* than accomplishing anything for themselves.

Our new renaissance, just like the previous one, defines not only a new cultural and commercial reality, but also a new kind of person. The New Renaissance Person.

The original Renaissance Man, as we might expect from what we already know about priorities in the 1500s, was a strident individual. For along with literacy and perspective came the abstract notion of the person as a separate entity, capable of having his own point of view. Sure, there were individuals before the Renaissance, but they existed mostly as parts of small groups—the identity and interests of the tribe or clan took precedence over those of any particular member. This idea of a human being as a "self" with independent will and capacity was pure Renaissance—a rebirth and extension of the ancient Greek conception of the citizen. And from it came all sorts of progressive notions, such as the natural autonomy of the individual, the importance of human agency, and the benefits of a meritocracy. The newly discovered—or perhaps "invented"—right to individual freedom was what eventually led to the French and American revolutions, the first modern democracies, and the notion of a republic. The values of freedom and individual rights we embrace and extend as Westerners, today, are based in some very particular beliefs about personhood, born in that original Renaissance.

Having spent so much time under the direct authority of the church, people hoped to enter a new age of self-reliant individualism. These "total personalities" were embodied by people such as Leonardo da Vinci, who was not only a painter but also an inventor and engineer; Michelangelo, who in addition to painting was an accomplished architect and sculptor; or Sir Walter Raleigh, pirate, knight, army commander, and New World explorer.

The irony, of course, is that all of this individual achievement was utterly dependent on central authorities. Both Michelangelo and

Leonardo worked exclusively within the patronage system. They were under the strict control of the court, the wealthiest of families, such as the Medicis, or the Pope. Sir Walter Raleigh's adventures and title were bestowed on him by the queen—and once that royal family was succeeded by another less friendly to his cause, he was promptly beheaded. So much for standing on one's own.

Renaissance individuality amounted to a competition for the graces and resources of the truly wealthy. As power became more centralized, individuals left their tribal and familial groupings to compete for how high they could rise in the greater system. We like to think of it as a high-minded meritocracy, but the rat race that ensued only strengthened the authority of central command. We learned to compete for resources and credit made artificially scarce by centralized banking and government.

Sure, competition has been a powerful motivator, particularly when enabled by capitalism; in a developing marketplace and on a level playing field, it can yield terrific innovation and growth. But measuring success individually took us only so far. By the modern age, our use of the "individual" as a model for a healthy existence has reached absurd proportions, and we've ceased being able to see ourselves any other way.

Freud told us that not only is each of us an individual with his own outlook and experience, but there's also another entity beneath that one, a subconscious, whose thoughts and intentions we can only discern through dream analysis or hypnosis. Great. Meanwhile, marketers reinforced our experience of ourselves as separate individuals— consumers deserving of at least one of everything we might desire. Why share when you can own? Notions such as self-sacrifice and civil society gave way to self-help and (nuclear) family values. For when we worry about our own well-being or that of our family, we have a great justification for our competitive behavior. After all, we've got mouths to feed and unformed personalities to protect. Sadly, however, by going it alone we're sunk before we begin. Very few people will ever be able to earn enough money to buy and provide everything they and their children might possibly need—and have a life at the same time. It really does take a village. Making oneself independent of need—independent of others—is itself a full-time job with limited returns.

But just as Freud's model of the individual-within-the-individual gave way to his student Carl Jung's idea of a "collective unconscious," linking us all just beneath the surface, the every-man-for-himself ethic of the consumer is giving way to a desire for community and connectedness. Just as the successful business learns how to provide social currency through which customers can interact, the successful person—the New Renaissance Person—defines himself not by his abilities, worth, or possessions, but by his connections to others.

Like the walled cities of the Renaissance and before, "self" has always been defined by a person's boundaries: the edges of the body or the limits on one's capabilities. Our new renaissance allows us to see these same boundaries, instead, as points of contact. A person is not the sum total of the abilities he contains, but the totality of his connections. Just as Web sites succeed not by their own strength but by the strength of their links, a person's abilities are extended to include those of all the people he can access. As Internet enthusiasts like to say, the power of a network is not the nodes, it's the connections. You are your address book.

This doesn't mean a person can't do anything himself. Each of his connections must go two ways. The tremendous access a New Renaissance Person has to the abilities of others is dependent on their ability to access *his*. Like a file-sharing program through which people can download files from one another's hard drives, the more files anyone has, the more files *everyone* has. The competitive paradox vanishes. The more people who "get it," the better. Just as it's useless to be the only person with a fax machine, it's pointless to be the only renaissance person in town. The more renaissance people we can create, the better.

Luckily for this proposition, our common understandings of personal freedom and point of view really have evolved. In a holograph, fractal, or even an Internet Web site, perspective is no longer about the individual observer's position; it's about that individual's connection to the whole. Any part of a holographic plate recapitulates the whole image; bringing all the pieces together simply brings greater resolution. Likewise, the tiniest detail of a fractal image reflects the whole system. Even the brain is now thought to work in a holographic fashion, with memories and functions shared by cells seemingly very far apart from one another.

Sciences ranging from quantum physics and chaos math to string theory all propose an interconnectedness where order and consciousness themselves emerge from networked systems, rather than the other way around. Even hard rationalists are exploring the possibilities of a measurable collective unconscious. Researchers at Princeton University have a developed a random number generator that responds, inexplicably, to events that generate widespread collective focus, from 9-11 to the tsunami in the Indian Ocean. Dubbed the Global Consciousness Project, it is dedicated to "registering coherence and resonance in the world."[1]

We are coming to appreciate that everything is connected to and reflective of everything else—and, moreover, actually defined by these associations.

That's why new models for both collaboration and progress have emerged during our renaissance, ones that obviate the need for competition between individuals and instead value the power of collectivism. People are already spending a significant portion of their time and energy adapting to these new models. Social networking tools such as Friendster, Linked-in, Dodgeball, and Meet-up not only give people the ability to connect with others, they also function as dynamic maps of a person's connections at any given moment. These personalized networks give the novice new renaissance player a sense of control over his inventory of available connections. The way a map of the country may have once delineated a landowner's extended sense of self, these maps of human contacts help people conceptualize the potentials for advice, support, and interplay.

The open source development model, shunning the secrecy of the competitive marketplace, promotes the free and open exchange of the codes underlying the software we use. In the examples we looked at earlier, everyone is invited to make improvements and additions, and the resulting projects are more nimble, stable, and user-friendly. Likewise, the development of complementary currency models, such as Ithaca Hours, allow people to determine together—without a mediating authority—what their goods and services are worth to one. They don't need to compete for currency in order to pay back a central creditor, so currency becomes an enabler of collaborative efforts rather than purely competitive ones.

Meanwhile, like children growing up into adulthood, we learn to depend less on central authorities for a sense of worth and security, as well. In part, this is by necessity. Whereas our parents could count on the first corporation that hired them to see them through to retirement, we have come to expect no such recompense for our dedication. Job security is an oxymoron, since only the independent contractor can spread his bets—and his associations—across a wide enough spectrum to offer himself any stability. The "company man" who does succeed is someone who shows more loyalty to the people he works with and for than to the company itself. And he's probably a better asset that way, too.

So, what kind of job does the New Renaissance Person have, anyway? It seems like another paradox: If he's a specialist, then he has surrendered to the categories of the central authority; if he's a generalist, then he hasn't really gotten into the box!

The New Renaissance Person is a specialist, but not necessarily in the categories or disciplines predetermined by the job market or the universities he's attended. He's a specialist in the path of exploration that has excited him most and given him the greatest opportunity to provide something meaningful to others. He can be a generalist, too, but to a New Renaissance Person even this becomes a core competence. The generalist crosses disciplines and areas of expertise in order to draw connections between them. He is the one who knows how to marry one company's expertise with another. The connector knows all there is to know about making connections, from the psychology of collaboration to the ability of the gingko plant to graft itself onto almost any other tree. Even the generalist goes deep, because—if he's in flow—that's where the fun lies.

The New Renaissance Person is not motivated by competition, gain, or even the desire for achievement, but by a quest for deep, playful inquiry and a desire to bring this renaissance sensibility to others.

Self-help gurus and motivation specialists miss the point. They're still bringing people up "Maslow's hierarchy of needs," from basic concerns like food and shelter up through emotional needs and to the ultimate goal of "self-actualization." But what use is self-actualization when the "self" is itself an artifact of another era?

The New Renaissance Person may as well be a golf pro as a businessman. He is simply someone who has achieved the new renaissance perspective, yet is willing to dive back into the affairs of real people and help them achieve this same level of liberation from the illusion of personal concerns and the need for competitive strife. In Buddhism, such a character is known as a bodhisattva. In the terminology of play theory, this character is the "spoil sport," who sees through the stakes of the game and calls our attention to their unreality. In aboriginal cultures, such a person was revered as a shaman, uniquely capable of seeing the connections between things that others could not, and taking troubled individuals on a journey beyond the frontiers of self.

Today, popular culture reimagines these capable characters as wizards, from Tolkien's Gandalf and Neo of *The Matrix* to the irrepressible Harry Potter. The wizard is aware of the subtle connections between things—connections that still seem invisible to everyone else. These are the kinds of figures who, as described by Buddhism, understand that the game occupying everyone's attention is unreal, yet still return for "joyful participation in the sorrows of the world." Like Nietzsche's "Overman," they have an "integral awareness" of our collective plight that gives humanity its best chance for evolution.

While the Renaissance invented the individual and spawned many institutions enabling personal choices and freedoms, our new renaissance is instead reinventing the collective in a new context. Originally, the collective was the clan or the tribe, an entity defined no more by what members had in common with each other than by what they had in opposition to the clan or tribe over the hill.

Networks add new dimensions to our potential relationships to one another. Membership in one group does not preclude membership in myriad others. We are all parts of a multitude of overlapping groups, often with conflicting or contradictory priorities. Because we can contend with having more than one perspective at a time, we needn't force them to compete for authority in our hearts and minds; we can hold them all, provisionally. That's the beauty of renaissance: our capacity to contend with multiple dimensions is increased. Things don't have to be just one way. We can embrace a spontaneous, emergent, and multifaceted reality.

As collaborators, we are no longer setting ourselves up for exclusion, conflict, or even the postponement of joy. We don't need to dangle the carrots of cash prizes, salvation, and spiritual enlightenment (or threaten with the corresponding sticks) in order to get others to join in our enterprises, because they are so much fun to do right now, for their own sake.

By the same token, our relationship to the human story changes, as well. Instead of aching toward conclusion, and seeing every global, business, or personal crisis as a sign of either impending catastrophe or paradigm shift, we evolve together as a natural course of events. We won't get those dramatic, cataclysmic jolts to look forward to, but neither will we need them. New threads and understandings simply emerge from our collective engagement, just as new traits and species emerge from our exchange of genomes.

Once we feel confident and competent enough to offer something of value to our fellows, we are free to recontextualize our enterprises and our very evolution as a team sport, rather than a competition. There's just one thing going on here, however many eyes and "I's" it may seem to have. Because, in the final analysis, there is no New Renaissance Person, just new renaissance people. We all make it, together, or none of us really does.

notes

PREFACE

1 Robert Peston, "Stirred but Not Shaken: Robert Peston on How the Saatchis Met Their Nemesis—and Then Bounced Back," *Financial Times* (London), January 11, 1997.

2 "Saatchi's Colourful History," *BBC News*, June 6, 2000.

3 Abrams, Abrams, "Ad Agency Acquisitions Increasing As Firms Seek World-Wide Market," *Wall Street Journal*, July 11, 1983.

4 Robert Peston, "Stirred but Not Shaken."

5 The Economist Staff, "The Demise of the Saatchi Brothers Was a Victory for Owners Over Founders," *The Economist*, January 24, 1994–January 6, 1995.

6 Janis Mara, "List Man," *Mediaweek*, August 21, 2000.

7 Ibid.

8 Donna Howell, "Craig's Online List of Stuff Became Popular Web Job Site," *Investor's Business Daily*, May 25, 2000.

9 Michael Bazeley, "eBay Buys 25 Percent Stake in San Francisco–Based Web Site Craigslist," *KnightRidder/Tribune Business News*, August 14, 2004.

10 Ken and Daria Dolan, "CraigsList.com Survived Dot-Com Bust by Putting Service First," *Dolans Unscripted*, Cable News Network (CNN), January 12, 2004.

INTRODUCTION

1   Bill Breen, "Sirius and XM Are Taking Strategy and Competition to the Skies in an Epic, Multi-Billion-Dollar Struggle to Dominate Next-Generation Radio," *Fast Company*, February 1, 2005.

2   Ibid.

3   Annys Shin, "At XM, Boldly Going; Under Hugh Panero, Satellite Radio Is a Hit. Just Ask Howard Stern and Mel Karmazin," *Washington Post*, November 29, 2004.

4   Bill Breen, "Sirius and XM Are Taking Strategy."

5   Gary Hill, "Journalist Says SEC Subpoenas Him on Stern, Sirius," *Reuters*, February 19, 2005, www.reuters.com.

6   Bill Breen, "Sirius and XM Are Taking Strategy."

7   Pamela McClintock, "Karmazin: We're Sirius and XM's Not; Topper Remains Upbeat at Bear Stearns Confab," *Daily Variety*, March 2, 2005.

8   Patrick Reilly, quoted in Bill Breen, "Sirius and XM Are Taking Strategy."

9   Bill Breen, "Sirius and XM Are Taking Strategy."

10   Ibid.

11   While this sort of observation may remind readers of Hegel and other pre-Fascist philosophers who saw the world as a single organism, please remember that they had much simpler conceptions of how the parts of a system relate. They had no knowledge of emergent systems and saw direction coming from the top.

12   As philosopher Fritjof Capra liked to say, "The rational mind is always in doubt."

13   We'll get to this more explicitly in Chapter Six, "Open Source Everything."

CHAPTER ONE

1   Joseph Tainter, "The Collapse of Complex Societies," 1988. In
Richard Heinberg, *The Party's Over: Oil, War, and the Fate of Industrial
Societies* (Garbriola Island, CA: New Society Publishers, 2003).

2   America, rich in fuel, served as an energy resource for Europe up until
the United States won independence—at which point Europe became
a technology supplier to the resource-rich United States.

3   Richard Heinberg, *The Party's Over: Oil, War, and the Fate of Industrial
Societies* (Garbriola Island, CA: New Society Publishers, 2003), 55.

4   Commerce Department Report, July 2003.

5   Hubbert's peak was named for a Shell Oil geologist, M. King
Hubbert. See *Hubbert's Peak: The Impending World Oil Shortage*
(Princeton: Princeton University Press, 2001), by Hubbert's colleague,
Kenneth S. Deffeyes. At first debated wildly by the energy industry, it
has proved itself quite true.

6   In 1865, William Stanley Jevons wrote *The Coal Question,* in which he
concluded that just as England's rise was a result of the ability to
exploit coal, its fall would be an inevitable result of the inability to
find more, indefinitely. His argument is deconstructed in Vaclav Smil's
Energy at the Crossroads: Global Perspectives and Uncertainties
(Cambridge, MA: MIT Press, 2003).

7   Or, as culture critic Walter Benjamin explained it, "World exhibitions
were places of pilgrimage to the fetish Commodity." Walter
Benjamin, "Paris—the Capital of the Nineteenth Century," in Walter
Benjamin, *The Arcades Project,* translated by Howard Eiland and
Kevin McLaughlin (Cambridge, MA: Harvard University Press,
2002), 165. Also see Karl Marx, *Das Kapital,* vol. 1, 163–177. Quoted
in Barbook, *New York Prophecies,* unpublished work-in-progress.

8   Richard Barbrook, "NEW YORK PROPHECIES: The Future Is
What It Used To Be." *Mute,* July 7, 2004. See www.metamute.com.

9   Using Taylor's methods, the Bethlehem Steelworks was able to cut its
workforce from 500 down to 140.

10 Actually, the assembly line was first used by Sears Roebuck and Co.

for its mail order factory. It was Ford that institutionalized the practice, after being inspired by seeing cows being transported on conveyor belts through a slaughterhouse. Some great background on this is available in the section on Scientific Management at the *Accel Team Website*, www.accel-team.com.

11   Richard H. Steckel, "A History of the Standard of Living in the United States," *Economic History Services Encyclopedia*, www.EH.net.

12   See the work of David Ricardo, James Mill, or Robert Torrens for more on Adam Smith's argument for the benefits of specialization extended to the power of free trade. One good text on this is Leonard Gomes, *The Economics and Ideology of Free Trade: A Historical Review* (Northampton, MA: Edward Elgar Publishing, 2003).

13   Sources for this statement include: Arcelor SWOT Analysis by *Datamonitor*, 2004. www.datamonitor.com; *The American Metal Market* (particularly September 15, 2003, and September 3, 2004); and statement of Keith Collins, chief economist, U.S. Department of Agriculture, before the U.S. Senate Committee on Appropriations, subcommittee on Agriculture, Rural Development, and Related Agencies, May 17, 2001. For Telecom, see FCC Commission En Banc Hearing of Monday, October 7, 2002, as well as then-chairman Michael Powell's statements on how mergers indicate glut of services, available through the FCC Web site at www.fcc.gov.

14   Bureau of Economic Analysis, Federal Trade Commission.

15   Booz Allen Hamilton study: "Airline Merger Integration" by Tom Hansson, Gary Neilson, and Sören Belin, January 2002.

16   Fleet Capital, "Why Lean Times May Be the Right Time for M&A," *Capital Eyes*, September 2003. Excerpted from a study by Boston Consulting Group.

17   Interestingly, the OpEd solicited by the *New York Times* from me on the subject, on the day of the announcement, was pulled from the page for its unnecessary "negativity" about the merger. It ran in the (London) *Guardian*, instead. See my commentary on the saga there: Douglas Rushkoff, "Signs of the Times: The AOL and Time Warner Merger Was Doomed from the Start," *Guardian*, July 25, 2002.

18   See articles and complaints, including: "People Magazine Cuts Five

Jobs; Cross-Divisional Volunteers' Period Has Begun." June 5, 2003; "Is Time Inc. Crazy?" October 18, 2001. Both are available on the New York Newspapers Guild Web site at www.nyguild.org. And David Lieberman, "AOL Time Warner Cuts 2,000 Jobs in Surprise Move," *USA Today*, January 24, 2001.

19   Jon Fine, "Crunchtime: Time Inc.," *Advertising Age*, May 7, 2001.

20   Editorial Staff, "Ms. Fiorina's Fatal Operating Error," *New York Times*, February 11, 2005.

21   Ibid.

22   Gregor Andrade and Erik Stafford, "Investigating the Economic Role of Mergers," working paper, 1999, Harvard Business School.

23   Poindexter Inc. is a leader in this field. It uses IP address, time of day, and referring links, among other data, to model probable profiles of Web site guests, and then call up banner ads meant for that market segment.

24   See my book *Coercion: Why We Listen to What "They" Say* (New York: Riverhead, 1999), 83.

25   Though often credited with inventing the dumbwaiter, Jefferson was really just responsible for significant improvements and its more widespread use in the home.

26   Gallup Poll, cited in Shoshana Zuboff, "From Subject to Citizen," *Fast Company*, May 2004.

27   This survey was conducted in 2000, before the market tanked and Wall Street lost 30,000 jobs, leading to a long series of investor lawsuits. See: Landon Thomas, Jr., "Depression, A Frequent Visitor to Wall St.," *New York Times*, September 12, 2004.

CHAPTER TWO

1   Seventeen percent of Americans believe the world will end in their lifetimes, according to a recent *Newsweek* poll cited by Frank Rich in his editorial, "Now on DVD: The Passion of the Bush," *New York Times*, October 3, 2004.

2   Invariably, the software applications developed by this community stressed communication over mere data retrieval—sharing over getting. They were egalitarian in design. IRC chats and USENET groups, for example, present every contributor's postings in the same universal ASCII text.

3   Several graduate students and I researched these results using the NexisLexis news search engine.

4   Drug Enforcement Agency Statistics, quoted in Adrianne Jeffries, "Prescription Drug Abuse," *Cherubs* (2003), a journal of the National High School Institute at Northwestern University.

5   For more on emergence theory and how it plays out in real life, see Steven Johnson, *Emergence: The Connected Lives of Ants, Brains, Cities, and Software* (New York: Scribner, 2001).

6   Interview with the author, in "The Persuaders," PBS *Frontline,* first aired November 9, 2004.

7   See Norbert Wiener, *The Human Use of Human Beings,* 2nd ed. (New York: Anchor Press, 1954).

8   A famous *Mother Jones* article of the period documented a sharp increase in Valium prescriptions at AT&T. For more on that article, as well as stories from employees on being dispensed "greenies" containing Valium by their supervisors, visit The Bell System Memorial, www.bellsystemmemorial.com/stories.html.

9   Shannon Quinn and Leslie Cintron, "If Technology Makes Our Lives Easier, Why Are We So Stressed Out?" *New York Times,* OpEd, September 9, 2000.

10   Thomas W. Gainey (of the State University of West Georgia) and Donald E. Kelley and Joseph A. Hill (of Francis Marion University), "S.A.M.," *Advanced Management Journal,* Fall 1999.

11   See Michel Foucault, *The Foucault Reader* (New York: Pantheon, 1984).

12   See my article, "The Power of Three: When Technology, Business, and Marketing Converge," *The Feature,* February 23, 2004, www.thefeature.com.

13   Tracie Rozhon, "Brand Names Are Paying the Price for a Change in Shopping Trends," *New York Times,* December 10, 2003.

CHAPTER THREE

1 Mitch Rattcliffe, "iPods get people laid and can improve their memories, too!" Mitch Rattcliffe Blog, December 9, 2004, www.ratcliffeblog.com/archives/000258.html.

2 Interestingly this same dearth of civic organizations accompanied the last great set of technological changes at the turn of the century, as the automobile, electricity, and telephones eroded the existing fabric of American society. For more on this, see: Bob Putnam, *Bowling Alone: The Collapse and Revival of American Community* (New York: Simon & Schuster, 2001).

3 See William Leach, *Land of Desire: Merchants, Power, and the Rise of a New American Culture* (New York: Vintage, 1994).

4 See, for example, the studies cited by the United Nations Platform for Action Committee AC, at http://unpac.ca/economy/consumers.html.

5 One fast-food restaurant designer claimed he could make a seat that was comfortable—but for only 20 minutes. See the chapter on "Atmospherics" in my book *Coercion: Why We Listen to What "They" Say* (New York: Riverhead, 1999).

6 Douglas Atkin, *The Culting of Brands: When Customers Become True Believers* (New York: Portfolio, 2004), 117.

7 See, for example, Caroline E. Mayer, "Nurturing Brand Loyalty: With Preschool Supplies, Firms Woo Future Customers—and Current Parents," *Washington Post,* October 12, 2003.

8 See Douglas Atkin, *The Culting of Brands,* for an excellent and detailed analysis of this and other cult brand phenomena.

9 John Entine, "Shattered Image: Is the Body Shop Too Good to Be True?" *Business Ethics,* May 1994.

10 Laurence Zuckerman, "Ambitious Low-Fare Carrier Names Itself Jet-Blue Airways," *New York Times,* July 15, 1999.

11 Douglas Atkin, *The Culting of Brands,* 65.

12 Michelle Krebs, "Saturn Just May Have a Future," *Global Auto,* January 20, 2005, www.globalauto.net.

CHAPTER FOUR

1 Roger Caillois took some of these ideas even further in his *Man, Play and Games* (Chicago: University of Illinois Press, 2001). He refined Huizinga's analysis by classifying the different categories of play, making them even more applicable to work and education. Both Caillois and Huizinga, however, took issue with anyone attempting to break the "sacred circle" by "corrupting" play with purpose.

2 *CFO* magazine, cited in Claudia H. Deutsch, "Where Have All the Chief Financial Officers Gone?" *New York Times,* November 28, 2004.

3 Ibid.

4 Shannon Quinn and Leslie Cintron, "If Technology Makes our Lives Easier, Why Are We So Stressed Out?" *New York Times*, OpEd, September 9, 2000.

5 Alain de Botton, "Workers of the World, Relax," *New York Times,* September 6, 2004.

6 Mihaly Csikszentmihalyi, *Flow* (New York: HarperPerennial, 1991), 148.

7 Ibid.

8 Don't confuse this with Marxism. Marx and his cohorts saw work and productivity as a privilege, not a chore. The human being, in his natural state, works hard and enjoys work. It's only the exploitation of this labor, or the omission of the workers' labors from the economic equation, that are to be questioned.

9 A psychedelic collective that traveled the United States by bus, and was immortalized in Tom Wolfe's *Electric Kool-Aid Acid Test* (New York: Farrar, Straus & Giroux, 1968).

10 Interestingly, as we'll see in Chapter Five, Shell wasn't able to emerge from these experiences unscathed. Like a college student coming down off a bad trip, Shell went on a desperate search for out-of-the-box saviors, and only recently restabilized.

11 GBN Web site, "History," www.gbn.com.

12 Pat Kane, *The Play Ethic: A Manifesto for a Different Way of Living* (London: Macmillan, 2004).

13 Mildred Parten, "Social Participation among Preschool Children," *Journal of Abnormal and Social Psychology,* 27 (1932): 243–269.

14 See Clay Shirky's writings on this and other subjects at www.shirky.com.

15 Howard Rheingold, "Toward a Literacy of Cooperation," course description, http://shl.stanford.edu/hum202_classnotes.html, December 13, 2004.

16 Of course it wasn't just Darwin's fault. Our mistake has been to understand Darwinian evolution as the battle for the survival of the fittest described in *Origin of the Species.* His later, lesser-known book *The Descent of Man* makes a very different case, explaining that human beings' evolutionary advantage is our ability to cooperate, and to use reason, love, and ethics in making our decisions.

17 Howard Rheingold, "Cooperation Strategies: An Interdisciplinary Map," Institute of the Future, 2005. (Available from the Institute of the Future, in San Francisco, by request.)

18 Richard Sennett, *The Corrosion of Character* (New York: W.W. Norton, 1998).

19 John Katzenbach and Douglas Smith, *The Wisdom of Teams* (New York: HarperBusiness, 2003).

20 Ibid. 38–39.

21 Ibid. 78.

22 Steve Jobs, *MacWorld,* 1984, from *MacWorld,* February 2004.

23 Steve Jobs, *MacWorld,* February 2004.

24 James P. Carse, *Finite and Infinite Games* (New York: Ballantine, 1987), 22.

25 Corie Brown, Interview, *All Things Considered,* with Jacki Lyden, NPR. May 11, 2002.

26 Mitch Potter, "The Mogul at Livent's Helm," *Toronto Star,* April 18, 1998.

27 Peter Bart, "Tenacious Tenpercenters," *Variety,* April 2003.

28   Robert Slater, *Ovitz: The Inside Story of Hollywood's Most Controversial Power Broker* (New York: McGraw-Hill, 1997).

29   Ibid.

30   Michael Eisner, "From the Desk of Michael D. Eisner," *Daily Variety*, February 27, 2004.

31   Robert Slater, *Ovitz*.

32   Laura M. Holson, "Eisner on the Stand, Describes Courting of Ovitz," *New York Times*, November 16, 2004.

33   Bloomberg News, "Ex-Disney Director Says Ovitz Was 'Like a Cancer,' " *New York Times*, December 8, 2004.

34   Robert Slater, *Ovitz*.

35   Rachel Abramowitz, "Meeting the Little People on the Way Back Down," *Los Angeles Times*, July 6, 2002.

36   Business Monitor International, Ltd., *Foreign Companies in Emerging Markets Yearbook*, February 5, 2004.

37   Richard Branson, Virgin Web site, www.virgin.co.uk (May 10, 2005).

38   Ibid.

39   Branson, in Sam Hill and Glenn Rifkin, *Radical Marketing: From Harvard to Harley, Lessons from Ten That Broke the Rules and Made It Big* (New York: HarperBusiness, 1999), 175.

40   David Tait in ibid.

41   Vincent Alonzo and Judy Quinn, "Cutting Loose," *Incentive*, May 1995.

42   Melanie Wells, "Feature," *Forbes*, July 3, 2000.

43   Writing programs that repeatedly make requests of a Web site's servers, overwhelming their capacity and disabling them from responding to real customer visits.

44   Randall Stross, "When Long Hours at a Video Game Stop Being Fun," *New York Times*, November 21, 2004.

45   Ibid.

46   Ibid.

47   Jonathan D. Glater, "Management: Seasoning Compensation Stew," *New York Times*, March 7, 2001.

48   Michelle Prather, "No Turning Back," *Entrepreneur*, August 2001.

49 John C. Beck and Mitchell Wade, *Got Game: How the Gamer Generation Is Reshaping Business Forever* (Cambridge, MA: Harvard Business School Press, 2004).

50 Benedict Carey, "Working Long Hours? Take a Massage Break, Courtesy of Your Boss," *New York Times,* September 7, 2004.

51 Dr. Peter Cappelli, Professor of Management, quoted in ibid.

52 Jeffrey Sanchez-Burks, "Friendlier Workers More Productive," *Journal of Personality and Social Psychology,* August 2003.

53 All three examples are from Melinda Ligos, "Unstuffing Those Stuffy Staff Meetings," *New York Times,* August 2, 2000.

54 Murray Weidenbaum, "A New Social Contract for the American Workplace," *Challenge,* January–February 1995.

55 Mary Williams Walsh, "Luring the Best in an Unsettled Time," *New York Times,* January 30, 2001.

56 Ibid.

57 David Koeppel, "The New Cost of Keeping Workers Happy," *New York Times,* March 7, 2004; and Milton Moskowitz, "20 Better Places to Work," *Mother Jones,* July/August 1997.

58 Alfie Kohn, "Challenging Behaviorist Dogma: Myths about Money and Motivation," *Compensation & Benefits Review,* March/April 1998.

59 Alfie Kohn, "In Pursuit of Affluence, at a High Price," *New York Times,* February 2, 1999.

60 Alfie Kohn, "Challenging Behaviorist Dogma."

61 Ibid.

CHAPTER FIVE

1 I'm not joking or exaggerating here. I brought in a computer hacker to teach a telephone company about switching software, an insurance actuary to show a mortgage broker how to calculate risk assessment, and a toy designer to teach a game company about the fundamentals of playability.

2   David A. Aaker, in Patricia Winters, "Giving Old, Established Brands an Updated Life," *Business Times,* February 23, 2000.

3   Candace Cornell, in Sherri Day, "Gap Picks Chief from Outside the Clothing Trade," *New York Times,* September 27, 2002.

4   Same-store sales are revenue increases or decreases for existing stores, as opposed to revenue coming from or lost by new stores.

5   Tracie Rozhon, "Designing a Brighter Future for The Gap," *New York Times,* May 2, 2004.

6   Ibid.

7   Kerry Capell and Gerry Khermouch, "Hip H&M," *BusinessWeek,* November 11, 2002.

8   Except for promotion of twice-yearly sales or the announcement of a new store. Such expenditures amount to less than .3 percent of revenue, compared with 3 to 4 percent typical of clothing chains.

9   Vikram D. Rao (Group Executive President, Madura Garments), "Fashion Vision Series," *Images 2005,* Fashion.com.

10 Andrew McAfee, Vincent Dessain, and Anders Sjöman, "Zara: IT for Fast Fashion," *Harvard Business School Case Study,* 2004.

11 Sean Elder, "Details Goes Bust," Salon.com, March 20, 2000.

12 Ibid.

13 Cynthia Cotts, "The Devil Is in the Details," Salon.com, May 1997.

14 David Carr, "Young Editor Finds a Voice As Fairchild Revives Details," *New York Times,* April 15, 2002.

15 Ibid.

16 Sean Elder, "Details Goes Bust."

17 Ibid.

18 Unnamed source, cited in Cotts, "The Devil Is in the Details."

19 According to Cynthia Cotts, in ibid. " '[Michael Caruso] is positively Venetian,' said a source who asked not to be named. 'He's the kind of guy you associate with stilettos and poison rings and people being thrown in canals.' "

20 Kate Fitzgerald, "Details in the Field: Men's Magazine Links Lifestyle with Sports via Fall Activities," *Advertising Age,* September 14, 1998.

21 Ibid.

22 Sean Elder, "Details Goes Bust."

23 Ibid.

24 Ibid.

25 Unless otherwise noted, the research in this paragraph is from David Carr's "Young Editor Finds a Voice As Fairchild Revives Details."

26 Ibid.

27 David Carr, "Most Wanted: Drilling Down / Magazines; Comeback Kids." *New York Times,* July 14, 2003.

28 David Carr, "Young Editor Finds a Voice As Fairchild Revives Details."

29 Ibid.

30 Leslie Koren, "City Hip in the Suburbs; At Home with Bill Wackerman," *The Record* (Bergen County, NJ), August 7, 2003.

31 David Carr, "Young Editor Finds a Voice As Fairchild Revives Details."

32 David Carr, "Most Wanted: Drilling Down / Magazines; Comeback Kids."

33 David Haffenreffer, "Details Mag Making a Business Comeback," The Biz, *CNNfn,* July 18, 2003.

34 Stock prices assume a company's future growth, and are measured in multiples of current earnings. A share price of $50 for a company earning $2 per share would mean a P/E of 25 times.

35 Sean Silcoff, "How Levi Strauss Lost the Battle for Cool," *National Post's Financial Post & FP Investing* (Canada), September 26, 2003.

36 Jane L. Levere, "The Media Business: Advertising," *New York Times,* August 8, 2000.

37 Ibid.

38 Thomas Cunningham, "Levi's Plans to 'Relentlessly Innovate,' " *Business and Industry,* June 17, 2002.

39 Strategic Direction Staff, "Caught in the Downward Trend: How Fiat, AOL, and Levi's Dealt with Failure," *Strategic Direction,* November 2002.

40 Jenny Strasburg, "Levi's Plans to Sell Dockers," *San Francisco Chronicle,* May 12, 2004.

41   Thomas Frank, *The Conquest of Cool* (Chicago: University of Chicago Press, 1997), 60.

42   Stephen Brown, "Teaching Old Brands New Tricks: Retro Branding and the Revival of Brand Meaning," *Journal of Marketing*, July 2003.

43   Karl Greenberg, "Giving a Small Car Big 'Tude," *Brandweek*, December 9, 2002.

44   Chip Cummins and Almar Latour, "How Shell's Move to Revamp Culture Ended in Scandal," *Wall Street Journal*, November 2, 2004.

45   Why they should have believed that the oil glut would be permanent, especially given peak oil predictions by the world's leading scientists, is strange and as yet unexplained. More likely, Shell's executives believed that Middle Eastern reserves would keep prices low until Shell's had run out.

46   Chip Cummins and Almar Latour, "How Shell's Move to Revamp Culture Ended in Scandal."

47   Ibid.

48   Ibid.

49   Ibid.

CHAPTER SIX

1   Eric S. Raymond, *The Cathedral and the Bazaar*, revised edition (New York: O'Reilly, 2001), 74.

2   Of course, the political process is not genuinely open source. It's about personalities and power, and soon Dean the Internet phenomenon and Dean the candidate contradicted each other, with disastrous results. Had Dean emerged organically from the process, rather than being grafted onto it, his candidacy might have maintained more coherence.

3   For an interesting discussion of the evolution of corporate power over the past four centuries, see the informative, if inflammatory, essay "Know Thine Enemy," by Joel Bleifuss, *In These Times*, February

1998; also at: www.thirdworldtraveler.com/Corporations/
KnowEnemy_ITT.html.

4 Congressional Research Service, 1994 report, quoted in Justin Ervin,
   Kurt Fenske, Daniel Foster, Jennifer Gogo, Peter Jacques, Rebecca
   Thomas, and Matthew Tunno, *Teaching Case Study: Wal-Mart or
   World Mart.* Flagstaff Activist Network, www.flagstaffactivist.org.

5 Ibid.

6 "Store Wars: When Wal-Mart Comes to Town," PBS, ITVS,
   television documentary. Research and transcripts available at:
   www.pbs.org/itvs/storewars/.

7 Constance L. Hayes, "What's Behind the Procter Deal? Wal-Mart,"
   New York Times, January 29, 2005.

8 W.D. Crotty, "Costco Clinches Another One," *Motley Fool,* May 27,
   2004.

9 Ann Zimmerman, "Costco's Dilemma: Is Treating Employees Well
   Unacceptable for a Public Corporation?" *Wall Street Journal,* March
   26, 2004.

10 Ibid.

11 Timothy J. Mullaney, "What Price Google?" *BusinessWeek Online,*
   August 17, 2004.

12 CBS *60 Minutes,* January 6, 2005.

13 G. de Fourquin, *Histoire économique de l'Occident médiéval* (Paris:
   Armand Colin, 1969), 192.

14 Bernard A. Lietaer and Stephen M. Belgin, *On Human Wealth: Beyond
   Greed and Scarcity,* galley edition (Boulder, CO: Human Wealth
   Books and Talks, 2004).

15 Bernard Lietaer and Stephen Belgin, *On Human Wealth.*

16 By the thirteenth century—the dawn of the Renaissance—this took
   the form of a wide array of centralizing reforms. Kings began to
   assume their authority by divine right. Through these monarchs and
   their militaries, the Pope began widespread repression of alternative
   religious practices. Kings including Louis IX and Philip IV outlawed
   all but royal currencies, and introduced a new "stealth" tax by slowly
   reducing the gold content of coins. Thus, inflation was born.

17   Richard Duncan, *The Dollar Crisis: Causes, Consequences, Cures* (Singapore: John Wiley & Sons [Asia], 2003).

18   Ernest Becker, *Escape from Evil*, reissue edition (New York: Free Press, 1985).

19   James Howard Kunstler, "Big and Blue in the USA," Orion Online, 2003; and David Loy, "Buddhism and Money: The Repression of Emptiness Today," *Buddhist Ethics and Modern Society*, no. 31, 1991.

20   "The Nestlé Boycott," *New Internationalist*, April 1982.

21   Margaret Webb Pressler, "DeBeers Pleads to Price-Fixing," *Washington Post*, July 14, 2004.

22   "The Cartel Isn't Forever," *The Economist*, July 15, 2004.

23   Bernard Lietaer and Stephen Belgin, *On Human Wealth*.

24   Quoted in ibid.

25   A very advanced peer-to-peer program, following along the lines of Napster, but where having files and sharing files are one and the same.

26   Bill Carter, "CNN Will Cancel Crossfire and Cut Ties to Commentator," *New York Times*, January 6, 2005.

27   According to INSTAT.com technology research. Accessed May 2005, by subscription only.

28   The exchange actually did this through its subsidiary PDR Services LLC and the Standard & Poor's Depository Receipt Trust.

29   Industry Week Staff, "Technology Leader of the Year," *Industry Week*, December 1, 2004.

30   Henry Chesbrough, *Open Innovation* (Cambridge, MA: Harvard Business School Press, 2003).

CHAPTER SEVEN

1   National Business Crime Information Network, quoted on www.pan-inc.com (May 1, 2005).

2   Susan Faludi, *Stiffed: The Betrayal of the American Man* (New York: HarperCollins, 1999).

3 Rob Walker, "Dirt Appeal," *The New York Times Magazine,* August 8, 2004.

4 Ibid.

5 Ibid.

6 Agence France Presse, September 15, 2004.

7 Ibid.

8 Ibid.

9 Christina Passariello, "Nestlé's Dispute with Perrier Could Be Coming to a Boil Soon," *Wall Street Journal,* March 17, 2004.

10 Claire Murphy, "Brand Health Check: Perrier," *Marketing,* June 30, 2004.

11 Business Day Staff, "The Insider," *Business Day* (South Africa), December 4, 2003.

12 Business Day Staff, "A Matter of Trust," *Business Day* (South Africa), December 4, 2003.

13 Chris Barron, "Diary of a Retail Revolutionary," *Sunday Times* (South Africa), November 11, 2001.

14 Raymond Ackerman, as told to Denise Prichard, *Hearing Grasshoppers Jump* (Cape Town, South Africa: David Philip, 2001), 38–39.

15 Ibid.

16 Linda A. Johnson "Protesters Target Cigarette-Maker Altria," Associated Press Newswires, April 29, 2004.

17 Mike Stobbe, Health Business Column, *Charlotte Observer,* January 3, 2004.

18 Linda A. Johnson, "Protesters Target Cigarette-Maker Altria."

19 Patricia Sellers, "Rising from the Smoke," *Fortune* (Europe), April 16, 2001.

20 Infact staff, "Kraft Looks to Fatten Profits at Expense of Global Health," Infact Press Release, April 27, 2004, www.infact.org.

21 From Ben and Jerry's Web site—www.benjerry.com—"Our Company" (May 2005).

22 From Obesity.org, updated February 2005, www.obesity.org/subs/fastfacts/obesity_US.shtml.

23 www.infact.org, quoting World Health Organization

study, "Global Strategy on Diet, Physical Activity and Health, 2005."

24   Kenneth Rapoza, "Will Big Business Gobble Up Ben and Jerry's?" Salon, December 16, 1999, www.salon.com, archives.

25   www.honku.org, 2003.

26   Sam Schechner, "The Roach That Failed," *New York Times,* Sunday July 25, 2004.

27   EXTOXNET: Extension Toxicology Network, Pesticide Information Profiles, http://Extoxnet.orst.edu, June 1996. A Pesticide Information Project of Cooperative Extension Offices of Cornell University, Oregon State University, the University of Idaho, and the University of California at Davis; and the Institute for Environmental Toxicology, Michigan State University. Major support and funding was provided by the USDA/Extension Service/National Agricultural Pesticide Impact Assessment Program.

28   Sam Schechner, "The Roach That Failed."

29   Henkel KGaA, Dusseldorf, exchanged its 28.8 percent stake in Clorox in return for several brands, including Combat, and $2.1 billion in cash. Clorox explained the deal would allow it to focus on core businesses.

30   See my book *Playing the Future* (New York: HarperCollins, 1997), soon to be rereleased by Hampton Press as *ScreenAgers,* for research and commentary on the absorption of branded media by children.

31   Amanda Griscom, "Got Sun? Marketing the Revolution in Clean Energy," *Grist Magazine,* August 29, 2002, www.grist.org.

32   Kenny Bruno, "BP: Beyond Petroleum or Beyond Preposterous?" *CorpWatch,* December 14, 2000, http://corpwatch.org.

33   Art Kleiner, *Who Really Matters: The Core Group Theory of Power, Privilege, and Success* (New York: Doubleday, 2003), 219.

34   Amanda Griscom, "Got Sun?"

35   Ibid.

36   Asmara Pelupessy, "The Green Screen," *AlterNet,* April 1, 2000, www.alternet.org.

37   www.patagonia.com (May 10, 2005).

38 "Israel in the Age of Eminem" is the name of a real study conducted mostly by pollster Frank Luntz. It is available online at www.jfunders.org.

EPILOGUE

1 The Global Consciousness Project is documented at http://noosphere.princeton.edu.

bibliography

Ackerman, Raymond, as told to Denise Prichard. *Hearing Grasshoppers Jump*. Cape Town, South Africa: David Philip, 2001.

Anchor, Robert. "History and Play: Johan Huizinga and His Critics." *History and Theory,* no. 17 (1966): 63–93.

Atkin, Douglas. *The Culting of Brands: When Customers Become True Believers*. New York: Portfolio, 2004.

Barbrook, Richard. New York Prophecies. Forthcoming. In progress online at www.debalie.nl/dossierartikel.jsp?dossierid=10123&articleid=22828.

Bateson, Gregory. "A Theory of Play and Fantasy," in *Play: Its Role in Development and Evolution,* Jerome S. Bruner, Allison Jolly, and Kathy Sylva, eds. New York: Basic Books, 1976.

———. "The Message 'This Is Play,' " in *Group Processes: Transactions of the Second Conference,* B. Schaffner ed. New York: Josiah Macy, 1956, 145–242.

Baudrillard, Jean. *Simulacra and Simulation.* Translated by Sheila Faria Glaser. Ann Arbor, MI: University of Michigan Press, 1994.

Becker, Ernest. *Escape from Evil* (reissue ed.). New York: Free Press, 1985.

Braudel, Fernand. *A History of Civilizations*. New York: Penguin, 1993.

Burckhardt, Jacob. *The Civilization of the Renaissance in Italy*. London: Penguin Books Ltd., 1990.

Caillois, Roger. *Man, Play and Games*. Chicago: University of Illinois Press, 2001.

Carse, James. *Finite and Infinite Games*. New York: Ballantine, 1987.

Csikszentmihalyi, Mihaly. *Flow: The Psychology of Optimal Experience.* New York: Harper & Row, 1990.

Debord, Guy. *Society of the Spectacle.* Detroit: Black & Red, 1977.

Deffeyes, Kenneth S. *Hubbert's Peak: The Impending World Oil Shortage.* Princeton, NJ: Princeton University Press, 2001.

Duncan, Richard. *The Dollar Crisis: Causes, Consequences, Cures.* Singapore: John Wiley & Sons (Asia), 2003.

Fourquin, G. *Histoire Economique de l'Occident Médiéval.* Paris: Armand Colin, 1969.

Frank, Thomas. *The Conquest of Cool.* Chicago: University of Chicago Press, 1997.

Fuller, R. Buckminster. *Operating Manual for Spaceship Earth.* New York, Dutton Books, 1969.

Gomes, Leonard. *The Economics and Ideology of Free Trade: A Historical Review.* Northampton, MA: Edward Elgar Publishing, 2003.

Guillory, John. *Cultural Capital.* Chicago: University of Chicago Press, 1993.

Hawken, Paul. *The Ecology of Commerce: A Declaration of Sustainability.* New York: HarperBusiness, 1993.

Heinberg, Richard. *The Party's Over: Oil, War, and the Fate of Industrial Societies.* Garbriola Island, CA: New Society Publishers, 2003.

Hill, Sam, and Rifkin, Glenn. *Radical Marketing: From Harvard to Harley, Lessons from Ten That Broke the Rules and Made It Big.* New York: HarperBusiness, 1999.

Huizinga, Johan. *Homo Ludens: A Study of the Play Element in Culture.* Boston: The Beacon Press, 1955.

Hyde, Lewis. *Trickster Makes This World: Mischief, Myth, and Art.* New York: Farrar, Straus and Giroux, 1998.

Jacobs, Jane. *Systems of Survival: A Dialogue on the Moral Foundations of Commerce and Politics.* New York: Vintage, 1992.

Johnson, Steven. *Emergence: The Connected Lives of Ants, Brains, Cities, and Software.* San Francisco: Scribner, 2001.

Kane, Pat. *The Play Ethic: A Manifesto for a Different Way of Living.* London: Macmillan, 2004.

Katzenbach, Jon, and Smith, Douglas. *The Wisdom of Teams*. New York: HarperBusiness, 2003.

Kleiner, Art. *Who Really Matters: The Core Group Theory of Power, Privilege, and Success*. New York: Doubleday, 2003.

Kubovy, Michael. *The Psychology of Perspective and Renaissance Art* (reprint ed.). Cambridge, MA: Cambridge University Press, 1986.

Kuhn, Thomas. *The Structure of Scientific Revolutions*. Chicago: University of Chicago Press, 1996.

Leach, William. *Land of Desire: Merchants, Power, and the Rise of a New American Culture*. New York: Vintage, 1994.

Lietaer, Bernard A., and Belgin, Stephen M. *On Human Wealth: Beyond Greed and Scarcity* (galley edition). Boulder, CO: Human Wealth Books and Talks, 2004.

MacCannell, Dean. *The Tourist: A New Theory of the Leisure Class*. New York: Schocken, 1976.

McKee, Sally, ed. *Crossing Boundaries: Issues of Cultural and Individual Identity in the Middle Ages and the Renaissance*. Turnhout, Belgium: Brepols Publishers, 2002.

Ong, Walter. *Orality and Literacy*. New York: Routledge, 2002.

Owen, Harrison. *Open Space Technology: A User's Guide* (2nd ed.). San Francisco: Berrett-Koehler Publishers, Inc., 1997.

Peters, Thomas J., and Waterman, Robert H. Jr. *In Search of Excellence: Lessons from America's Best-Run Corporations*. New York: Warner Books, 1982.

Putnam, Bob. *Bowling Alone: The Collapse and Revival of American Community*. New York: Simon & Schuster, 2001.

Raymond, Eric S. *The Cathedral and the Bazaar* (revised ed.). New York: O'Reilly, 2001.

Rheingold, Howard. *Smart Mobs: The Next Social Revolution*. New York: Basic Books, 2003.

Roberts, Kevin. *Lovemarks: The Future Beyond Brands*. New York: Powerhouse Books, 2004.

Roston, Murray. *Changing Perspectives in Literature and the Visual Arts*. Princeton, NJ: Princeton University Press, 1987.

Rushkoff, Douglas. *Coercion: Why We Listen to What "They" Say*. New York: Riverhead, 1999.

———. *Media Virus: Hidden Agendas in Popular Culture*. New York: Ballantine, 1994.

———. *Cyberia* (2nd ed.). Manchester, U.K.: Clinamen Press, 2002.

———. *Open Source Democracy*. London: Demos, 2003.

———. *ScreenAgers*. Cresskill, NJ: Hampton Press, 2005.

Russel, Peter. *The Awakening Earth: The Global Brain*. London: Routledge, 1982.

Sennett, Richard. *The Corrosion of Character*. New York: W.W. Norton, 1998.

———. *The Fall of Public Man*. New York: W.W. Norton, 1977.

Slater, Robert. *Ovitz: The Inside Story of Hollywood's Most Controversial Power Broker*. New York: McGraw-Hill, 1997.

Sloan, Alfred P. Jr. *My Years with General Motors*. New York: Doubleday, 1963 and 1990.

Smil, Vaclav. *Energy at the Crossroads: Global Perspectives and Uncertainties*. Cambridge, MA: MIT Press, 2003.

Sutton-Smith, Brian, and Kelly Byrne, Diana, eds. *The Masks of Play*. New York: Leisure Press, 1984.

Teilhard de Chardin, Pierre. *The Future of Man*. Translated by Norman Denny. New York: Harper & Row, 1969.

Wiener, Norbert. *The Human Use of Human Beings* (2nd ed.). New York: Anchor Press, 1954.

Wightman, W.P.D. *Science in a Renaissance Society*. London: Hutchinson, 1972.

acknowledgments

As a new father, I have to admit this book wouldn't have been possible without the support of my wife, Barbara, who went through pregnancy and early motherhood while I went through research and rewrites. Her love, patience, and tolerance made this work possible, and I am forever in her debt.

I'm also deeply indebted to the wonderful interns and research assistants whose ongoing collaboration with me over the past three years gave me access to information, ideas, and inspiration far beyond what I would have been able to muster on my own. Thanks to Menaka Nayyar and Melissa Johnson for their diligence and enthusiasm, as well as to the members of my Narrative Lab at New York University's Interactive Telecommunications Program: Lían Sifuentes, Wiley Bowen, Michael Horan, Alyssa Wright, and Dan Melinger, who each brought unique perspectives and passion to this project.

Thanks to Joost Raessens and Frank Kessler, of Utrecht University, who have given me the support and guidance to ground the ideas in this book within a larger context of thought and study. And thanks to Lance Strate and the Media Ecology Association for giving me a forum in which to experiment with the most radical of these ideas, out loud.

Great thanks is also due to my editor, Marion Maneker, who believed in this work and helped me hone a lifetime of thought into a coherent message, and my agent Jay Mandel, who has believed in the relevancy of these ideas, sometimes more than I have myself. For rising above and beyond the call of duty at every opportunity, Edwin Tan has a friend in me, forever.

As for everyone else who has contributed to this book and the thinking that led up to it, please accept my humble thanks. You know who you are, and how much I appreciate your counsel, cajoling, and challenges.

Most of all, thanks to you, dear reader, for engaging with these ideas and making room for this on your shelf and in your day. I hope you find it worth the ride.

index